MW00675617

Feb 1996

For Moris Lippman

with warm regards

M-O.

# Myth
# and
# Madness

Mortimer Ostow

# Myth and Madness

*The Psychodynamics of Antisemitism*

**Transaction Publishers**
New Brunswick (U.S.A.) and London (U.K.)

Copyright © 1996 by Transaction Publishers, New Brunswick, New Jersey 08903.

All rights reserved under International and Pan-American Copyright Conventions. No part of this book may be reproduced or transmitted in any form or by any means, electronic or mechanical, including photocopy, recording, or any information storage and retrieval system, without prior permission in writing from the publisher. All inquiries should be addressed to Transaction Publishers, Rutgers—The State University, New Brunswick, New Jersey 08903.

This book is printed on acid-free paper that meets the American National Standard for Permanence of Paper for Printed Library Materials.

Library of Congress Catalog Number: 95-36973
ISBN: 1-56000-224-7
Printed in the United States of America

Library of Congress Cataloging-in-Publication Data

Ostow, Mortimer.
    Myth and madness : the psychodynamics of antisemitism / Mortimer Ostow.
        p. cm.
    Includes bibliographical references and index.
    ISBN 1-56000-224-7 (alk. paper)
    1. Antisemitism—Psychological aspects.  I. Title.
DS145.O84 1995
305.892′4—dc20                                                     95-36973
                                                                        CIP

# Dedication

This book is dedicated
to **my colleagues**
who participated in this project so devotedly
over the years in the hope of contributing
to the defeat of antisemitism,
to our inspiring, learned
and faithful guide and leader,
**Yosef H. Yerushalmi,**
and to the memory of my close friend and teacher,
**Gerson D. Cohen,**
an extraordinary scholar and heroic Jew.

# Contents

*Foreword*                                                    ix

*Participants*                                                 x

*Introduction*                                                 1

1. The Project, its Background,
   and its Presuppositions                                     3

2. Study of Clinical Data                                      43

3. Mythology                                                   63

4. Antisemitic Myths                                           95

5. The Pogrom Mentality                                       151

6. Conclusions                                                175

   *Bibliography*                                             181

   *Index*                                                    187

# Foreword

This is a report of a nine-year study of the psychodynamics of anti-semitism undertaken by the Psychoanalytic Research and Development Fund. The study consisted of the presentation to each other and discussion of case material and other data relevant to the subject by a group of psychoanalysts.

This book does not record the transactions of our study group, nor does it report all of the opinions voiced by the participants. The discussions, by design, ranged far and wide, covering not only individual psychodynamics and group psychology, but also history, religion, literature, politics, philosophy, and intellectual and cultural history. Many insights were recorded that we found interesting and fruitful.

However, as a practical matter, we decided that the major findings of our group could be presented only if one person reported his own insights, inferences, and conclusions, inspired by the group analysis of the case material and the other data. As organizer and leader of the group during its nine years of work, I undertook that task and what I offer here is my impression of what we learned and my conclusions. I am sure that each of us would have written a different book, but I suspect that almost all of the observations and many of the conclusions would overlap considerably. The differences would probably lie chiefly in the emphasis.

I am grateful to all of the members of our group who attended the sessions so faithfully over the years and contributed so earnestly. I am especially grateful to Professor Yosef H. Yerushalmi, a distinguished scholar of Jewish history, who was invited to serve as our resource authority, but who became far more than that, a source of inspiration, encouragement. and wisdom in addition to information. Without his historical and academic expertise, and his practical orientation, we would have gone off the track at many points. My wife, Miriam Ostow, helped to clarify my thoughts on these matters by long hours of discussion, and improved the style and precision of the manuscript. I wish to thank Professor Naomi Cohen for her help with American Jewish history, and Professor Michal Bodemann, who read the manuscript with the eye of a sophisticated sociologist and made many helpful suggestions. I am grateful also to my daughter-in-law, Carmen Ramos Ostow who accurately transcribed all seventy-five sessions with care and served as secretary of the group. She was always a cheerful and encouraging presence and contributed helpfully to the discussions. Finally, I should like to thank the Psychoanalytic Research and Development Fund that sponsored this study, its officers and members, and its lay leadership, individuals who over the years have made possible our many activities with grace and generosity.

Mortimer Ostow

## Participants

*Mortimer Ostow, M.D.*, chairman, Sandrow Visiting Professor Emeritus of Pastoral Psychiatry, Jewish Theological Seminary of America; president, Psychoanalytic Research and Development Fund; attending psychiatrist, Montefiore Medical Center, New York City.

*Jacob A. Arlow, M.D.*, past president, American Psychoanalytic Association; former editor-in-chief, Psychoanalytic Quarterly; clinical professor of psychiatry, New York University College of Medicine.

*Martin Bergmann, Ph.D.*, clinical professor of psychology, New York University Post-Doctoral Program; training and supervising analyst, New York Freudian Society.

*Kenneth Calder, M.D.*, past president, American Psychoanalytic Association; past vice president, International Psychoanalytical Association.

*Joseph Coltrera, M.D.*, clinical professor of psychiatry, New York University Medical Center, training and supervising psychoanalyst, Psychoanalytic Institute, New York Medical Center.

*Sidney Furst, M.D.*, professional director, Psychoanalytic Research and

Development Fund; training and supervising Psychoanalyst, New York Psychoanalytic Institute.

*Alexander Grinstein, M.D.*, president, Sigmund Freud Archives; training and supervising psychoanalyst, Michigan Psychoanalytic Institute; clinical professor of psychiatry, Wayne State University of Medicine.

*John Hartman, Ph.D.*, clinical associate professor of psychology, Department of Psychiatry, University of Michigan; faculty member, Michigan Psychoanalytic Institute.

*Milton Jucovy, M.D.*, faculty, training and supervising psychoanalyst, The New York Psychoanalytic Institute; past president, The New York and Long Island Psychoanalytic Societies; past president, The New York Psychoanalytic Institute; co-editor, *Generations of the Holocaust.*

*Curtis Kendrick, M.D.*, assistant professor of psychiatry, New York Medical Center; member, American Psychoanalytic Association.

*Eugene Mahon, M.D.*, practicing psychoanalyst, adults and children, New York, New York; assistant clinical professor of psychiatry, Columbia College of Physicians and Surgeons.

*Peter B. Neubauer, M.D.*, clinical professor of psychiatry, New York University; editor, *Psychoanalytic Study of the Child.*

*Winfred Overholser, M.D.*, former associate professor of psychiatry, Cornell Medical School; practicing psychoanalyst, New York, New York.

*Bernard Pacella, M.D.*, president, American Psychoanalytic Association; clinical professor emeritus of Psychiatry, College of Physicians and Surgeons, Columbia University; board of directors and secretary-treasurer, Sigmund Freud Archives, Inc.; board of directors, Freud London Museum.

*John Sours, M.D.,* * child and adult psychoanalyst; training and supervising child and adult psychoanalyst, Columbia University Psychoanalytic Center for Training and Research; supervising child analyst, New York Psychoanalytic Institute.

*George Wiedeman, M.D.,* * training and supervising psychoanalyst emeritus, Psychoanalytic Institute; Marion E. Kenworthy Professor Emeritus of Psychiatry, Faculty of Social Work, Columbia University.

*Annemarie Weil, M.D.,* * training and supervising psychoanalyst, (adolescents and children), New York Psychoanalytic Institute; Consultant Child Development Center.

*Yosef Hayim Yerushalmi, Ph.D.*, Salo Wittmayer Baron Professor of Jewish History, Culture and Society, Columbia University.

*deceased

## Guest Participants

*Helene Bass, M.S.W.*

*Elisabeth Brainin, M.D.*, psychoanalyst in a child guidance clinic, Vienna; psychoanalyst, private practice; training and supervising psychoanalyst, Viennese Psychoanalytic Society.

*Karen Brecht, Dipl. Psych.*

*Janine Chasseguet-Smirgel*, Doctor of Letters and Humane Sciences; training analyst, Paris Psychoanalytical Society; former vice president, International Psychoanalytical Assn.; former Freud Memorial Professor, University of London.

*Alvin Frank, M.D.*

*Gertrud Hardtmann, M.D.*

*Muriel Morris, M.D.*

*Norman Rosenblood, Ph.D.*, psychoanalyst; member, Toronto Psychoanalytic Society; member, Canadian Psychoanalytic Society; member, International Psychoanalytical Assn.; associate professor of English.

*Edith Schwartz, Ph.D.*

*Samy Teicher, Dipl. Psych.*

# Introduction

The persistence of antisemitism and its current resurgence after a brief post-Holocaust suppression, challenge those of us who believe that we understand something of human behavior to apply our expertise for the purpose of discerning the causes of antisemitism and perhaps suggesting an approach to combatting it. This book reflects my response to the work of a study group addressed to the subject, organized and supported by the Psychoanalytic Research and Development Fund. We hoped that the application of the psychoanalytic method to case material, and the application of psychoanalytic theory and thinking to the data of history and to available cultural products, would yield new insights into the phenomenon. We did arrive at some new formulations that we believe are valid, and that add a dimension of comprehensibility to our subject. We believe too that we have arrived at some idea of the way in which the various causative influences relate to and reinforce each other.

Why now? Now, because antisemitism must always be on the agenda of all of us who have a concern for the welfare of human society: many people care. It must be on the agenda especially of Jews who are in a position to help.

Needless to say we are not reassured by the fact that for American Jewry, this might well be called a golden age.[1] There have been few occasions in the past when Jews have enjoyed the prosperity, the prestige, the freedom to participate in national and community life in every way to the extent that they enjoy these in the United States today. And although they are aware of persisting pockets of antisemitism, they feel themselves comfortably at home as appreciative and loyal citizens. They do not quail before occasional manifestations of antisemitism and feel that they have the right to demand corrective action by appropriate agencies. Nevertheless we all know that Jews have enjoyed similar golden ages in the past, in Babylonia, in Spain, in Italy, in Poland, for example, and yet changes in the political, economic, or military situation have

1

brought each golden age to an end, whereupon antisemitism revived. Antisemitism seems to be a phasic phenomenon and at no point can we remain confident that it has been permanently overcome. Even now, at the close of this project, nine years after its inception, antisemitism has become more active, more threatening, and less a matter of history than it seemed then.

## Note

1. The term golden age is, of course, not precisely defined. Some historians see the golden age of American Jewry as having begun in the 1930s as the Roosevelt administration, in its struggle against economic depression and then in its pursuit of World War II, took advantage of the intellectual abilities, education, ambition, and identification with America, of the children and grandchildren of the Jewish immigrants of late nineteenth and early twentieth century. With them, the American Jewish community achieved status and power. When, on the other hand, soon after the Kennedy assassination, the liberal agenda that had united the country for the previous three decades, lost its grip on the public, individual, rival constituencies evolved, not all of which were congenial to Jews. It was not long afterwards that the earliest postwar expressions of antisemitism began to appear in the public arena. In other respects, numbers, wealth, power, and cultural development, the Jewish community has continued to flourish.

# 1

# The Project, its Background, and its Presuppositions

We anticipated that the psychoanalytic method could usefully be applied to the phenomenon of antisemitism since antisemitism seems to be largely irrational. Its ubiquity and persistence cannot be explained by any realistic considerations. Of course we do not contend that antisemitism is to be attributed only to the outcome of psychic conflict, that it has no roots in the material world. Historians tend to attribute both individual antisemitic sentiments and active persecution to economic and political rivalry, to opportunism, to the struggle for resources, for power, and for status. Salo W. Baron, the doyen of Jewish historical scholarship, attributed antisemitism to "dislike of the unlike" (1976). However, he continues in that essay to list a variety of historical situations in which material rivalries augmented antisemitic religious mythology so as to bring about persecution. Benjamin Ginsberg focuses almost entirely on material rather than psychological motives (1993). Leon Poliakov, in his four-volume history of antisemitism (1965, 1973, 1975, 1985), attempts to combine the material with the psychologic. Studies of antisemitism are being published today at a rapid pace, each author presenting his individual point of view.

Antisemites often justify their prejudice by offering myths that persist in form and remain similar in content or intent over generations and centuries, in many places, and in diverse cultures. When analysts turn their attention to antisemitic issues that come up in the course of psychoanalysis undertaken for whatever reasons, they invariably find that these issues are dealt with in the same way that other issues are dealt with, namely, they are used in transference projections as well as for defense and for instinctual gratification.

3

We initiated this investigation now because we believed that the psychoanalytic approach has, in recent years, achieved a new sophistication and a new appreciation of the influence of developmental events, of the interplay of the individual and group, the influence of cultural background and the opportunities and hazards of the material world in the determination of adult behavior. These advances in psychoanalytic understanding come, paradoxically, at a time when the value of psychoanalysis as a therapy is being questioned, and when it is being displaced by psychiatric drug therapy for the treatment of certain mental illnesses, and reinforced by it for the treatment of others. Our project exemplifies the application of psychoanalytic thinking to social and cultural issues; applied psychoanalysis the discipline is called. Sigmund Freud initiated this subdiscipline in his many papers on the origin and nature of human society, and pointed the way to its use to elucidate creative works.

## Psychoanalytic Interpretations of Antisemitism

Strangely, although antisemitism as a powerful prejudice prevailed in Central Europe where it influenced the lives of the founders of psychoanalysis, they showed little interest in applying the psychoanalytic method to the problem. A study of the minutes of the early meetings of the Vienna Psychoanalytic Society (Federn and Nunberg, 1962) discloses that the word antisemitism does not appear in the index. There are relatively few references to Jews, and none vaguely appreciative except the remark by Freud "(Werner) Sombart has neglected a basic difference; otherwise he would have seen that the old Jewish religion has rendered a great service in the restriction of *perverted* sexuality, by guiding all libidinal currents into the bed of propagation" (vol. 3, p.273). Aside from Freud's many references to antisemitism in a number of papers, psychoanalytic literature was relatively silent about the matter until the Nazi period. When European psychoanalysts reached safety, a few of them undertook an essay, or in a few cases even a book, on the subject. For the most part, these offered explanations based upon the common defense mechanisms of displacement and projection, yielding the scapegoat theory and Oedipal determination. Some spoke of the influence of Christian mythology, specifically the charge of deicide and the symbolism of the mass. Others attempted an approach via group psychology.

Allusions to antisemitism appear in many autobiographical sections of Sigmund Freud's writings. In *The Interpretation of Dreams*, (Freud, 1900), both the dream entitled "My Uncle With the Yellow Beard" and "My Son, the Myops" deal with Freud's reaction to antisemitism. At the very beginning of his autobiography (Freud, 1925) he writes, *"Ich bin Jude geboren und Jude geblieben."* He asserts, in other words, his resistance to pressure for conversion. In his address to B'nai B'rith (1941), he talks about his feelings of belonging to the opposition and doing without membership in the "compact majority."

In other writings he offered some etiologic considerations. In a footnote to the 1919 essay on Leonardo da Vinci, he suggests that antisemitism may be derived, in part, from the unconscious equation between circumcision and castration, the latter inducing the response of horror. In fact, as early as 1909, in the Little Hans paper, he suggests that the Jews are despised because of circumcision since "the deepest unconscious root of antisemitism is the castration complex." In 1921, in his essay on Group Psychology, he wrote that every intimate relation between two peoples that persists for some time, leaves a sediment of feelings of aversion and hostility. He speaks of "an insuperable repugnance" of the Aryan for the Semite. Notice that he doesn't mention the converse. In *Civilization and Its Discontents* (1930), he observed that hostility against intruders permits an outlet for aggression that arises within small cultural groups. The narcissism of minor differences makes cohesion between members of a community easier. Therefore the dream of Germanic world dominion called for antisemitism as its complement.

In *Moses and Monotheism* (1939), Freud gave a list of etiologic factors responsible for antisemitism. The Jews disavow the murder of the father, God, while the Christians admit it. Jews are considered aliens. They are a convenient scapegoat for communal hostility. They are different from their hosts but only slightly so. They are successful despite oppression. Unconscious roots of antisemitism include Christian jealousy of the Jews for proclaiming themselves *the chosen people*. Circumcision is a disagreeable reminder of castration. The Christians blame the Jews for imposing their own religion, Christianity, upon them.

All of Freud's comments about antisemitism were written before the Holocaust, and in fact before the Holocaust was imaginable. *Moses and Monotheism* itself might be regarded, although it was begun in the 1920s, as having been inspired and directed towards the gathering Holocaust.

In fact, a friend of mine, a distinguished student of Jewish history, was persuaded that *Moses and Monotheism* contains two messages, an exoteric one with which we are familiar, and simultaneously an esoteric one. The latter he contends, is a response to antisemitism and a defense of the Jews. He bases his argument partially on the fact that one can recognize in the text a point by point refutation of Werner Sombart's anti-Jewish arguments in his 1911 book *The Jews and Modern Capitalism* in which he attempted to document the thesis that the Jews are responsible for the disruption of the medieval economic system and for laying the foundations of capitalism.[1] When my friend came to this conclusion, he was not aware of the discussion of Sombart's book that had taken place at the meeting of the Wednesday evening Vienna Psychoanalytic Society in 1911, as soon as the book appeared, with comments by many members including specifically by Freud.

Following the Holocaust many other analysts turned their attention to antisemitism. Erik Erickson in an article that appeared in *Psychiatry* in 1942, entitled "Hitler's Imagery and German Youth" (Erickson, 1942), wrote that in times of national anxiety, Jewish relativism threatens provincials who then cling to traditional absolutes that had been neglected in periods of freedom. Jewish power is felt by these provincials to be "penetrating" rather than "overpowering." The Jew makes relativism a means of racial self-preservation. He contrasts the Germans who are geographically encircled within Europe, with the Jews who are dispersed throughout Europe.

Ernst Simmel edited a volume of essays in 1946, entitled *Antisemitism, A Social Disease*, (Simmel, 1946). In this volume Douglas Orr contributed a paper, "Antisemitism and the Psychopathology of Daily Life" (Orr, 1946). He contends that the masochism of the Jews and their need for punishment may provoke antisemitic attitudes in non-Jews. Antisemitism may also arise as a result of the displacement of hostility onto strangers as a projection of undesirable traits since minorities may threaten the repressions of the majority. He suggests that one undo the strangeness of the Jews by education about Jews and about antisemitism.

Simmel contributed a paper to the volume, entitled "Antisemitism and Mass Psychopathology" (Simmel, 1946). He writes that some individual antisemitism may be derived from latent homosexuality that requires hate as a defense. Group regression may bring about a mass psychosis. Antisemitism may be provoked as a result of projection of deicidal wishes, specifically the wish to devour the lamb of God. The Eucharist, he says, is closer to human and animal sacrifice than any Jewish practice. Jews can become potentially international as well as intranational enemies. He too recommends education about the psychology of hatred in normal individuals, that athletic competitions be promoted and spiritualized, that the vulnerability of the public to propaganda be taught, and that disturbed individuals be educated further. Because within a democratic group, the ego is not dissolved, he recommends stringent government protection for all minorities.

Frenkel-Brunswik and Sanford, again in the same volume, published an initial report of their study of the antisemitic personality. They observed that antisemitism is associated with: unthoughtful support of the status quo; little concern with political issues; the association of ethnocentric purity with the rejection of other minority groups; cultivation of a composed, decorous, well-groomed appearance and concern with social standing; a resentment of "prying" investigations such as the authors'; an absence of interest in the individual's inner life; and conscious expression of affection for parents and respect for authority. (A contrasting, non-antisemitic group showed less self-satisfaction and more open criticism of parents.) On projective tests, antisemitic personalities demonstrated aggressive themes, cruel fantasies, and cynicism, with a lack of affectionate themes. By contrast with non-antisemitic groups, the antisemites saw dangers arising externally rather than from their own ego defects. They saw religion as a source of support rather than as a source of ethics. They admired patriots and people with power rather than artists, scientists, and humanitarians. They were moralistic and conventional. They exhibited an aversion to expression of emotion, and they projected their feelings onto others who were uninhibited. They exhibited a fear of losing control over their thoughts. They expressed concern with sex crimes that deserve punishment. They expressed little guilt. Beneath a surface admiration, they concealed hatred and criticism of parents. They tended to judge by stereotype, distinguishing between good and evil people. They exhibited paranoid tendencies. There was some concern with unusual psychic experiences. They were concerned with dominance as opposed to submission. Projecting the evil upon outside groups facilitated their efforts to integrate their own personalities. The non-antisemitic group acknowledged the evil impulses within themselves. Antisemitic males exhibited conscious masculinity but unconscious passivity and dependence. A liberal attitude toward one's own instincts was associated with a liberal attitude toward minority groups.

A paper by Fenichel, "Elements of a Psychoanalytic Theory of Antisemitism" (Fenichel, 1946) emphasized scapegoating and projection as a basic mechanism, and added too that it is common for individuals to fear the victim of their hostility.

Ernest Jones in 1951 wrote on "The Psychology of the Jewish Question" (Jones, 1951). He suggested that antisemitism derived from a rejection of dark pigmentation which is associated with feces, that it appeared when the population of Jews exceeded the concentration that could be tolerated by non-Jews, that antisemitism could be attributed to the separateness of Jews which is associated with a superiority complex. He also related it to Jewish aversion to violence and to the Jewish practice of circumcision, both contributing to castration fear on the part of their neighbors. He, who spoke of himself as the *shabbos goy* of the psychoanalytic community, proposed that the Jewish community destroy itself by assimilation, thereby demonstrating ambivalence, both philosemitism and antisemitism which we shall discuss below.

Loewenstein, in 1951, wrote a book, *Christians and Jews: A Psychoanalytic Study* (Loewenstein, 1951). He reviewed different social influences and individual psychodynamic mechanisms contributing to antisemitism. He considered the history of antisemitism and looked into Jewish history as a source of the origins of "Jewish traits." Judaism and Christianity, he proposed, form a cultural pair. The Jews are therefore integral to Christianity. The dynamics of the Christian revolution against Judaism two thousand years ago are paralleled by conflicts of early childhood. The Jews represent the father who must be rebelled against.

Ackerman and Jahoda published a small volume entitled *Antisemitism and Emotional Disorder: A Psychoanalytic Interpretation* in 1950 (Ackerman and Jahoda, 1950). They studied secondhand reports of psychotherapeutic treatment, in some cases psychoanalytic treatment, of forty antisemites, including eight Jews. They came to a number of interesting conclusions. The transference facilitates the appearance of antisemitism in the analysis of antisemitic patients with Jewish analysts. Most clearly, antisemitism is associated with psychopathic or paranoid personalities. The emotional predisposition to antisemitism is associated with: diffuse anxiety and exaggerated vulnerability; identity diffusion, including feelings of inferiority and homosexual tendencies derived from problems with passivity; poor interpersonal relations; the need to conform, associated with difficulty in submitting to the group; an inability to obtain emotional gratification from the outside world; poor development of conscience associated with a failure of repression. They suggested genetic, that is, psychogenetic contributions to antisemitism: parental discord; rejection by parents, resulting in the envy of Jewish family life. The rejection also produces a diminution of self-esteem, increased dependence, and repressed hostility resulting in sub-missiveness and displacement of hostility. Parental rejection was also frequently associated with ambivalent fixations around toilet training. There were unresolved Oedipal struggles. Defenses employed by antisemites include: projection; denial; aggression (replacing anxiety); emotional withdrawal, opposition (presumably negativism), displace-ment (of hostility from others onto Jews), reaction formation (produc-ing overt philosemitism), an absence of sublimation, a need for success to compensate for felt inferiority, introjection as a means of identifica-tion with the elite. They observed that group pressures provide for so-cial determination of stereotypes and social determination of antisemitic behavior. They also considered Jewish antisemitism, "liberal anti-semitism," and antisemitism in family life.

A splendid review of the literature on the nature and causes of preju-dice, by John Duckitt of the University of Witwatersrand, (Duckitt, 1992)  draws attention to the fact that the specific focus of research has changed systematically from decade to decade in this century. He points out that in the nineteenth century, the targets of prejudice, for example, blacks and colonials, were considered racially inferior. In the twenties and thir-ties of this century, psychologists, especially in the United States, began to question these attitudes as derogatory, unfair, and irrational. He re-lates this shift in "scientific attitude" to the rise of a black civil rights movement in the United States, and to challenges to the legitimacy of colonial rule by Europeans.

In the thirties and forties psychodynamic theories were offered. Preju-dice, says Duckitt, was seen as the result of the operation of universal psychological processes such as defense mechanisms. Externally arising frustrations and deprivations created inner conflicts that required defenses. By the fifties however, in response to universal revulsion at Nazi antisemitism, the emphasis shifted from common dynamic mechanisms to particular deformed personality structures that favor such mechanisms.

During the sixties and seventies the emphasis shifted from the individual to the group as psychologists seemed to lose interest in the problem of prejudice and sociologists and social psychologists took it up. Prejudice reflected conformity to group values as evidenced not only by voiced opinions but by prejudicial behavior. As resistance developed to attempts to undo irrational bias, students emphasized realistic conflicts of interests.

Duckitt continues his analysis by observing that in the eighties one began to appreciate that prejudice was inherent in the very structure of all groups. Group cohesion demands unrealistic appreciation of one's own group and depreciation of neighbor's groups.

This perceptive and comprehensive review concludes with the suggestion that at least four basic processes and forces combine to generate prejudice. First, Duckitt notes, prejudices are generated by certain universal psychological processes. Second, group dynamics exploit this potential for prejudice to create group prejudicial consensus. Third, mechanisms for transmission of these ideas guarantee their spread through the group. Fourth, small individual differences modulate the susceptibility of the individual to group influence.

John Hartman called my attention to this analysis after the first draft of this book had been completed. The reader will observe how closely our own nine-year study, begun in the early eighties, recapitulated the sequence of issues enumerated in Duckitt's review. Although we approached the subject as psychoanalysts, we have at various points, concerned ourselves with each of the forces and processes that he considered basic and elementary.

An excellent review of the history of the psychoanalytic studies of antisemitism until very recently, is given in volume 2 of the series on Current Research on Antisemitism sponsored by the Zentrum fur Antisemitismusforschung at the Technical University of Berlin. This series is edited by Herbert A. Strauss and Werner Bergmann and this volume contains recent articles from the psychologic literature, including a section specifically devoted to psychoanalysis. It was edited by Bergmann who also prepared excellent summaries of this literature.

Although the psychoanalytic professional literature has been proliferating rapidly, studies of the psychodynamics of antisemitism have been very few. These various studies associate antisemitism with specific dynamics, or with personality profiles or intergroup relations. None of them attempts an integrated approach to the problem and none of them attempts to relate the psychologic factors to the actual history of antisemitism. One misses also a psychologic study of antisemitic myths and any distinction between antisemitic attitudes and the pogrom mentality. We ambitiously hoped to achieve a broader and more multifaceted examination of the problem of antisemitism. Our approaches included all of those included by Duckitt in his review, and others. The reader will decide how well we have fulfilled our ambition.

Just as our project was terminating in 1990, Professor Gavin Langmuir of the University of California published two books, *Toward a Definition of Antisemitism*, and *History, Religion and Antisemitism*. These, it seems to me, stand out sharply from among the many others not only by the originality of the historical research and the breadth of social and historical perspective, but also by the clarity of his psychologic perceptions.

Langmuir distinguishes between xenophobia and chimeria. The former responds to actual encounters with the real stranger and concern with actual or potential damage. Chimeria, or chimerical fantasies, deal with the chimerical, unrealistic fantasy image of the Jew based upon the Christian's inner needs without reference to reality. Xenophobia, he says, prevailed in medieval Europe before the end of the eleventh century, and the chimeria thereafter where it gave rise to the well-known medieval persecutions.

The Jew is seen as a source and reinforcer of Christian doubt and disbelief. Order would be restored to the cosmos and certainty to the mind of the individual if the Jewish disturber and disbeliever were eliminated. The visible behavior of the Jews was irrelevant, they were a "hidden menace." The crusaders felt "reconnected with their God from whom they had felt estranged."

Although we worked from different though overlapping data, he and we came to some similar conclusions. As the reader will see, we both deal with reality and fantasy, history and myth, doubt and certainty, manifest and hidden.

## Method

Our study group had hoped to probe more deeply and systematically than had been done in the past in order to discern the relevant issues in greater detail and to construct a more specific and more coherent chain of causation. Seventeen analysts participated[2], all experienced and thoughtful, and all of whom shared an interest in the subject of antisemitism and prejudice in general. About half of the group was Jewish, and among the non-Jews, an African-American participated during the first half of the project. The members of the group were selected not only for their experience and skill and interest, but also for their congeniality with each other.

We assumed that non-Jewish analysts might have greater access to antisemitic patients and to the antisemitic sentiments of non-Jewish patients who were not clearly antisemitic. We assumed that they might think about the subject somewhat differently from the Jewish analysts. We were privileged also to have as a regular participant, Professor Yosef Yerushalmi, a distinguished scholar in the field of Jewish history and Jewish historiography, who was extraordinarily helpful, not only as a resource person, but also as a commentator on methodology and on the application of the psychoanalytic method to historical material.

We met about eight times a year at monthly intervals for two hours, so that in the nine-year period there were seventy-five meetings. Each of the meetings was recorded and transcribed, and the transcriptions were studied, summarized, and abstracted, so that the material could be studied and reviewed one or more times.

Since we believed that as clinical psychoanalysts we were competent only in the study of psychoanalytic case material, we addressed ourselves in the first instance to that. When, after some time it appeared to us that many of the important determinants of antisemitism lay, not within the individual but in the dynamics of the community, we studied selected historical materials, current literary productions, classic myths and whatever else Professor Yerushalmi or others could suggest. For the final year of the project we were fortunate to obtain the active participation of Dr. John Hartman, a person who had achieved skill and distinction both as a psychoanalyst and as a sociologist, with a special interest in the subject of prejudice. He tried to orient us to a sociologic perspective on the problem of prejudice and he reviewed with us some relevant formulations. Nevertheless, despite Yerushalmi's encouragement to apply the principles of psychoanalytic hermeneutics to the nonclinical materials that were available, and despite Hartman's encouragement to examine sociologic data and hypotheses from a psychoanalytic point of view, the study group decided to limit its activities in these realms to introductory and tentative suggestions.

During the course of our work we were afforded the opportunity to examine some relevant observations made by colleagues from France (Janine Chasseguet-Smirgel), from Germany (Gertrud Hardtmann and Karen Brecht), and from Austria (Elisabeth Brainin and Samy Teicher), and discussions introduced by them became a part of our data and our formulations.

Inevitably the Holocaust, its causes, its nature, and its consequences were introduced into the discussion frequently. We did not hesitate to study the materials that we obtained for the light that these might throw on antisemitism, the subject of our interest. However, we tried to distinguish clearly between antisemitism as a general issue and the Holocaust as a specific, in fact, unique manifestation. We did give some thought to the etiologic background of the Holocaust, what triggered the events, the method by which virtually the entire population of Germany and the lands that it occupied became co-opted into the project of murdering Jews. And we have taken cognizance of the aftermath of the Holocaust: complexes prevailing among Jewish survivors and other Jews and complexes prevailing among non-Jews, especially in Germany and its allies, that have followed in its wake. However, we have not actively pursued the effects of the Holocaust on the survivors and their descendants, the responses to the physical and psychic trauma, even though two of the leaders of this particular field of study, Martin Bergmann and Milton Jucovy participated actively in our group. Perhaps the most important lesson that we learned from contemplating the Holocaust is the importance of apocalyptic thinking and of a fundamentalist reorganization of society in converting antisemitic prejudice into antisemitic persecution.

## Definition

As soon as our discussions started, we realized that we had no commonly accepted definition of antisemitism. Obviously the term antisemitism refers to prejudice against Jews. The term is generally understood to be an inappropriate one. It is generally attributed to a Jew hater in late nineteenth-century Germany by the name of Wilhelm Marr[3] who contended, as did many German intellectuals of that time, that Jews were members of a different race, the Semites,[4] and were therefore not acceptable as full members of German society. Antisemitism followed as the natural consequence. It is interesting that, based upon a false premise, the term has nevertheless found almost universal acceptance—

even among Jews. Other terms that have been proposed, such as Jew-hatred or anti-Judaism, have not replaced it. In this book I shall spell the term without capitals and without hyphen, thus indicating my rejection of the racial implications of the term. It is a poor compromise, adopted only in order to comply with general usage.

What qualifies as antisemitism? Granted that Nazis who kill Jews because they are Jews are, by any definition, antisemites. We would have to agree too, that even in the absence of persecution, active discrimination to the detriment of the Jew, would imply antisemitism. But suppose a non-Jew finds Jews unpleasant and avoids contact with them when he can, but takes no action against them nor speaks ill of them. Is such a person antisemitic? If he is, what would one say about sincere non-Jewish friends, who, if only because they harbor a sympathetic interest in Jews, are aware of differences, differences in interests, differences in the structure of the family and the strength of family attachments, differences in interest in the State of Israel and in social loyalties, such as loyalty to fellow Jews? Does that awareness of differences mean that they are prejudiced? And suppose on some occasion, our genuine friend, miffed by a Jew, momentarily finds himself thinking in stereotypes, but then when he realizes that he is doing so, immediately corrects himself with a genuine feeling of dismay? And what about the truly virtuous individual who is never aware of any antisemitic thoughts whatever, but in analysis reports dreams that reflect hostility to Jews? I believe that most would agree that there is no one who is completely without prejudice. At what point do we draw a line and say that on the one side of this line antisemitism prevails, and on the other it does not?

There is no problem recognizing extremes of antisemitism and of philosemitism. However sentiments vary on a continuum and even if it were possible to devise a measure of such prejudice, it is clear that we would find no natural break in that continuum.

The problem is complicated further by two additional issues. First, both philosemitic and antisemitic sentiments are seldom if ever unopposed by modifying or contradictory feelings, so that any attempt at a hypothetical, diagrammatic representation would require at least a two-dimensional or a vector scheme. Second, prejudicial sentiments are seldom constant over time. Remember Martin Luther's swing from philosemitism to virulent antisemitism when he found that Jews did not respond positively to his invitation to convert. Marr himself started as a philosemite, became an active antisemite, and then, subsequently dropped his antisemitism (Zimmerman, 1986). The man who, in our series of cases, exhibited the most intense and active antisemitism, a few decades later told his analyst that he was "finished with that foolishness." There may be oscillations even over a period of days, weeks, or months. An individual, on his own, may have no interest in Jews one way or the other, but in the presence of antisemitic friends or at his antisemitic club, may permit himself to be co-opted by the sentiments of those around him. Or he may be pleased or angered by an experience with Jewish friends or associates or strangers. Or he may respond to news of Israeli behavior of which he disapproves, such as the 1982 incursion into Lebanon, with reflections on Jews. So that in many people, as our case histories demonstrated, antisemitic sentiment waxes and wanes in response to either inner mood changes or external circumstances.

At one point in our deliberations, it seemed to us that, for the study of the dynamics of individual antisemitism, we had much to learn from studying anti-Jewish thoughts in non-antisemitic individuals, because in them the antisemitism was minimally complicated by hostility and the need to discharge aggression. Loewenstein in his book, *Christians and Jews*, (1951) quotes a letter from a former patient, written presumably soon after the Israeli War of Independence in 1948, in which, although he had never regarded himself as an antisemite, he nevertheless reveals considerable ambivalence about Jews, which he now regrets.

Obviously, we found no formula that overcame these ambiguities. In practice we spoke of antisemites in the case of individuals to whom hostility to Jews was important. We spoke of antisemitic sentiments in the case of individuals who did not display clear evidence of active antisemitic hostility.

## Antisemitism as a Prejudice

Is antisemitism just a prejudice, not different in quality from other prejudices, or is it something *sui generis?* If one asks that question of a historian, he might reply that it differs from other prejudices in its ubiquity, its duration and persistence, in the grievousness of its consequences, and in its being embedded in the mythology of Christianity. One could maintain that the same qualities apply to prejudice against African-Americans too, except for the last, but that would be replaced by the widespread historical as well as current feeling among many whites that African-Americans are in some way inferior to whites. From the point of view of mythology, it appears that black is considered negatively with respect to white, signifying degradation, depression, defeat, immorality, wickedness, danger, and death. So that antiblack prejudice possesses its own uniqueness. From a phenomenologic point of view we would have to concede, I think, that there may be little difference between one prejudice and another, but that antisemitism is more firmly embedded in the matrix of the prevailing social mythology and lends itself more readily to the reinforcement of fundamentalist and apocalyptic regression—with fatally different consequences. We shall see that psychodynamically, antisemitism is indeed unique or at least different from most other prejudices with which we, in the Western world, are familiar.

## Antisemitism and Psychopathology

Our methodology led us to the study of antisemitism in patients who had come to psychoanalysis for treatment of illness. We generally assume that the psychodynamics that prevail in illness are the same as those that prevail in health, except that in illness, satisfactory resolution is not achieved. Instead of realistic compromise or sublimation, a symptom ensues, or some other form of pathologic behavior. Similarly, we assumed at first that antisemitism could be understood as an externalized effort at solution of a conflict. To the extent that antisemitism is socially disruptive and inconsistent with usual concepts of ethical behavior, it could be considered an inappropriate response and hence pathologic. We soon realized however that in certain segments of society, antisemitism was encouraged, and within that segment, socially compliant. That being the case, we had no basis for considering it pathologic or even anomalous unless we assumed that our own views of socially desirable behavior are absolute and universally true. Accordingly, we revised our views, seeing antisemitism now simply as an aspect of human behavior that we in our study group considered undesirable, but that was not necessarily pathologic, especially when it was limited to prejudice or discrimination rather than persecution.

We recognized too that within other societies, such as the Nazi society, even antisemitic persecution could not necessarily be seen as pathologic. Reprehensible, barbarous, horrible, and degraded, yes, but pathologic, perhaps not. On the other hand, it was also true that antisemitic prejudice might reflect an attempt to resolve conflict or to control affect by externalization, by displacement or by projection, thereby pathologically distorting reality. Delusional antisemitism is pathological no matter in what society, at least to the extent that delusional thinking on any subject is pathologic for that society.

## Are Jews Responsible For Antisemitism?

Antisemites often fortify their views and behavior by contending that Jews make themselves obnoxious or unacceptable in one way or another, They exhibit bad character; they undermine society; they conspire against or prey upon their neighbors. Sometimes these antisemites can point to obvious instances in which the behavior of individual Jews was indeed undesirable and unneighborly, the greedy slumlord, the cheating storekeeper, the Wall Street manipulator.[5] The readiness to find fault is obviously the result of an existing antisemitic attitude that is seeking rationalization and justification. The prejudiced attitude is betrayed in generalizing individual misbehavior into a group stereotype. In other instances, the condemnation is so broad and so fictitious, as for example, the claims of *The Protocols of the Elders of Zion*, that no consideration need be given to a reality basis.

Jews are not passive objects; they often play an active role in history and in so doing they are likely on occasion to act against the interests of their neighbors and hosts. For example, blacks and Jews differ in their opinions of the propriety of the principle of affirmative action. While that circumstance warrants attempts to resolve the conflicting interests or to compromise them, it justifies antisemitism only when a readiness for it already exists.

In our case material we did encounter criticism of Jewish behavior but in the context of the patient's antisemitic attitude it was clear that in each instance the criticism was intended to justify that attitude.

## Jewish Separatism

Perhaps the most authentic Jewish behavior that is taken amiss is Jewish separatism. Judaism, from its Biblical roots, has encouraged a

self-conscious, determined attempt to hold the Jewish community cohesive and separate. To this date, Jewish ritual encourages that separatism. The Jew who observes the laws of kashrut will not eat in homes or
restaurants where these laws are not observed, so that his social contacts with non-Jews will be limited. As Shylock said to Bassanio, "I will
buy with you, sell with you, talk with you, walk with you {and so fol-
lowing} but I will not eat with you, drink with you, nor pray with you"
(*The Merchant of Venice*).

Nevertheless, there were periods and places in Jewish history that
saw close fraternization between Jews and Christians, so close that it
was discouraged by religious authorities. When Jews were shut up in
ghettos, their own tendency to separatism was powerfully reinforced by
separatist regulations that were imposed upon them. In societies that do
not impose separation upon Jews, their cohesiveness is taken as provocation by neighbors who seek rationalizations for their antisemitism.

One of the most troublesome aspects of Jewish separatism—even for
their philosemitic friends, is the Jewish doctrine of election. That Jews are
encouraged to think of themselves as "the chosen people" is misunder-
stood as an attempt to degrade their neighbors rather than to encourage
pride in their own community and a sense of intimacy with their God. We
may distinguish two circumstances under which resentment occurs. From
a Christian religious point of view, the Church is seen as superseding
Israel as God's elect community. For those subscribing to this view, Jews'
persistence in their claim of election can only be seen as perversity that
invokes resentment. We shall have more to say about the role of Church
doctrine in the genesis of antisemitism below. Secondly, many Christians
who are not concerned with Church doctrine resent Jewish claims of
chosenness. One non-Jewish patient was described who could be considered antisemitic by no criterion whatever. He favored Jews as friends and
colleagues, and welcomed a Jewish daughter-in-law into his family. Yet
he complained about Jewish self-confidence that he associated with the
claim of chosenness. He resented too their exclusiveness and resistance
to intermarriage. One would not be surprised to hear that he had a problem with self-confidence and was comfortable only in a select and limited
company. He might be said to have a subclinical social phobia. Feeling
that he belongs nowhere, he envied Jews who belonged to a cohesive
community and saw their self-confidence and separateness as traits that
he unconsciously envied but consciously saw as a fault.

On the other hand, in communities in which Jews have assimilated, or attempted actively to accommodate, they have been criticized as "pushy" and have been accused of attempting to invade the Christian community stealthily and to undermine it or take it over. This was a view that we heard from time to time from our forty-six patients. We must concede, I think, that when one's mind set calls for antisemitic sentiments, it can be rationalized by whatever behavior is being exhibited by the proximate Jewish community, whether separatism or accommodation or assimilation.

However, there is a way in which Jews are indeed responsible for facilitating antisemitism. I am referring to the defection of self-hating Jews who convert and then turn against the Jewish community. Sander Gilman's *Jewish Self-Hatred* (1986) tells the story of some of the more significant of these instances, the well-known Jews who became enemies of the Jewish people and did serious damage. Gilman proposes the idea that in hating other Jews, the self-hating Jew is externalizing the qualities within himself that he finds hateful. My own clinical experience complies with that hypothesis. Even today, many Jews who have opted out of the Jewish community share the antisemitism of their new co- religionists. In any case I shall make no effort to deal with Jewish antisemitism here.

How have Jews responded to antisemitism? This is a subject that we did not examine closely. I mention it here because it is relevant to the question of the contribution of Jews to the encouragement of antisemitism. In general, one can easily recognize three modes of response: Jews can defensively idealize Judaism and tighten the Jewish community and intensify its separatism; they can defensively attempt to undermine or otherwise attack the institution that degrades them; they can attempt to opt out of the Jewish community and into the major surrounding community, altering their manifest identity in the process, and sometimes turning aggressively against the community of their origin (cf. Rothman and Isenberg). All of these responses can and on occasion have earned the condemnation and enmity of the antisemites who elicited them and have used them to justify their antisemitism. This too is an issue that we have not attempted to examine.[6]

When reality issues, such as the African-American/Jewish difference over affirmative action or the Arab/Jewish differences over the existence of the State of Israel, create rivalry or hostility, the rival invokes and mobilizes the antisemitic sentiment that pervades the Western world, even when it has been latent and substantively irrelevant to the current issue. Our black patient who had Jewish competitors, when in the antisemitic mode, invoked the usual antisemitic stereotypes.

For reasons that we have yet to discuss, throughout their history, Christians have recurrently found it urgently necessary to invite, seduce, induce, harass, or persecute the Jews in the hope that they will convert to Christianity. Their refusal to do so in sufficiently large numbers has been a realistic provocation to many Christians, as for example, in the well-known case of Martin Luther. On the other hand when, as in fourteenth- and fifteenth-century Spain, they did convert in large numbers, they were discriminated against and persecuted as "new Christians."

### Jews, Psychoanalysis, and Antisemitism

As psychoanalysts, we like to think that our discipline is objectively scientific and neither dependent upon nor modified by any personal or social considerations. And yet historians of science will have no difficulty in citing instances in which the motivation and nature of scientific developments were determined by the social circumstances in which they arose. The influence of the needs of the industrial revolution upon the evolution of thermodynamics and the needs of the military upon the creation of all kinds of technologies are two obvious examples that come to mind. The influence of religion upon the healing professions, their motivation, form, and content is another. Not only is it true that to this day many hospitals bear religious denominational names, though funded and governed by sectarian supporters, but in addition religious institutions and considerations influence, if they do not actually constrain, such developments as techniques for overcoming sterility, genetic therapies, and the distribution of medical care. Yet these cultural influences do not invalidate the science, the development of which they have influenced. In the same way the validity of psychoanalysis is not limited by its having been created in a given social context, namely the antisemitism of *fin de siècle* Vienna. Another aspect of the relation between psychoanalysis and antisemitism is reflected in the common perception that psychoanalysis is a "Jewish science."

The decade between 1886 and 1896 saw two important changes in Freud's outlook and commitment. First he acknowledged and became concerned with the antisemitism of his society and resolved to deal with it by retreating into the Jewish community and its organizations for support. He saw that his professional advancement and the recognition of his achievements were limited by the antisemitism of his Christian colleagues and he absented himself from the Vienna Society of Physicians (see Klein). In 1886, he married but expressed resentment against participating in a religious marriage ceremony. In 1897, he joined the Vienna chapter of the International Order of B'nai B'rith. Here he became active, serving in several capacities and shortly organized a second chapter of B'nai B'rith for Vienna. Second, this was the decade during which Freud, decisively though with difficulty, turned away from neurology and the hope that studying the structure of the brain would yield insights into mental function (Ostow, 1990). The papers that he wrote during that decade reflect his troubled ambivalence, and in 1895, having completed the Project for Scientific Psychology, he discarded it unpublished and continued his psychoanalytic studies, unconcerned with anatomic and physiologic considerations. The first psychoanalytic concepts were voiced during that decade and in 1897 his first public presentation of these concepts was made before the B'nai B'rith Society.

This was the fourth decade of Freud's life and it marked a definitive turn to commitment to the Jewish community and to the discipline of psychoanalysis. These two commitments were joined at birth.

It was not until 1902 that Freud's activity in B'nai B'rith began to decline. It was then that he formed the first psychoanalytic circle and thereafter both the discipline of psychoanalysis and the movement occupied him completely. But his interest in Judaism, its religion and history, as well as the Jewish community, found expression in his writing. He recounted Jewish jokes in his essay "On Wit and Humour" (1905) as though he were trying thereby to learn the differences between Jews and others. In the discussion of his dreams (see especially, "My Uncle with the Yellow Beard") he referred to his thoughts about dealing with antisemitism, namely, should a Jew encourage his children to emigrate? He understood much of the opposition to the new discipline as inspired by antisemitism. "Rest assured," he wrote to Abraham, "that if my name were Oberhuber, in spite of everything, my innovations would have met with far less resistance" (Abraham and Freud, 1965). He selected Jung as his successor initially and at least partially because he hoped that Jung's leadership would prevent the labeling of psychoanalysis as a Jewish discipline. In many places he offered brief ideologic comments on the origins of antisemitism as we have observed above. Finally, his last work in the field of applied analysis, that is, *Moses and Monotheism* was devoted to the elucidation of the problem of the origin of the characteristics of the Jews and the Jewish community, and incidentally, the causes of antisemitism.

From its outset the psychoanalytic movement was Jewish, that is from 1902 when the psychoanalytic circle was formed, until 1907, every one of the twenty-some members was Jewish. In 1907, Carl Jung and Ludwig Binswanger became the first non-Jews to attend a meeting of the circle. In 1908 the circle welcomed its first non-Jewish members, Rudolf Urbantschitsch and Ernest Jones. The exclusive Jewishness of the early organized movement is explained by the fact that Freud's professional associates at the time were Jewish, and by the fact that the B'nai B'rith became the recruiting ground for the new movement.[7]

Despite the fact that psychoanalysis has developed in an antisemitic atmosphere, and despite the fact that antisemitism had left its imprint on Sigmund Freud and his early colleagues, outside of Freud's writings we find little in the psychoanalytic literature about the subject. I find that little short of amazing. A number of early analysts presumed to offer dynamic explanations for various Jewish religious rituals and doctrines. These are not among the most distinguished accomplishments of psychoanalysis. About antisemitism itself we find relative silence. I doubt that it was because they thought that antisemitism was essentially a group phenomenon and therefore individual psychodynamics had little to contribute to the subject. Sigmund Freud did indeed make a contribution to the psychodynamics of antisemitism. More likely they took its existence for granted as a given of their society, not relevant to the practice of psychoanalysis, much as we currently hesitate to offer psychodynamic explanations for political attitudes in the course of our work with our patients.

In the early 1930s, with the growing prominence of the Nazis in Germany, a beginning interest in the subject became evident and in 1939 *Moses and Monotheism* appeared, a work initiated in the early 1920s but not completed or published until just before Freud's death. While it purports to deal with the development of the Jewish people and to demonstrate that its current practices and beliefs derive from its early history, in fact, it defends the Jews against the accusations of their detractors.[8]

As I observed above, a number of Jewish analysts, having arrived in the United States or at other sanctuaries, each wrote an essay on antisemitism, appealing to obvious and standard mechanisms associated with prejudice, most of which had already been alluded to by Freud. However, the past two decades have seen a manifestation of interest in the traumatic impact of the Holocaust on survivors and their descendents in the psychoanalytic world and elsewhere (see Bergmann and Jucovy, 1982). The issue of antisemitism as a proper object for psychoanalytic study received a strong push on the occasion of the 1985 Congress of the International Psychoanalytic Association in Hamburg, the first such Congress since the Holocaust, on German territory. While there was enough opposition to the site of the meeting to have deterred a number of analysts who said that they might have attended a meeting located elsewhere, other analysts used the occasion to deal with the issue of antisemitism, its etiology and consequences, and current status, as a matter of legitimate professional concern. Discussions on the subject of the psychoanalytic study of antisemitism have been appearing more frequently in recent years as interest has been increasing, not only among Jewish analysts, but among their non-Jewish colleagues as well, and not only in the United States but in Europe and Latin America too.

The attitude of psychoanalysts to Judaism and Jews and to the Jewish religion is not irrelevant to our discussion of psychoanalysis and antisemitism. If one examines the writings of the early analysts toward religion and especially the Jewish religion, one finds almost exclusively negative comments. Religious observance is treated as a neurosis, a practice encouraged by Freud's relating it to obsessive compulsive neurosis. As I noted above, in the minutes of the Vienna Psychoanalytic Society, the only positive comments about the Jewish religion were made by Freud (Federn and Nunberg, vol. 3, p.273). The application of psychoanalytic analysis to ritual and liturgy results in only derogatory conclusions as for example, in the works of Reik and Abraham (Ostow, 1982). One may infer from this material that the early Jewish analysts had only contempt for their observant coreligionists, many or most of whom were East European Jews. The second and third generations of psychoanalysts have dealt no more kindly with religion than their forebears and mentors. Until very recent times—and in some places even now—religious belief, interest, and affiliation are looked upon with suspicion if not with disrespect, and are considered, at least tacitly, reason for refusal of advancement of a candidate or practicing analyst in professional organizations. I have no data about this point, but it has seemed to me that observant Jewish psychoanalysts are treated less generously in this regard than observant non-Jewish analysts. On the other hand, the revulsion against the Holocaust and the creation of a Jewish state in the past half century have permitted many analysts to assert an interest in Jewish affairs without having to take any interest in religion. The paradigmatic case is the secularism of most Israeli analysts. Asecular interest in Jewish affairs has become popular among Jewish analysts in recent decades, so that the 1979 Congress of the International Psychoanalytic Association was held in Jerusalem, and, under the leadership of Dr. Martin Wangh, psychoanalysts raised enough money in the late 1970s and 1980s to endow a Sigmund Freud Chair at the Hebrew University and to provide funds for its support. Indeed a sympathetic secular interest in Zionism and in Jewish political and social affairs was expressed in action by Freud and a few other analysts , mostly of the second and third generations, but was not initially shared by most Jewish analysts. A friend of mine who was a medical student in Vienna in the early thirties, visited Freud annually to accept his regular contribution for the support of the local Zionist youth organization. With respect to the early generations of analysts, if we consider their general derogation of the Jewish religion and its practitioners; their failure to express an interest in Jewish affairs and Jewish destiny until the confrontation with Nazism made these issues unavoidable; their reductionistic and simplistic efforts to "analyze" Jewish religious ritual and liturgy with which they were barely familiar, while simultaneously taking no psychoanalytic interest in antisemitism with which they were very familiar, we are forced to infer the existence of a degree of Jewish shame and self-hatred.

Returning to our argument, psychoanalysis has been associated with Judaism not only because of the circumstances of its origin but also for the following reasons. First, psychoanalysis and Judaism have shared a common fate. At its birth, psychoanalysis had to contend with the antisemitic forces that faced the Jews who promoted it. Thereafter, psychoanalysis flourished wherever the Jewish community flourished. Confronted with Nazism, psychoanalysis suffered along with the Jews, and survived only because its center moved westward as they did. Even today psychoanalysis is welcome and permitted to flourish only where and to the extent that Jews are. One might say that the tolerance toward each is a measure of the humanitarianism of the host community. In a sense each stands for humanitarianism and benefits from the humanistic attitude. But more directly, the commoness of their fate is based upon the fact that the discipline was created and promoted by Jews, that many of its distinguished scholars have been Jews, and that to this day, in most localities, Jews constitute a disproportionately large fraction of its members. The spread of psychoanalytic practice to Protestant Middle America, to Catholic Latin America, and its rebirth in a resurgent, tolerant Germany, has done little to dissipate the association of psychoanalysis with Judaism.

The second reason has to do more with the discipline than with the disciples. Classical Jewish scholarship has been an exegetical scholarship. Talmudic[9] and Midrashic[10] comments and arguments are each addressed to a specific verse in Scripture or to a specific verse in a previously written commentary. The prooftext conveys sanction to a new interpretation. It is because of this format that these later writings are often described as commentary on Scripture, whereas they actually use Scripture as a point of departure from which to make an argument that is relevant to the time and place of their composition. The psychoanalytic technique too is an exegetical one. A psychoanalyst examines everything his patient presents to him, reports of actual events, free associations, dreams, not only for their explicit meaning, but also for a hidden meaning, not obvious to the patient himself. The analysis is performed upon these texts by means of the application of a set of exegetical principles. For example, allusions are considered as valid as direct statements if not more so. Images are examined for their symbolic significance. One looks for displacement of emphasis, for externalization of inner conflict, for projection, internalization, reaction formation, and the effects of other classical defensive operations. At one point Karl Abraham described Freud's procedure as "essentially Talmudic." One might object that very few of the early analysts were familiar with Talmudic discourse. However the idea of exegetical study is well known as the Talmudic method.

Third, the same criticisms have been directed against Judaism and Jews and against psychoanalysis and psychoanalysts—usually by people who are antagonistic to both. Psychoanalysis is said to sanction immorality, to promote it, and thereby undermine civilization and Christian morality. This accusation is based upon obvious and usually deliberate

misunderstandings. The analyst argues that some forms of mental illness are brought about by the unsatisfactory resolution of unconscious
conflicts, many of them sexual in nature. He argues further that bring-
ing the conflict, both the original unconscious impulses and the oppos-
ing forces, into consciousness, can facilitate a realistic resolution, and
thereby alleviate the manifestations of the illness. The critic misreads
the encouragement to make the forbidden impulse conscious as encouragement to act upon it, and so he sees analysts as encouraging all forms
of immorality.

In the same way antisemites frequently greatly exaggerate the difference between Christian and Jewish ethics, promoting the myth that Jews
do not value and do not abide by the conventions of Christian morality.
Antisemites frequently contend that Jews are representatives of Satan,
eager to lead virtuous Christians into temptation and sin. They buttress
their arguments by reference to Jewish contributions to the creative arts
and to political and social liberalism, where indeed they have achieved
distinction. They overlook the fact that Jews have achieved equal distinction in the hard and soft sciences and that non-Jews have also contributed generously to the creative arts, and that creative art does not
necessarily conduce to immorality. The Jewish community is quite het-
erogeneous and those Jews who promote a greater openness in social
thinking and behavior are not, in doing so, reflecting traditional Jewish
values, although concern for the welfare of all members of society, mutual
responsibility and justice, and equity are well-known and celebrated
prophetic ideas. On the other hand, as I observed above, many Jews
respond to their being relegated to a marginal position in society, by
trying to undermine the system that defines them as marginal. Some of
their political activity can be viewed as so motivated. The antisemite
feels equally threatened by the psychoanalytic encouragement of self-
knowledge, and by the Jews' attempts to escape their marginality and
confuses the two.

## The Search For Case Material

Given the relation between psychoanalysis and Judaism in terms of
history of origins, character of discipline, and popular mythology, it
follows that one cannot expect analysis to serve as a truly disinterested
instrument for the study of antisemitism. As our project was essentially

a psychoanalytic one, an effort to apply the methods of depth psychology to the study of antisemitism, it became necessary for us to explore the limitations that the current practice of psychoanalysis entails.

From the point of view of both the patient who has any feelings about Jews, either favorable or unfavorable, psychoanalysis is a biased therapy. Antisemites are not likely to be attracted to it, even when the analyst is not Jewish. As our project was originally set up, we deliberately arranged to select for our membership Jewish analysts and non-Jewish analysts in equal number. We hoped in this way to balance the pro-Jewish biases of the former with the more dispassionate views of the latter. Obviously the device did not guarantee objectivity inasmuch as the non-Jewish analysts on the panel served because they were eager to be helpful in overcoming antisemitism. We also hoped that the non-Jews would be able to provide more plentiful case material than the Jews, who, we knew, seldom encountered pronounced antisemitism in sessions. In fact, we were surprised to find that the non-Jewish analysts too encountered little explicit antisemitism in their practice. Both Jewish and non-Jewish analysts reported that their practices were comprised of Jews and non-Jews in a ratio of about three to two. Nevertheless we had all observed that occasional patients insisted upon seeing only a non-Jewish analyst just as a number of anxious Jews insisted upon only a Jewish analyst.

We looked to our German and Austrian colleagues for more ample case material. We had not anticipated, though in retrospect we should have, that most of their patients had considerably stronger views about Nazism than about Jews. Frequently they were torn between submitting to the demands of their conscience in denouncing Nazism and antisemitism on the one hand, and of affirming loyalty to their parents who as often as not had been Nazis. The issue for them was really quite different from normal antisemitism or philosemitism, normal at least as we see it in the United States.

A second issue that complicated case finding was the fact that many psychoanalysts whether Jewish or non-Jewish, were not comfortable dealing with antisemitism, and therefore ignored it when they could. They feared liberating it into the analytic discourse. Some colleagues who practice group therapy told us that they deliberately abort discussion of antisemitism for fear that it might disrupt the group. Because antisemitism was ignored or minimized, we lacked associations, dream material, and genetic sources that might have thrown light on its psychodynamic basis. Therefore much case material was thin and uninformative. Why associational data were ignored was not self-evident. Presumably the Jewish analysts felt defensive and did not wish to seem so to their patients. The non-Jewish analysts also dealt with the subject fairly diffidently. They did not see it necessarily as an indication of pathology and psychoanalysts in general hesitate to deal with social or political issues in psychoanalysis for fear of imposing their own biases upon the patient. It follows that some psychoanalysts reported more about antisemitism explicitly dealt with than others. After we encountered this problem and discussed it, our members agreed that when they encountered the issue again, they would deal with it more explicitly and with greater interest. Anti-black prejudice was dealt with no more forthrightly than antisemitism, presumably for similar reasons. Our colleagues from Austria reported that the psychoanalysts shared some of the conflict and ambivalence of their patients and so tended to respect the anti-anti-Nazi feelings of some of them; or to lean over backwards too far in sympathizing with and justifying their Jewish patients.

We resolved the problem of inadequate case material in the following way. We considered some cases of patients who reported antisemitic fantasies and sentiments although they were not really practicing antisemites, that is, we studied the antisemitism of non-antisemites. We studied and discussed *Sophie's Choice* by William Styron and some stories from the collection of *Memoirs of an Anti-Semite* by Gregor Von Rezzori. Both books deal with antisemitic prejudice from an apparently friendly point of view. The latter deals with the author's conscious ambivalence toward Jews, expressing openly both antisemitic and philosemitic views, and trying to account for them on the basis of personal background and experience. The former falls into the category of works that can be considered communally shared vehicles for repressed, hidden personal prejudices and antisemitic or at least ambivalent attitudes. We discussed some of the essays written on our subject by our European colleagues, describing their experiences. Finally, we did obtain reports of a number of suitable cases.

Discussion of this material made us all aware of the fact that psychoanalysts presume a certain range of social and political opinions among patients, and within that range, do not analyze such opinions and prejudices. We take notice when a patient's response is inconsistent with group ideology. The presuppositions vary at different times and in different places. Our discussions with our German and Austrian colleagues made it clear that they regularly deal with issues that we scarcely recognize. We learned that we should attempt to familiarize ourselves with the political and social orientation of our patients, to analyze it to the extent that it is discordant with that of the surrounding population among whom the patient lives and with whom he identifies.

These considerations made us think more systematically about the circumstances under which patients are likely to introduce current events into their analytic sessions. When an event exerts a traumatic impact, for example, by virtue of its intensity, the patient is more likely to report it than an event that is not seriously traumatic. An incident that lends itself to the activation of one of the subject's active conflicts is likely to be reported. Patients who seek gratification in action within and upon the outside world are more likely to report incidental events. External events may be used as a defense against anxiety arising from internal conflict. An external event may be reported when it arouses a memory of a childhood trauma. External events are not reported when an individual's energies are exhausted in narcissistic concerns.

## Developmental and Dynamic Issues

In our pursuit of the mental mechanisms motivating prejudice in general and antisemitism in particular, we must address ourselves to the evolution of individual responses to the inner processes of maturation and to the outer circumstances of opportunity and danger. Prejudice is not a phenomenon imposed upon the adult, but rather the result of a number of processes initiated in the course of the unfolding of the personality. Obviously a full investigation of this subject would require a review of everything that psychoanalysts and developmental psychologists know about human development. Equally obviously I am not qualified to write such a review nor would it be appropriate for this book. In preparation for considering the data that we accumulated, I shall attempt to set down here briefly a few of the developmental mechanisms that I have found most relevant to our work.

Let us consider first the general ways in which we deal with the challenges of our worlds, both inner and outer. Anna Freud (Freud, A., 1981) points out that starting in very early childhood we are better prepared to deal with the dangers of the external world than with those of the internal world. She lists all of the common defenses employed against inner turmoil: denial, externalization, projection, internalization, isolation, and rationalization. The normal ego functions of attention, perception, memory, reason, reality testing, secondary process thinking, and understanding of causality make it possible for the child to orient and alert himself to danger from the outside world. One common defense of childhood, externalization, serves to make internal danger seem to be external and thus less threatening. She observes further that even in the period of latency, that is, the interval between age four or five and puberty, when the intense strivings of the Oedipal period are relatively subdued and better controlled by the ego, the child is not able to relinquish or relax his defenses. Adolescents on the other hand, seem more interested in internal mental processes; they desire insight. But again externalization occurs: "Thoughts, wishes, fantasies, fears, and judgments are translated into concern with cosmic, political or philosophical matters. They are, thus, as far removed from the personal sphere as possible. Obviously, such adolescents hope to understand what happens in themselves in the less frightening terms of the world at large." Most adults are scarcely more insightful but even those who are, under stress, regress in mental function to more primitive modes including the employment of such externalization defenses.

The attempt to externalize is so powerful that it prevails not only over external reality when the latter offers no basis for inner misery, but it ignores it even when it does. For example, during the plague of 1348, it was clear that it was an epidemic that was causing widespread death. But the populace, suffering the pain of loss and the fear of their own death, found it necessary to attribute the catastrophe to an external agent, the Jews. This despite the fact that it was evident that the Jews were dying from the plague as well, and that there was no conceivable way they could have caused the epidemic. Again, Hitler and his Nazis found their support among the population suffering economic privation and undertook a war of conquest in order to overcome it. But the inner distress that was caused by the economic stress had to find a more personal, animate cause, the Jews. The Jews were considered responsible for the economic depression and for the war and the defeat. In other words, given inner distress of whatever source, whether internally or externally provoked, the cause for that distress must be attributed to an external destructive force. As I shall note again below, the antisemite has two sources of pain, two enemies: whatever external real inimical force maybe discernible, and an illusory one contrived to explain the existence of the former and the suffering it creates.

The external world, of course, provides us with trauma, accident, injury, illness, but also love relationships, gratifying work, and membership in our own community as well as encounters with communities other than ours. We devoted several meetings to the subject of group membership because group membership and group motivation make the difference between sentiment and persecution. When the child arrives at the stage of latency, he or she encounters other children in the playground, in the classroom, at the homes of neighbors and friends. His maturing drives lead him to seek out such contacts, to make friends and to play with them. At the same time, these friends and their parents present as strangers, and as such, they seem not only attractive but sometimes as dangerous. Obviously many factors contribute to determining how the stranger will be greeted, including the child's mood, his or her maturational readiness for dealing with strangers, the circumstances under which the meeting occurs, the response to the new, and so on. It is at this point that we see the first groups begin to form. Groups of two or three and more cohere but usually manage to exclude others. In fact, the issue of inclusion and exclusion often causes gratification or grief among these children.

In a book entitled *You Can't Say You Can't Play*, Vivian Gussin Paley, a kindergarten teacher, reports the prejudices of latency-age children and their responses to her efforts to overcome them. Unfortunately, she considered it irrelevant to try to ascertain the basis for the selection of one or another child as the victim of prejudicial exclusion from the group. From her account it seemed to me that at times it was black children who were rejected by white children, but that is not clear. What is clear is that the children almost insist upon the right to reject. "But what is the whole point in playing?" one little girl asked when the teacher introduced the topic of overcoming prejudice. These observations force one to conclude that as early as kindergarten, it becomes important for some children to exclude others and by so doing, to victimize them. Perhaps it is an expression of the same tendency that finds expression within the family as sibling rivalry (Paley, 1992).

Usually the group coheres around the qualities that the individual children have in common so that they exclude one or more children who may differ in some visible way. What is important is the fact that exclusion and rejection start with group formation and must be seen as an intrinsic part of it.

We shall discuss the psychology of group formation in chapter 5. However here I should like to anticipate that discussion by noting that clinical experience suggests that to the individual, the group symbolizes mother, presumably because it provides a sense of security and protection. This observation has been made by several analysts independently, for example, Chasseguet-Smirgel (1985) from the individual point of view and Scheidlinger (1974) from the group point of view. Starting with latency, groups function as a home base and refuge, but also as a source of strength and morale. In the primitive, fundamentalist type group, the members identify with each other and with the group, so that group membership becomes a salient part of their identity. In that mutual identification of the members of the group with each other, they find the security they seek (Freud, 1913, 1921).

The capacity and desire to identify with a group are normal. In pathology, one may be unable to identify, or be too ready to identify.

We ordinarily think of identification as the experience of feeling at one, or united with someone who shares the contemporary world with us, or behaving as though we were that person. But it is clear that we also often identify with figures from the past, an ancestor, a distinguished historical figure, or with past members of our own group. In that case we obtain a sense of continuity with the past. That leads us to the notion that to maintain continuity is actually one purpose of identification with whatever group encompasses both ourselves and the object of our identification. The experience of continuity and the experience of identification are subjectively the same and serve the same function. If these suppositions are correct, then identification with the historical group as well as with the contemporary group conveys the assurance of retaining the infantile feeling of remaining attached to mother.

Returning to the latency groups, in perhaps every instance, it consists either exclusively of boys or exclusively of girls. Gender homogeneity seems to be an essential element in the overall homogeneity of the group. Boys identify more easily with other boys, and girls more easily with other girls. One can speculate about the reasons. Perhaps the anatomy of the other gender is visually repugnant. That repugnance is not overcome until puberty and its endocrine changes create sexual desire. Whatever the explanation the regularity of the phenomenon is impressive. Parenthetically and paradoxically, the little boy ensconced in his all-male group experiences the kind of comfort and security that unconsciously remind him of his comfort in his mother's embrace. The group is the mother substitute. Achieving this kind of substitute gratification in the group, the little boy can take steps to distance himself from his mother. Membership in the group encourages identification with his father. On the other hand, girls in the female group can identify more fully with their mothers. Their attraction to their fathers would tend to draw them out of the group commitment. Later, when sexual desire commences, the transition to heterosexuality is marked by the phenomenon of the girls' identifying with each other in their common devotion to an individual male idol or to a specific group of men. Sooner or later increasing sexuality pulls the children out of their exclusive same-gender orientation, and the same-gender groups weaken. In early adolescence, mixed-gender groups begin to appear as the single-gender groups fade. The groups develop common interests, for example: athletic competition. Clubs focus on mutual interests such as stamp collecting. Groups organize to engage in dramatic productions or choral singing. With increasing maturity, mixed-gender groups organize around common communal concerns, political, religious, community oriented, scientific, or artistic.

Gender homogeneous groups become fraternities or sororities. Groups adopt a definite social point of view. They may form along the fracture lines of society and so acquire strong prejudicial commitments. Discrimination becomes a characteristic aspect of their functioning and under certain special circumstances, they may proceed from discrimination to persecution. It is for this reason that militant ideologic movements emphasize the recruitment of adolescents into parallel youth organizations. The acceptance of group discipline, ideology, and, as we shall see, mythology, involves the setting up of superego[11] structures that may be congruent with the superego nuclei established under parental influence, or that may be inconsistent with these. Such group superego structures may supersede early parental influence and lead to behavior that may be thoroughly inconsistent with it, as we saw in the extreme case of the behavior of the Nazis.

In adult life we join with and disaffiliate from groups in accordance with our changing interests. Some of these may be common gender groups, but most are mixed.

Under stress, we tend to regress to the kind of group that resembles the earliest groups of childhood. In these regressive adult groups, the feeling of group identity becomes more important than the common external interests. In some, but not all of these groups, gender homogeneity or gender dominance again prevails. These are often all-male groups from which women are banished or pushed to the periphery.

The element that interests us especially is the demand for homogeneity in the primitive group. The exception, the anomaly, the unique is excluded. The exceptional quality may be a matter of skin color, of obesity, of language or accent, or disability or disfigurement. Here we find probably the earliest manifestations of prejudice. When the difference between gentile and Jew is salient in the community, that may become the basis for exclusion even at such an early age. Given our interest in prejudice in general and antisemitism in particular, a question that interests us is: under what circumstances do the normal or common adolescent and adult groups retain or regress to the intolerance of difference that prevails so absolutely in the latency groups?

Let us turn now to the sources of distress that elicit the defensive measures, individual and group, that we have been considering. We shall find that they all lend themselves to prejudicial thinking and acting.

Of course reality, though it promises gratifications, threatens all of us with accident, injury, misfortune, illness. We may lose a loved person, we may lose our jobs, our community may fragment and wither. Though, as Anna Freud tells us, we are better organized to deal with externally imposed insults than with inner pain, nevertheless, when we do not succeed in escaping a serious blow, we experience inner pain. When the pain exceeds a certain degree of intensity, an individual threshold, inner defenses take over.

The most familiar such defense perhaps is denial. Denial in some instances permits optimism that can be life saving. However, in other cases, it deters effective remedial action. In earliest infancy when, presumably, the child is unable to distinguish inner from outer causes of distress, the cry will normally call a child's mother to provide prompt relief. The readiness to call a parent for rescue continues to prevail during most of childhood. During adolescence, however, when the inner struggle to achieve independence reaches its height, the victim may hesitate to call for help. Nevertheless at all stages in life, when confronted with a desperate situation, even the most rational among us hopes—and many of us believe—that rescue will come at the hands of a messianic figure, if only we call or entreat or behave in the right way. The messiah, the supernatural rescuer, is the image of the infant's mother reconfigured to comply with the conventionally accepted religious imago.

The complement to the rescuer is the imago of a source of evil. The source of evil for the infant may be the unresponsive mother herself, or a fantasied malicious individual who defeats the mother, or a rival, perhaps a sibling or the father, who distracts the mother. Even when the injurious agent is visibly external, the pain causes the child to attribute the absence of relief to a fantasied hostile force deliberately targeting the individual out of malice or in punishment for some real or imagined misbehavior. As we noted above, the child is now left with two enemies, the realistic one and the fantasied one. Even when the impinging agent is external, the locus of the pain is internal and the child may respond to his experience of both as though they are external. Here again we have an infantile mechanism that is not eradicated, merely suppressed, with the passage of time. Under stress, mental regression occurs, and otherwise reasonable adults too search for a source of evil. What this has to do with prejudice and persecution and specifically antisemitism, is that encouraged by the teachings of the early Church, Christians in many ages have assigned that role to Jews. We shall elaborate this issue below.

The individual's interests are impinged upon by rivalry from the outside. If there is indeed a rival for the mother's love and affection, the child, even during its first year will become aware of it. Actual rivalry may threaten or damage our interests at every phase of life. When the rival is dealt with realistically, whether tolerated, compromised with, or combatted, we have no problem. Prejudice results when the rival is assigned the role of a supernatural—or unnatural—source of evil. Rivalry has been a source of difficulty in many societies in history. However, when it has caused malicious stereotyping, and the rival has been endowed with diabolic characteristics, persecution has followed.

Some dangers are usually virtual, that is, unreal, though on occasion they may become actual. The stranger reaction of age six to nine months is now generally recognized. Starting at that time the infant who has already begun to distinguish between the face of its mother or caregivers and the faces of others, now becomes fearful in the presence of the latter. Child analysts attribute this phenomenon to danger created by the infant's incipient mobility. If the infant did not distinguish automatically and effectively between its mother and strangers, it might pursue the latter and so encounter danger. Curiosity and an interest in the novel is restrained by stranger anxiety so that the infant is protected against unwise exploration. This anxious response to the presence of the stranger binds the child to the nuclear family. As the child matures, cognitively informed caution gradually displaces the automatic stranger anxiety and in a dynamic relationship with normal curiosity, governs the child's approach and distancing behavior.

However the stranger's potential for good and evil persists through adult life so that, as we shall see below, the stranger becomes a mythical figure. Where a virtual source of evil must be found, the outsider, the new immigrant, the stranger who lives outside the walls may be labeled as that source and may be persecuted as such. In the absence of that need to externalize the source of evil, the stranger may be greeted as an object of benign curiosity, as a potential friend and ally. The interplay between familiar and strange, and in the strange between benign and malignant, leads us to the device of the family romance which we shall examine below.

The term strange applies to at least two distinguishable concepts: first, the unfamiliar which we have just discussed, and second, the unnatural or unexpected. The latter category includes the anomalous, the discordant, the inappropriate, and the misplaced. In the literature of child psychiatry, some percepts are labeled discrepant in the sense that "they activate a cognitive schema but cannot be assimilated into it" (Lewis, M., 1971, p. 414). Thus the discrepancy experience could arise from the unreadiness of the child's cognitive apparatus as well as from the unexpectedness of the stimulus. It would seem to me that the contrast between what is presented and what is expected is maximized when the presentation is "unnatural." That term, of course, cannot be rigidly defined, for it does not imply any specifiable, logical criteria. Yet there are *Gestalten* that elicit alarm reactions from animals and humans alike: a dead or mutilated conspecific, or a combination of features that does not occur in nature, such as the creatures of myth and fantasy, composites of elements of various natural creatures, chimeras. The unnaturalness often seems to acquire the characteristics of the supernatural. But it is not only demons that inspire alarm. Angels too are composite creatures. When encountered in myth they are usually greeted with alarm and awe, and the human who encounters them must be assured of their benign nature—when they are indeed benign. Horror of the unnatural, weird, and uncanny persists into adult life, attenuated perhaps, but seldom completely obliterated. A disabled or mutilated person is called a cripple who in his unnatural appearance is unsettling so that the observer becomes anxious and antagonized. When the appearance of the newcomer is strange in this sense, he becomes a threatening figure and elicits a hostile response.

We know little about the origin of aversions and preferences. Strongest during childhood, many are attenuated later in life. They seem to overlap with or metamorphose into what we call taste, aesthetic preferences. And we know that taste, in music and art for example, changes in the history of the culture as well as in the history of the individual.

When an individual or group becomes the object of prejudice, making the victim look strange stigmatizes him as dangerous and a target worthy of degradation. In the history of antisemitic persecution we find many attempts to make the Jew seem strange or anomalous: by forcing him to wear distinctive and ugly clothing, by requiring him to wear a prominent identifying badge, by representing him as ugly and weird in caricature. Trachtenberg (1943, pp. 44ff.) records a number of bizarre physical characteristics that were attributed to Jews, especially in the Middle Ages. Jews, it was believed, had horns and a tail and in this way resembled the devil with which they were associated. Jews were characterized by a foul odor, the *foetor judaicus*. Jewish men were said to menstruate. Yerushalmi (1971, pp. 123ff.) quotes a Spanish court dignitary of the seventeenth century, Dr. Juan de Quinones de Benavente who described these and other idiosyncracies in a treatise on Jews.[12]

A form of strangeness that I have not mentioned is chaos, disorder. Unpredictability is a major source of anxiety, and orderliness reassures us. We see a hypertrophied need for order in the autistic child, and the anxiety that appears when his concept of orderly structure is violated. The experiences of anomaly that I have been discussing are usually individual. However, a breakdown in social structure creates the anxiety of unpredictability in the entire population and so is inclined to favor group cohesion and regression.

In a book intriguingly entitled *Purity and Danger,* Mary Douglas elaborates the concepts of pollution and taboo (1966). Dirt, she says, is matter out of place. While the concept of pollution relates to violation of orderly structure, it is disorder of a specific kind. Pollution means that the sacred is violated by contact with an impurity. More specifically, certain substances are considered impure because they are excretions or secretions of the body or because they are associated with disease or death. In some cultures, these impure fluids include any flux whether normal or pathologic, such as menstrual blood, semen, and even saliva. If we look for ethologic antecedents, we may associate the need to avoid pollution with the animal's instinctive aversion to fouling its own nest. On the human level, the toilet training of the infant may be seen as the paradigm of the avoidance of pollution. Soiling of the parents' living space is forbidden and is likely to bring retribution. Every religion publishes clear-cut rules against the polluting violation of its sancta. If these are violated, the community will suffer.

This concept too relates to the phenomenology of antisemitism. The idea that the Jews contaminate the blood of their Christian neighbors appears, as we shall see, in Spanish antisemitism of the fifteenth and sixteenth century and again in *Mein Kampf* and other Nazi documents. Apparently in each case, the existing distress of the host population was interpreted by them as a form of disease caused by impurity, and the impurity was being introduced by the Jews. Notice that the concept of impurity and disease are combined here. The Jews are held responsible for the physical or emotional illness of the population among whom they live, whether by poisoning wells in the Europe of 1348, or contaminating Spanish blood in the fifteenth century, or German blood in the twentieth century, or by injecting black babies with HIV virus as a black American demagogue recently proclaimed.

Mental pain can arise from entirely internal sources. Such pain may come about because of miscarried internal regulation of emotion. Normally when we tend toward depression, a corrective mechanism is activated so as to move us back to an equilibrium position. Similarly when we tend toward euphoria, we are automatically corrected to median position. Ordinarily this mechanism operates silently and permits only slight mood swings. However, when the regulation is imperfect, we may be left with a state of depression, mild or more severe, that has no discernible external cause. As we observed above, the usual response is to assign responsibility for the distress to some external cause, a source of evil often identified with a population that is the victim of prejudice. This phenomenon seems to have occurred frequently in the history of antisemitism.

No less illusory is the classical Jewish position that suffering is the consequence of sin. Although it is illusory, it usually leads to socially constructive rather than destructive behavior.

Consideration of case reports in which individuals gave expression to antisemitic sentiments left us wondering at each point how the patient acquired these sentiments. There was no question but that in every case, the patient's individual antisemitism was congruent with that of the community to which he belonged. However it was not always evident that it was group sentiment that determined the individual's prejudice. It sometimes seemed that the individual attached himself to a specific antisemitic group because it suited his own prejudices. In those cases, he brought his prejudices to the group rather than vice versa. In many cases, the patient's antisemitism resembled that of one or both parents and could be attributed to their influence. In others the patient became actively antisemitic though he reported that his parents had not influenced him in that direction, having set an example of tolerance.

Parental influence is generally not very subtle. It expresses itself in dinner table conversation. It is imposed upon the child by warning him against certain friends and by determining which friends could be invited to the house. We had no data about when this influence was exerted, but presumably it was not limited to any one brief period in childhood. We also had no data about whether the influence was exerted by teaching or by example. Did the children obey their parents or did they identify with them, or both? Or was that difference irrelevant?

I have in this section pointed out certain developmental and dynamic mechanisms that come into play in the evolution of prejudice and persecution, and especially prominently in antisemitism. I have drawn attention to a number of sources of distress, realistic, virtual, and subjective, and have described the individual response to them by externalization, and the group response, namely, group regression to the need for homogeneity and intolerance of deviation and less a matter of history than it seemed then.

## Notes

1. As we shall see, for some promotors of antisemitic views antisemitism is a phasic phenomenon. Sombart's opinions of the Jews were phasic, or ambivalent, often negative, sometimes positive.

2. In toto. We started with fifteen. The total number involved was seventeen. Because of losses and acquisitions, there were fifteen at the end of the project.
3. The history of the term and its vicissitudes are given by M. Zimmerman (1986). Although Marr is often said to have had Jewish antecedents, Zimmerman finds no evidence supporting that contention. Zimmerman's biography tells us that Marr actually oscillated between philosemitism and antisemitism—as many antisemites do.
4. For a discussion of the concept of a "Semitic race," see B. Lewis, (1986), who demonstrates that it is derived from the concept of a Semitic set of languages but that it has no other demonstrable basis in fact.
5. Similar views are expressed by Jews who like to believe that antisemitism could be eradicated if Jews would behave better.
6. The subject of the Jewish response to antisemitism has been treated extensively in the following: Roskies, D.G.(1984) *Against the Apocalypse,* Cambridge, MA: Harvard University Press; Mintz, A.(1984) *Hurban: Responses to Catastrophe in Hebrew Literature,* New York: Columbia University Press; Reinharz, J.(1987) *Living with Antisemitism: Modern Jewish Responses,* Hanover, NH: University Press of New England; Schorsch, I.(1972) *Jewish Reactions to German Anti-Semitism, 1870–1914,* New York: Columbia University Press and Philadelphia: Jewish Publication Society; Baron, S.W. and Wise, G.(1977) *Violence and Defense in the Jewish Experience,* Philadelphia: Jewish Publication Society. See also Ostow, M.(1980) "The Jewish Response to Crisis," *Conservative Judaism,* vol.33, no. 4. pp. 3–25.
7. Elisabeth Brainin adds: In 1938 nearly 65 percent of all medical doctors in Vienna were Jews, because until the end of the last century there was a *numerus clausus* and then they could study and universities were open for everybody. It was nearly the same percentage of Jewish lawyers. Doctors and lawyers were professions where one could work independently in one's own office, without being employed and they had a high social standing. That was also an important reason why the first analysts were Jews.
8. For a discussion of the implications of *Moses and Monotheism,* see Yerushalmi, Y.H.(1991) *Freud's Moses: Judaism Terminable and Interminable,* New Haven: Yale University Press.
9. Judaism as we know it today is a religion based upon rabbinic teachings which were formulated in a collection called the Mishnah as a series of principles during the first two centuries before, and the first two centuries of the Common Era (a nondenominational term that designates that period of history that begins with what in Christian tradition is called Anno Domini). These principles were then elaborated and interpreted in a series of discussions and debates from the beginning of the third to the end of the fifth century. This material is called the Gemara. The word Talmud applies either to the combination of Mishnah and Gemara or to the Gemara alone. These documents contain the basic teachings of rabbinic Judaism.
10. The term Midrash designates a genre of rabbinic literature which is exegetical in form but homiletic in intent. It is structured as a series of commentaries on Scripture. The various collections of Midrashim date from before the Common Era to the thirteenth century.
11. The superego is the hypothetical psychic structure that sets ideals and judges behavior in the light of these ideals.

12. The fact that these features were not observed by Christians who had immediate contact with Jews, did not dispel the stereotype. Stereotypes are myths and myths are not invalidated by reality. Even today antisemites distinguish between individual Jews whom they know and consider friends, and Jews as a group who bear the mythical, undesirable traits. See for example the letter of Loewenstein's patient, page 80.

# 2

# Study of Clinical Data

Despite the paucity of clinical material, by advertising our interests in various ways, we were able to study ten case histories in some depth, five men and five women, and in addition considered four cases less intensively, three men and one woman. Five others, all men, were mentioned briefly.

Our conclusions would be more persuasive and more interesting if these data could be presented here. However, considerations of confidentiality preclude publication and so I shall merely describe the findings in general, illustrating specific points with brief vignettes.

The cases were presented by our own group primarily, but we were also fortunate to have been given some material by colleagues, including some from abroad. For this favor we are indebted to Drs. Alvin Frank, Helene Bass, Muriel Morris, and Edith Schwartz from the United States; Norman Rosenblood from Canada; Elisabeth Brainin and Samy Teicher from Vienna; Karen Brecht from Heidelberg; and Gertrud Hardtmann from Berlin.

Only one of the patients presented to us was so committed to antisemitic activity and active identification with Nazis and neo-Nazis that he sought them out and attended neo-Nazi meetings. Two others did not hesitate to join like-minded friends in complaining about Jews or excluding them from their neighborhoods and organizations, but antisemitism was not a major item on their agenda. In two other cases, it was clear that the patient was using antisemitic comments in order to provoke the analyst. Both patients indulged in perverse sexual gratifications. Their antisemitism was prominent but was only one aspect of their generally perverse and hostile character.

For the American cases, in the absence of active antisemitism, there was little occasion for the discussion of antisemitic sentiments

43

during the course of their analytic treatment. By contrast, for the European cases, their attitudes toward Jews, for or against, could scarcely be avoided, since in all instances the patient's parents had been involved in the antisemitism of the Nazi period, one way or another. In two American instances, the appearance of antisemitic sentiments in the manifest content of dreams surprised the dreamer for neither had consciously realized that he or she was harboring such emotions. In fact, in one case the dreamer continued to deny that his dream expressed any antisemitic stereotypes. In other cases, antisemitic comments were made during analytic sessions, generally without much intensity and without the patient's or the analyst's attributing much importance to them.

### General Observations

We found that those patients who exhibited the most militant or active antisemitism, were people who had difficulty in controlling their anger in general. They seemed to fall into such diagnostic categories as borderline personality disorder or adult attention deficit disorder. None of our patients was considered psychotic. One is not likely to encounter many psychotics among analytic patients. Only the most militant, the patient who associated with neo-Nazis, was thought likely to participate in an active antisemitic political movement if one existed within his reach. We inferred that a problem in the disposition of aggressiveness might conduce to militant antisemitism.

Some individuals, as we observed in the previous section, seemed to have difficulty in resolving inner conflict without displacing it onto the outside world. Most of us have difficulty with Oedipal problems, with rivalry, with self control, and we try to prevent these problems from inducing inappropriate behavior. Others however, can deal with these problems only when roles are assigned to other individuals, with whom one can experience the conflict in real life. This type of person is especially likely to find antisemitism a convenient issue around which he can attempt to resolve the conflict.

For a number of individuals, the antisemitism was "ego syntonic" but "superego dystonic." That is, they acknowledged antisemitic sentiments, they "owned" them, but they felt guilty and ashamed of their sentiments. This attitude, probably a fairly common one in the United

States, is clearly articulated in a letter sent to Dr. Rudolph M. Loewenstein, a distinguished psychoanalyst, by a former patient after the Israel War of Independence in 1948.

My reactions to the recent Jewish successes in Palestine have come as somewhat of a surprise and relief to me. There had always been a conflict between a more or less socialist point of view, as well as sympathy for the underdog, and an undercurrent of anti-Semitism, which as we know came from "way back." I took no position on the Palestinian question. Jewish nationalism was no solution. Of course under the circumstances, one couldn't help favoring the Jewish side, for all the various objective reasons, and then common justice demands that one... but then it was always common justice demanding that one... it was never any real sympathy for the Zionist cause.

I just knew it was going to be just another one of those lost causes. They were going to get pushed around as usual and sold down the river. And I hadn't done anything about it. I wasn't going to do anything about it. But it still gave me a bad feeling. They were always on the spot, sort of hopeless, helpless, on my conscience, with their hand outstretched and maybe looking in my direction. It was rather uncomfortable.

All these stories about Haganah and Irgun being well organized and representing a certain strength, were just stories. When the showdown came they'd be a pushover. It all seemed out of character and contrary to precedent. I thought of the Jews as eternal foreigners, city people who belonged behind a counter in some buying and selling game with a pretty high rate of profit in their favor. Not a very wholesome lot. Then always being herded into rather disreputable and dirty ghettos or worse, concentration camps—innocently of course. Always running with their tails between their legs from one tragedy to another. Everybody's stepchildren. I felt sorry for them and knew they were wronged. But I couldn't possibly identify with people like that. I couldn't really feel anything for their fool cause. Too many shopkeepers and too damn many martyrs!

Then there were all the other Jews—the super-Jews one heard so much about—all the big names. Most fields of science, the arts and politics seem slightly overloaded with "distinguished" Jewish names. I never resented their success. In fact I rather enjoyed the rather exotic touch and it more or less illustrated what I would have liked to believe, that they were just as good as anyone else. If they seemed a bit better, I didn't really mind, it just made all that business about the ghettos and concentration camps harder to bear. The point is, that it didn't bring them closer to home either. Einstein or Freud or any of those over talented individuals don't remind me much of the people I know any more than those martyrs or the little greaser behind the counter. The fact of course that I do know a lot of Jews is beside the point. They were just friends, and my antisemitism, except in a very veiled form, was usually felt, or directed, against the Jews I didn't know. When I thought of "Jews" I just didn't think of regular ordinary people. They didn't have a history either, except of being kicked around, and they didn't have a country where you could "place" them like other people.

Then a few weeks ago, as the Palestinian situation began to reach a crisis, news of Jewish successes kept filling the papers. It was more than just resistance. These incidents began to look more and more like real military victories. Newspaper reporters discussed the relative military strength of both sides, with the general consensus of opinion putting the balance in favor of the Jews. This was a relief from the high-minded appeals of the liberal press. Maybe they were well organized after all...well equipped. I looked at the illustrations of the training camps with new eyes. They had suddenly become respectable...not a few desperadoes but a people with an army like everyone else, fighting for national independence. From what the papers said it looked like a pretty good outfit. With half a break they could probably clean up on the Arabs. The bastards weren't a pain in the neck any more! They were just regular guys with a tough job on their hands.

I thought of the old Bible stories...the Promised Land, the Siege of Jericho, King David and all that. It was part of my history too. I'd been brought up on that stuff. But somehow I had never been able to reconcile the hero tales of the Children of Israel with my other conception of the Jews. Now it all began to make sense. These were really the people the Bible was talking about. I didn't have to feel sorry for the Jews any longer. I could feel with them. I know how my grandmother would have felt. And I do too. "We stand at Armageddon, and we battle for the Lord." (Loewenstein, Rudolph M., *Christians and Jews: A Psychoanalytic Study*, International Universities Press, Madison, CT, pp.22–24. 1951, reprinted with permission)

For some others, the antisemitism was "ego dystonic." They rejected the idea that they harbored any antisemitic thoughts. One patient who was described to us was amazed when an explicit reference to the Holocaust appeared in one of his dreams, following a disappointment by a Jewish girlfriend.

Evidently, neither antisemitism or philosemitism is an unmixed sentiment.

## Transference, Externalization, Displacement, and Projection

Most Jewish analysts and occasionally non-Jewish analysts too, encounter antisemitic comments on occasions when the transference turns negative. Typically at a certain point in the analysis, a male patient may come to feel that he is in danger of some form of persecution or abuse or homosexual seduction or rape by his male analyst. At that time he might comment on the analyst's Jewishness, or the Jewish origins of the analytic profession and its founders. At that time, he might recall that he had been warned that Jews might take his money or take advantage of him in some other way. In one such instance, the patient reported becoming aware that he was passing a Jewish institution as he drove to his analyst's office. As he did so, he imagined that a circumcised Jew would castrate him and have intercourse with his wife. Commonly the occasion might be an actual conflict of interest such as the question of raising the fee in a long-lasting treatment.

A Christian clergyman had been taken into treatment by a Jewish analyst at a low fee, as a courtesy, out of respect for his calling and in view of his limited resources. At one point in a generally successful treatment, he inherited a sum of money that permitted him to purchase a vacation home in the country. The analyst suggested that he might consider raising the fee though to a sum that was still less than the analyst's usual fee. The patient agreed promptly but on the occasion of the next session, he reported a dream that clearly represented classical antisemitic views that Jews were greedy, although the term Jew is not mentioned in the manifest dream content, and although the patient denied the sentiment. It is not irrelevant that the patient's father had been a moderately successful businessman who had wished his son to follow in his footsteps. The son started to prepare for a career in business but a conflict, the nature of which never clearly emerged, caused him to abandon that route and opt for a career in the church, which of course, provided a standard of living clearly lower than that of his parents. The request to raise the fee not only called upon his financial resources, but also revived the old struggle with his father about the importance of money and about a vocation. The dream involved the typical accusation of Jewish materialistic preoccupations with money.

The occasion for turning against the analyst might be a feeling of special warmth and affection. The patient might invoke his fear of his own father, whether as an Oedipal threat or, in a negative reaction to his love for his father. These negative feelings originally generated in the son/father relation are now transferred onto the analyst. Both the father's hostility and his love might be perceived as threats. Whatever indoctrination the patient had had as a child about the dangers posed by Jews, will then be recalled and mentioned in the analysis. In most instances an Oedipal constellation was clearly visible. I recall from my own clinical experience that when non-Jewish patients were doing well and pleased with the analysis and me, they would voice philosemitic sentiments, and when they were doing badly, they would voice antisemitic sentiments. To generalize, when the analyst is seen by the patient as a transference image of the threatening Oedipal father, his Jewishness is likely to be noted.

Sometimes a challenge would come from an authority figure who was Jewish, someone other than the analyst. In such cases, the analyst's

Jewishness was nevertheless likely to be mentioned in a pejorative context. Under similar circumstances a female analyst too could be drawn into the antisemitic net, and some of our women colleagues reported such incidents.

Rivalry with a contemporary, colleague, competitor, when the rival is Jewish, is no less likely to invoke antisemitic sentiments than challenge by an authority figure. That is, sibling rivalry can evoke antisemitic feelings as effectively as Oedipal rivalry. We see this in both professional and business competition. This kind of rivalry is likely to give rise to accusations that Jews are materialistic and money hungry, reflecting the Christian religious characterization of Jews as carnal rather than spiritual. In one instance an occasion drew a non-Jew's attention to the fact that his new non-Jewish wife's previous lover had been Jewish. It was then, after years in analysis with a Jewish analyst, that he first made critical remarks about Jewish men, and observed that his analyst would not be welcome at his parents' country club.

Antisemitic thoughts are generated as often by feelings of being excluded as by other forms of rivalry. Commonly a non-Jew will make Jewish friends and associate with them with good will and generosity of spirit. At some point he or she may experience rejection by a Jew. A romantic attachment might come to an end because the religious difference precludes marriage. The non-Jew might perceive that even though his friendship is valued, nevertheless he is regarded or treated differently from Jewish friends and colleagues. The consequent resentment might assume antisemitic form. At times the feeling of exclusion might become inappropriately intense compared to the relatively minor provocation. Jewish separatism certainly gives rise to such feelings of rejection and to the antisemite's complaints that Jews are exclusive, that they consider themselves superior and really believe that they are the chosen people.

In a particularly poignant example of this mechanism, a seven-year-old child first commented on the items of Jewish decor that she encountered in her analyst's office, but only after she became aware that the analyst had children of her own when one of them had intruded into her session. Drawing upon sources of antisemitic information that she had not previously disclosed, she announced that she was "allergic to Jews," that they don't believe in God, that they "go down" rather than up and that "their country does bad things to other people." The child had been sensitized to separation and exclusion by the early divorce of her parents and by several moves from one continent to another within her brief lifespan.

A Polish Catholic who had been denied a job as a school teacher, probably because her heavy accent would have made it difficult for young children to understand her, came to believe that the Jews on the board of education had conspired to exclude her. She had been brought up in Poland on antisemitic notions but, because of her personality difficulties, associated almost only with Jewish friends, and complained that they did not trust Poles as friends and therefore would not fully accept her.

Sometimes Jews become the recipients of certain negative qualities of the individual's parents, so that the ambivalence toward the parents is partially defused. By coincidence, two of the case histories reported to us dealt with patients each of whom had been exposed in childhood to mothers who had been preoccupied in a major way with fecal soiling and fecal odors. In one instance, the mother was psychotic and would not permit the toilets in the house to be flushed so that feces accumulated and a foul odor pervaded the house. In the second instance, the mother had a rectovaginal fistula so that she was unable to prevent the emission of flatus and fecal odors. The two patients were quite different from each other in every way. Nevertheless both families considered themselves aristocratic and looked down on others condescendingly, and especially upon Jews. In each case the anomalous and intense sensory impact of the mother upon the child presumably left the child overwhelmed and impaired in ability to escape the mother's influence in the course of development. As a result, the mother's image as a loving protector became associated with and contaminated by the image of a persecutor. Such a child, therefore, will have to struggle to dissociate these two images even into adult life. If one can displace the negative component of the image of the mother onto another individual, the tension of the ambivalence is relieved. We assume that this ambivalence problem characterizes many of those instances in which a flawed parent exerts an excessively intense influence upon a vulnerable child even before intrafamily rivalries, sexual and sibling, complicate the child's developmental emancipation. The parents of both patients spoke of Jews as undesirable contaminants, sources of pollution who had to be avoided, kept away. One of the patients insisted that his analyst too had a foul odor. It was clear that the parent's negative qualities were transferred to Jews generally and to the analyst particularly.

These two cases made it clear that the negative qualities attributed to Jews were influenced by the individual's complexes that, in many instance, had been determined by traumatizing or other childhood experiences, and that often the Jew had become the receptacle for accusations that had initially been leveled at the parents.

These two case histories also suggested to us that the accusations made against Jews might reflect aspects of the patient's psychic development. I have just described characterizing the Jews as degraded, inferior, and literally smelly, that is, as anal. Traits attributed to Jews by other patients of our series, suggest oral fixation, namely, greediness, obesity, alcoholism, and stealing. Similarly, we inferred that the phallic level was the focus in patients who saw Jews as excessively sexual, as ravagers of Christian women, as pushy and intrusive. The most mature patients cast their antisemitic accusations in Oedipal terms. Jews were excessively ambitious, intellectual, domineering, and self confident.

So we became aware that Jews were seen sometimes as Oedipal rivals, sometimes as sibling rivals, sometimes as degraded and unworthy, sometimes as individuals who do not exert sufficient self-discipline and permit themselves all kinds of excesses, sometimes as individuals who are self-righteously moralistic, sometimes as separatist and exclusive, and sometimes as presumptuous intruders. The accusations leveled at Jews were determined less by their actual behavior than by the behavior to which the patient had been subjected in the past at the hands of his parents, that he experienced as traumatic, and that he now attributed to the Jew.

It is important that Jews remember that when antisemitism prevails in the community, there is no Jewish conduct or life-style that will undo that antisemitism. Whatever they do will be misinterpreted and chalked up to their discredit. As I write these lines, I read in the newspaper that George Soros, an American Jewish businessman of Hungarian descent, has been making large philanthropic contributions in his native Hungary and other parts of Eastern Europe in particularly thoughtful and imaginative ways. His behavior is interpreted by the antisemites as his attempt to obtain control of government and public institutions in conformity with the classical antisemitic canard to the effect that "the Jews" are engaged in a worldswide conspiracy to dominate the world and to destroy all Christian institutions, a myth given form and cachet by the *Protocols of the Elders of Zion* (see chapter 4).

## Family Romance

The consistency of one observation struck us. We encountered no adult patient in this series who had not at one time enjoyed a close friendship with one or more Jews or who had not experienced romantic involvement with Jews, or both. Perhaps this fact should not surprise us because we are dealing with a population, most of whom had merely voiced some anti-Jewish comment in the course of analysis. Few of them would be called antisemites. That being the case, we should expect to find that in most instances their attitudes were at worst ambivalent rather than hostile to Jews. Nevertheless, the consistency of this observation is striking and makes one wonder whether there is an important regularity here. Obviously we are not considering individuals who permit themselves to be co-opted into an antisemitic movement without having had any personal experience with Jews. We shall discuss that issue below. That is a different phenomenon from the appearance of antisemitic sentiments in individuals in response to their own current experiences. That antisemitism can represent merely one aspect of an ambivalence, for many psychoanalytic patients as well as for others, is suggested by the well-known instances of Martin Luther in sixteenth-century Germany and Mohammed in seventh-century Arabia. In both instances these leaders reached out to the Jewish communities and in both instances they reacted with vicious hostility when their invitations to convert were rejected. (Poliakov, 1974 and 1961). Wilhelm Marr was a philosemite as a young man, a leader in the antisemitic movement in middle life, and no longer antisemitic in later years. Observation discloses that in a number of instances the alternation between philosemitism and antisemitism occurs not once, but several times during an individual's lifetime.

In a paper entitled "Family Romances," Freud (1909) called attention to the fact that some children imagine that the parents with whom they are living are not their real parents. That fantasy, he suggested, represents an effort to disengage from the parents in the course of development. The fantasy "real" parents are grander in some way, wealthier, more accomplished, more distinguished than the inferior people who pretend to be their parents. This fantasy that they belong to another family may compensate for disappointment caused by the contrast between the realistic current image of the actual family and the memory of the image of the far more impressive family that the child thought he possessed when he was younger. The family romance fantasy also serves to remove from interdiction, thoughts and wishes for sexual contacts that would violate incest barriers. In this essay, Freud did not discuss any behavioral consequences that flowed from these fantasies.

I believe that family romance fantasies give dramatic expression to the tendency to move outward from the original family into a neighboring family or community, quite as Freud suggested. It is this tendency that encourages exploratory excursions into friendships with neighboring children, including some visibly different from themselves, some disapproved of by the parents. When they are not co-opted into the exclusive, homogeneous, intolerant latency groups of which we spoke above, white and black children, Western and Oriental children, gentile and Jewish children, tolerate each other; they find each other more interesting than their own siblings and than other children exactly similar in background and characteristics. We heard quite regularly from the patients whom we studied that they recalled close and warm friendships with Jewish children whom they encountered in their neighborhood, often over the protests of their parents.

Curiosity and the attraction to the different, the other, interplay dynamically with the fear of strangers and the need to retreat to the exclusive group.

The family romance might be motivated not merely by the usual tendency to migrate out, away from the family; additional factors might encourage it. One of our patients, an adopted child, felt unwelcome to her adoptive parents and sought a more hospitable environment among her Jewish friends. In a number of instances, a Jewish man or woman was approached as an exogamous object, affording the gentile partner the opportunity to avoid symbolically incestuous attachments. The foreign individual and his or her associates might offer an escape from the actual or symbolic Oedipal or sibling rivalry. A child who feels abused or neglected by his true parents might seek in the outsider a more affectionate parent. In the case of one of our patients, moving from a Nazi to a democratic environment after World War II made him ashamed of his parents and eager to find friends and respect in a neighboring Jewish community. This mechanism presumably prevailed among some of the children of Nazis. In the case of the seven-year-old girl mentioned above, she was attracted to a kindly, maternal female analyst, having had the experience of parental separation at age three, her mother's subsequent remarriage, and a number of residential dislocations.

Generally in this group of patients, the friendships with Jews was broken and the tendency to befriend outsiders was discontinued at some point. Or there may have been several alternations up and back in their attachments to children of different backgrounds. Or the individual might have emerged without fixed prejudice, but ready to assume either mildly philosemitic or antisemitic attitudes as situations arose. Following the antisemitic rioting of blacks against Lubavitch Hasidim in Brooklyn during the week of the 19th of August, 1991, the *New York Times* (28 August) printed an "About New York" column dealing with the children of Crown Heights. In an interview, the director of the Brooklyn Children's Museum, is quoted as having said that although the museum attracted both black and Hasidic children, and the preschoolers played together, the staff had become increasingly aware that the older children were profoundly alienated from each other. This observation supports the generalization that (pp 57ff.) latency children and adolescents both tend to form exclusive and prejudicial groups.

Seldom did attitudes freeze in either direction indefinitely. Even the most active of our "antisemites" thirty years later had abandoned his antisemitism.

While a number of the patients who were reported to us described early friendships with Jewish children, we heard no accounts of a deliberate selection of or preference for Jews. I did encounter one such instance. A gentile man who had devoted much of his life to defending the Jewish people and the State of Israel told me that he remembered an incident that had occurred at the age of two or three. His mother was holding him in her arms as they looked out the window at the houses opposite, across the alley. He observed through a window in one of these houses, a group of men wearing hats, all facing in the same direction and swaying to and fro. He asked his mother who they were and he remembers her saying "Jews." In this memory he recalls having decided at that moment that he liked them and that he would try to be close to them.

Childhood memories that seem to anticipate some important change in attitude, are usually found in analysis to be distortions of an actual event. The distortion is an attempt to screen what may really have happened, something possibly traumatic or problematic in some other way and to make it seem to have a significance that determines a subsequent change. We call such memories screen memories. The memory that was reported to me by this man probably falls into the category of screen memory. However, I don't have the data that would permit me to guess at what was being screened. Nevertheless, the intent is clear and it did indeed presage his major life interest.

The retreat from the philosemitic excursion was frequently triggered by a significant event. One man turned against Jews after his Jewish girlfriend jilted him for a Jew. A woman who had always had favorable attitudes toward Jews as an adult, became resentful when she encountered instances of exclusiveness, pronounced self- confidence, and expressions of their feelings of chosenness.

One black patient was attracted to Jews because of their intellectuality, but reacted against them when he came to feel that he could not compete with them. He was especially hurt when he experienced actual discrimination by a professional associate who was Jewish. But he became noisily and aggressively antisemitic when black separatism and black antisemitic aggressiveness sanctioned and reinforced the antisemitic aspect of his ambivalence.

The little girl whom we mentioned, gave vent to antisemitic views when the analyst's son intruded upon her session.

To supplement the case studies we turned to literary works including personal memoirs. *Memoirs of an Anti-Semite*, by Gregor Von Rezzori, a native of Bukovina, recounts a number of incidents in each of which his friendly interest and association with Jews, was violated by a specific experience, leaving him with antisemitic rather than philosemitic sentiments. In the first, as a thirteen-year-old boy, he was sent to live with an aunt and uncle, having been expelled from school where he was found to have been unable to learn and where he exhibited a tendency toward violence. In the village where the aunt and uncle lived, he adapted to a bucolic but essentially lonely life. He discovered his uncle's fraternity gear and pretended that he was a member of the old drinking and dueling fraternity. His loneliness was alleviated by the discovery in the village of a Jewish boy his own age and the two became friends even though he envied his companion's self confidence and brash manner. However the friendship gave way to envy and jealousy when it became clear that the Jewish boy was an accomplished pianist and on that account, became a protege of the author's aunt. In revenge, he impulsively injured his friend's hands, ending the philosemitic flirtation. Note in this story the author's personality problem that may have fallen into the category that we now call attention deficit disorder, and that often incorporates impulsive hostility. His way of dealing with the disappointments that his problem brought about because of the handicaps it imposed, was to fantasize himself living in another world and to tend to cross boundaries. The boundary crossing tendency we found in a number of our patients who exhibited philosemitism early in life. It facilitates the family romance fantasies that I mentioned above.

The second story describes the author as a nineteen year old, finding his way into adult sex life and encountering Oedipal problems. A Jewish man appeared in the story as someone who cheated him and prevented his consummating a liaison with a street gypsy girl whom he had paid. Then he found himself erotically attracted to a Jewish woman, despite his ambivalence toward Jews. The affair went well for a while, but came to grief when he tried to make her real self comply with his idealized version of her and she resisted that change. The Jewish man is the Oedipal obstacle to sexual fulfillment. The Jewish woman is the exogamous partner, the disguised mother who, after a while, loses her charm, as guilt and shame overcome the author.

In the third memoir, the author, now twenty-three, betrayed a Jewish woman friend, but for no reason other than his inability to resist the temptation to boast of a make-believe sexual adventure. He had helped the Jewish woman with a project that had no sexual significance, but he pretended to a non-Jewish male friend that he had scored sexually with her. He was embarrassed to admit that he had been helpful to a Jew merely out of friendship without sexual payoff.

The fourth episode describes the author's state of mind during the immediate prewar years, and the conflict between his affection for his Jewish friends and his contempt for antisemitism on the one hand, and his loyalty to his parents and community on the other. The story is called "Troth" and deals with conflicting loyalties.

In the final story, as an aging man, Von Rezzori reflects on his irregular life, his lack of any consistent career, his three marriages, his one child who died very young, and his sense of loyalty to his noble heritage. All of this was anticipated by the personality problem that became evident in the first story. He had never achieved any consistent sense of identity and had never come to terms with his ambivalent antisemitism. He had lived in many places. His first wife was Prussian, his second, the mother of his child, Jewish, and his third, current wife, Italian. He had tried to make a virtue and profession out of his preference for fantasy over reality and attributes the failure of his marriage to his Jewish wife, to her insistence upon reality, and denunciation of his preference for fantasy, the very issue that had terminated his affair with his Jewish lover in the second story. His antisemitism he attributes to his loyalty to his parents, and to "sick jealousy." He sees himself as a Jew in his little Jewish son. He plays with the idea of a racial Jewish mentality. Antisemitism appears in his recollection of the bitter quarrels with his Jewish wife, and the disenchantment and antagonism that followed the exciting romance.

These stories illustrate clearly the author's conflict between anti-semitism and philosemitism. Specific incidents of envy, frustration, rivalry, disappointment, reinforced antisemitic sentiments. However, his own personality and background created the conditions that favored his ambivalence. The stories tell us that he had difficulty learning and behaving at school, despite an obviously very high intelligence and skill in writing. He grew up in an aristocratic family, traditionally antisemitic, but although he loved his parents and felt loyal to them and their values, nevertheless he seemed to have believed that he could not live up to their expectations. He responded to his sense of incompetence by departing from the world in which he felt incompetent. He enjoyed having been sent to live with his aunt and uncle at thirteen when he was expelled from school. He retreated into a world of fantasy, and that retreat facilitated his writing. He traveled from place to place and from community to community. The personality distortion that was responsible for the disruption of his life also made the control of hostile impulses difficult for him. He regretted the occasional unfortunate lapses. In Eastern Europe, in Germany, and in postwar America he repeatedly came into close contact with Jews to whom he was attracted as exotic aliens and as intellectuals. At the same time he was antagonized by his envy of them, by their separatism, and by his loyalty to his ancestors. As a reflective person and as an intellectual, he repudiates and mocks conventional antisemitic mythology, but he cannot resist the obligation to remain faithful to the traditions of his forebears, and especially of their antisemitism.

Family romance is usually terminated, at least temporarily, when the subject comes to feel that his positive interest in Jews represents disloyalty to antisemitic parents. That point is made repeatedly by von Rezzori. One patient who complained loudly and frequently to her analyst about her parents, on other occasions accused him of sitting in judgment over them, whereas he, a Jew, was not worthy of being in their company.

The conflict of family romance versus loyalty to parents has become an important issue for the children of Nazis and Nazi sympathizers. Facing the incontrovertible facts of the Holocaust, these adult children are deeply ashamed of the behavior of their parents and they identify with the Jewish victims. On the other hand, personal, family, and community crises occur that create feelings of disloyalty and unfaithfulness, and the subjects are then torn between their conflicting feelings. A gentile German man had been literally horrified by Holocaust films as a child and strongly identified with the Jewish victims, to the point of naming his daughter Sarah, the name that every Jewish woman in Nazi Germany was obliged to assume. However, when his father became terminally ill, he felt impelled to speak to him about his activities during World War II for the first time, and thought that he had denied Nazi sympathies. Shortly thereafter the man saw the film *Shoah* and reacted to it by declaring that everyone was at fault, the Jewish victims as well as the Poles and fascists (the East German code word for Nazis).

### The Transmission of Antisemitic Sentiments

How were antisemitic sentiments conveyed to our patients? The method most commonly reported was simple indoctrination by parents. Some individuals remembered casual comments warning them against Jews. Others recalled more serious discussions to the same effect. The parents also served as role models. The children observed that they avoided social contact with Jews. They also discouraged their children's friendships with Jews during the school year and would not permit them to invite Jewish friends to the house. Some patients recalled parental attitudes of complete tolerance, but they acquired antisemitic prejudices from their friends or community groups. For example, a black patient described his parents as completely free of prejudice, but he was incited to become antisemitic by black separatist and belligerent groups. Early religious teaching was cited by some. At least one woman remembered a coloring book in Sunday school depicting the Jews crucifying Jesus. Needless to say no one growing up in the Christian world can be untouched by negative Christian doctrine regarding the Jews and its various derivatives, religious and secular. We shall have considerably more to say about the mythologic basis of antisemitism in the next chapter. None of our patients reported child to child transmission but members of our group informed us that, in Catholic parochial schools especially, antisemitic sentiments and myths were commonly passed around among the students.

### Antisemitism and Criticism of Israel

We must also record the political encouragement of antisemitism. Chapter 5 will deal at greater length with group issues. But we easily see how political issues can influence the level of antisemitism. As an example, the religious antisemites in the United States have adopted the Arab political position, whereas the Arabs have adopted traditional Christian antisemitism. Both come together, for example, in the Arab distribution of the *Protocols of the Elders of Zion*, which was promoted by Christian antisemites in the political turmoil of turn-of-the-century Russia.

Antisemitism has acquired a new face recently—it presents itself as antagonism to the State of Israel. As such, it exploits whatever political issues can be used to denounce Israel, Jews, and their state.

The association is expressed clearly and innocently by the seven-year-old child whom I quoted above (p. 48). She expressed her personal aversion to Jews (she said she was "allergic" to them), her accusation that they don't believe in God, and that "their country does bad things to people." Obviously she was putting together comments she had heard from adults.

Antisemites complain that not all criticism of Israel can be construed as antisemitism. However, it clearly represents antisemitism if: the accusations are clearly false; the criticism comes from individuals who never voice noncritical comments about Israel; Israel is held by others to stricter standards than other countries. During the course of our project, Israel became involved in its Lebanese War. At that time individuals, many who had never expressed any antisemitic sentiments or in fact any sentiments about Jews found themselves indignant about Israel's behavior, unsympathetic to the situation that had brought the invasion about, and amazingly self-righteous. In the first half of 1984, the German psychoanalytic journal, *Psyche*, published a series of letters, all of them controversial, concerning psychoanalysis in Hitler's Germany. Professor Rolf Vogt of the University of Bremen in a letter dated 27 March 1984 addressed to Dr. Helmut Dahmer, editor of *Psyche*, concluded his letter with the following account:

> And again, I cannot be the uninvolved observer. I have experienced on myself these unconscious processes for which I can not imagine any more appropriate expression than tribal loyalty. Although I was just six years old when the war ended and although my family was clearly opposed to National Socialism and hence I am in this respect not under a particular pressure of family identification, the plain fact that I grew up as a German in the Federal Republic of Germany may perhaps suffice to explain what I want to report now.
>
> When the massacres in the two Palestinian camps in Beirut that were not prevented by the Israeli army became known, I felt, in addition to the horror, simultaneously a just barely perceptible sense of relief. I followed this up and heard myself saying inside, "The Jews are not better than we are either." The fact that it had been so spontaneously natural for me to place myself via that "we" close to the Nazis was shocking to me and I began slowly to understand that I had, hitherto unconscious, specific feelings of guilt referring to the Nazi period. And that it was for this reason that I had felt relieved when I had in my mind made murderers of the Israelis.
>
> Since then I have experienced many an object lesson in this by way of my own person as well as others. What happened at the fall meeting of the German Psychoanalytic in Wiesbaden in 1983 in connection with a lecture by Hillel Klein from Jerusalem is a case in point. It was a crushing experience for me to realize on that occasion that we psychoanalysts are hardly capable of even perceiving our unconscious feelings of guilt connected with the Nazi period. Let alone of dealing with them. However, I saw a ray of light that the meeting was too deeply affected emotionally after Klein's lecture from passing over smoothly to the order of the day.
>
> I am convinced that these unconscious feelings of guilt concern a specific syndrome that must not be regarded simply as a displacement substitute for something else. This syndrome produces the most tenacious resistance to truly facing the Nazi past and its effects that even today still determine our thinking and feeling. (Vogt, 1984)

In many cases it was clear that criticism of Israel for its incursion into Lebanon, was less the result of objective political analysis than the exploitation of a political opportunity to voice antisemitic sentiments that had heretofore been suppressed, whether knowingly or unknowingly.

Needless to say in most instances more than one of the influences that we have been discussing, played a role. The existence of one or more of these preconditions for antisemitism made the individual susceptible to others. A person who acts out conflicts and who has poor control over his aggressive tendencies will welcome parental, religious, and community encouragement of antisemitism and political occasions to attack the State of Israel.

## Conclusion

In summary, this section examines the case histories of nineteen patients who were seen in psychoanalysis or psychotherapy. Only three or at most four of these individuals could be called true antisemites. The others had merely expressed prejudicial sentiments on occasion and were, at worst, ambivalent. In most instances, we were studying antisemitic sentiments expressed by non-antisemites. In this group of patients, no diagnostic entity predominated. They would seem to be a representative cross-section of present-day psychoanalytic patients, mostly patients with personality disorder and of these, mostly borderline personality disorder. Perhaps depression and cyclothymic personality were less well represented than one would have expected, but I doubt that the difference, if there was any, has any significance.

The few patients who perceived themselves to be active antisemites exhibited a problem in the deployment of unusual degrees of aggressiveness.

Among all of the patients we found problems in the resolution of the Oedipus complex, or problems in the resolution of sibling rivalry, or problems in effecting emancipation from traumatizing parents. These issues too, are encountered frequently in analysis and do not set this group apart from a random collection of modern analytic patients.

In the case of some of these people, full-blown family romance fantasies were employed to help with resolution of ambivalence toward parents and with emancipation from them. And we found some suggestion that this fantasy is often associated with the tendency to cross social borders. It was the family romance fantasy and the retreat from it that seemed to explain the alternation of philosemitism and antisemitism.

In most instances, the antisemitic sentiments that appeared during treatment, were directed initially toward the analyst. That happened often when the transference became negative, usually when the psychoanalyst was seen as an Oedipal threat or rival or a sibling rival. On such occasions the patient might withdraw from and repudiate the analyst as a family romance fantasy object. However antisemitic sentiments appeared and were reported also when similar problems were encountered outside the treatment situation itself, when the rival or family romance object was a Jew.

Since the purpose of our project was to learn something about the genesis of antisemitism, we must now ask why specifically antisemitism appears as a consequence of these reality problems and dynamic conflicts. Why not some other prejudice? In the first place the antagonist may have been a Jew. But the fact is that the actual religious or ethnic background of a rival is not held against him nearly as commonly or as consistently in the absence of communal stereotypes. While blacks are the objects of social stereotyping in the United States and in some parts of Europe, and Catholics in some Protestant communities, and Orientals in many places, the readiness to stereotype Jews is found all over the Western world. The negative cultural stereotyping of Jews has persisted for two millenia in most of Europe and the Western Hemisphere. It seems that the readiness to entertain antisemitic sentiments is determined not only by the reality of the rival's religious or ethnic background, but also by a need to invoke certain mythic influences that prevail within the community. In fact, the complaints about Jews, in our small sample and in the general population, as well as in antisemitic propaganda, tend to fall into stereotypes. Jews, we hear, are greedy, grasping, ambitious, pushy, standoffish, arrogant, excessively self confident, money loving, materialistic rather than spiritual, disloyal, dirty vermin, or naturally gifted. The stereotypes of antisemitic attacks override the variety of personalities and personality disorders found in the individuals in our sample. It seems likely therefore that when an unpleasant incident occurs in which a Jew is the opposite number, a ready-made stereotype, a communally accepted and sanctioned myth, is called into action and creates an illusion that seems to carry the force of reality. I believe that this is one of the most important inferences that we can draw from our experience. Antisemitism is generated when there is a real, current, though relatively minor reason for hostility toward Jews and when, at the same time, an antisemitic myth is invoked from the myths that circulate, masked or unmasked, in the surrounding society. The relative importance of these two components varies from occasion to occasion and infrequently, one alone may suffice.

On the other hand, the phenomenon of family romance fantasy implies a mythic philosemitic stereotype. In fact, there have been periods—and the interval since World War II in the United States has been one such period—when Jews have enjoyed a "golden age" such as tenth to fourteenth century in Spain and thirteenth to fourteenth century in Poland. At times Christians had to be admonished by Church authorities against fraternizing with their Jewish neighbors. We tend to lose sight of the reciprocal alternation between philosemitism and anti-semitism in a community as well as on an individual level.

The next chapter will deal with the origin and function of myths in general and chapter four with myths relating to Jews.

# 3

# Mythology

The group experience with the case histories that we considered made us aware that with respect to antisemitic sentiments, individual differences of personality characteristics and psychodynamic structure were, in almost every instance, overridden by certain commonalities in the hostile comments about Jews. Obviously, whatever the occasion for thinking or voicing these sentiments, they drew upon some negative opinions about Jews that seemed to prevail in the general population, and that resemble in some ways, opinions about Jews that have been voiced throughout Christendom. For such ideas to have persisted this long and to have diffused this widely, they must have served one or more important psychic functions. Consequently, we must expect that they will be given up reluctantly if at all. Therein lies the mystery of the tenacity of antisemitism.

The making and the use of myths by individuals and groups is a complex phenomenon that has been studied extensively by sociologists and cultural anthropologists. In what follows I confine myself to the psychology of myth. A myth, from our point of view, is an account of how some real or illusory aspect of the real world came to be, something respecting the life of the individual, the group, the world, or the cosmos.

While we ordinarily think of myths as group products, we each, as individuals, cherish personal myths. For example, a woman remembered that her father had been very difficult with her when she was a child and that her mother had protected her against his hostility. The analytic material clearly pointed to the opposite, that is, that it was the mother who was abusive and that she kept the child and father separated. When my patient related this discovery to her brother, he expressed scepticism, but when he discussed this new formulation in his own analysis, he found that it resolved many of his problems. The myth was created by the mother in order to explain the children's unhappiness and to deny her own mischief; it was accepted and preserved by the children in order to idealize her. The idealization was needed because in fact she was an unhappy and hostile mother who had kept the father away from the children, and yet the children had to believe that they had a loving mother.

A man reported that when he was a child, his father had such a bad temper that in a rage he destroyed a costly article. What happened in fact was that this man's little brother had broken something costly and had become extremely disturbed. The father, in order to demonstrate dramatically that the child's feelings were more important than material objects, had deliberately broken a second object in the presence of the child.

In each of these cases, significant events or experiences were distorted in memory so that what was actually benign was interpreted as hostile or the hostile was reinterpreted as benign. The distortion had the effect of protecting the child against the distress caused by reality. It justified illusion.

In the case of the individual, we usually speak of a "screen memory" rather than a myth but these two have much in common. In general although we use the term screen memory when we speak about a specific, discrete incident, and myth when we speak of a connected account, the two terms overlap considerably. A myth, then, is an account that may be basically untrue as an account of objectively viewed events, though it may incorporate some veridical elements.

What is the purpose of a myth? A myth rationalizes and justifies an emotional attitude that is important to maintain. Psychoanalysis contends that alongside of conscious mentation, we are governed by a set of unconscious affects and motives that create fantasies that reconcile the conscious with the unconscious. Though we maintain the illusion that our actions are determined by conscious thoughts and intentions, in fact, much of our behavior and especially, much of our important behavior, is determined by unconscious motivation. We manage most of the time to keep these two systems, conscious and unconscious, from conflicting, especially by creating rationales, false explanations for behavior whose explanations we really do not know. A myth is a plausible story concocted to explain and validate unconscious attitudes and wishes. An unconscious wish or fear or the defense against it is mentally translated into the sphere of reality where it becomes an illusion; it is perceived as reality. The myth bridges the gap between fantasy and reality.

Let me develop this point a little more fully. This suggestion that a myth is a plausible story that rationalizes and justifies a strongly held view is a special case of the general principle of double registration. That principle holds that apperception takes place when a percept is superimposed upon an emotionally meaningful idea (Ostow, 1955, pp. 402f.). Freud (1900, pp. 565f.) spoke of the "duality of perception" and Nunberg (1955, pp.348f.) elaborated that concept. It was Freud's idea that when an instinctual need is aroused, the organism by its motor activity, strives to achieve a state in which the initial gratifying experience is repeated. Generalizing from that, one can say that the significance of a percept is judged by how closely it resembles the hoped for state of gratification or promises to bring it about.

The myth, of course, plays an important role in human affairs because it is a communally shared and communally active fantasy. It is not merely an idea, a story. It possesses cogency and motivates behavior, either instigating action or defending against inner drives or outer reality. It may generate despair or hope and may result in surrender or enterprise.

While we ordinarily think of myth as a group phenomenon, we must not forget that it starts in the mind of the individual. I don't know that anyone has ever traced the evolution of a myth. We can try to understand only what function it serves. I imagine that at some point an articulate and imaginative individual conceives of a fantasy that seems to resolve an unconscious problem that he shares with his community. The myth makes the resultant attitude seem reasonable even though the problem to which it responds may remain unconscious.

Let us examine one of the myths that we shall discuss below, namely the myth that Jews regularly drain the blood of a Christian child and use it for ritual purposes. I shall present there some evidence suggesting that the libel started against the background of relative overpopulation and relative inadequacy of food supplies. Given that reality and the ubiquity of Oedipal intergenerational rivalry, and given also the recurrent cannibalistic overtones of the mass, it would be surprising if the thought did not occur to a number of parents that it would be helpful if there were no children to feed, or worse, that it might even be helpful to eat the children. Infanticide, after all, was openly practiced in the ancient world and cannibalism has been known to occur under situations of great privation. By an ironic twist, Tacitus complained that the Jews "regarded it as a crime to kill any late-born child."[1] However infanticide was not an option that could be entertained consciously in the twelfth century. To defuse the tension created by the reality need and the inadmissible resolution and the guilt aroused by that, one could attribute the bloodthirstiness to a malevolent agent. The Jew was perceived in the Christian world at that time as just such a presence, an ally of the devil. Accusing the Jew of seeking the blood of a Christian child would appeal to many parents all of whom found themselves in the same situation, and so what originated as an idea of one or more individuals was over time accepted by the community.

Langmuir (1990), a distinguished University of California historian, has studied carefully the ritual murder accusation of 1144 in Norwich, England. A twelve-year-old boy, William, was found dead in a wood. Immediately thereafter his family accused the Jews of the murder. Their story was bolstered by a dream reported by the child's aunt. Two weeks before the incident, she said, she dreamed that, while she was in the marketplace, Jews rushed at her, surrounded her, broke her right leg with a club, tore the leg off her body, and ran away with it. Whatever it was that she feared at the time, in the dream she blamed it on the Jews. After the murder, she and the inhabitants of Norwich interpreted the dream as proof of Jewish guilt. Doubtless the readiness of the family and the neighbors to attribute the murder to the Jews in the absence of any real evidence, suggests that this readiness preexisted the murder.

However the matter might have attracted little notice were it not that a monk, Thomas of Monmouth, heard the story in 1150, examined the witnesses, and concluded not only that the Jews had murdered William, but that they had crucified him. He arranged to have William's body translated in stages to the cathedral. He managed also to have the tomb become a source of miraculous healing. He wrote a *Life* of William. Starting in 1150, miraculous cures were attributed to the tomb. The rumors of the alleged crucifixion and cure spread widely and by 1170 had crossed the Channel. Langmuir charges Thomas with having created a myth that affected Western mentality from the twelfth century on. I would suspect that he merely gave voice and authority to a myth that was already circulating, or provided the content to people who were ready for the myth. That this myth was so readily accepted and that it spread so easily indicates that it met the needs of both the community and its individual members.

Even more generally, the prevailing affective disposition determines how we interpret what we perceive. The depressed individual sees everything in his life as frustrating and threatening. When after a few weeks of antidepression drug therapy that individual recovers to normal mood or perhaps slightly higher (to a normal condition that we call hypomania), the world seems rich with all kinds of possibilities and opportunities. Again, it is a commonplace observation in psychoanalysis that when an individual has lost a loved one, by death or otherwise, he will often imagine that he sees that individual in one or more strangers who are encountered every day. The invocation of a myth influences expectations and apperception in the same way. The memory of each of us that when, as infants, our tears brought rescue by a loving parent, inclines us to expect that as adults too a messianic savior will come to our aid when we are in trouble. When the community validates that wish by institutionalizing it as a myth, we attribute reality to it. This mechanism is even more easily recognized in the case of the group myth. If, for example, it becomes important to unify a community and to motivate its members to support it more vigorously, then leaders will invoke the myth that it is under serious attack by another group and that the attacking group has been a historic enemy. By calling attention to a few real incidents and fabricating others, the accusation can be made plausible. Reality testing is the first victim of instinctual need. Moreover, since we look to group opinion to validate our own concepts of reality, group myths easily pass the reality test.

The current antisemitism of the African-American community in the United States illustrates the creation and use of myth. Encouraged by recent and belated gains that African-Americans have achieved in civil rights, in obtaining equality before the law, and equality of opportunity and education, the African-American community has mobilized itself to fight to close the gaps that still exist. (The attempt to maximize gains has been called the revolution of rising expectations, but I have not been able to ascertain who coined that felicitous term.) The mobilization is reinforced by promoting the myth that there is a specific, unitary community that is trying to victimize the African-Americans and undermine their efforts. The Jews are designated for that role since they are a relatively small community in the United States and since they have been characterized as the main principle of evil in Christendom for two millenia. The blacks need two enemies, one real and one mythical. The contention that Jews have historically supported black struggles for equality more vigorously than any other group is vehemently denied, minimized, or disparaged because that support seems incompatible with the idea of "black power" and deprives them of an important mythical enemy.

Myths deal primarily with either or both of two issues, origins and danger. On a group level, myths of origin are virtually universal, myths about the creation of the world and its contents, myths about how religions and ethnic groups began: the exodus from Egypt, the American Revolution, the founding of Rome and of Berlin. Myths of escape from danger are equally famous: the British victory over the Spanish Armada, the biblical story of Esther who saved the Persian Jews from extermination. On the individual level, the family romance, that is, the child's idea that he was really born into another family, belongs in the category of myths of genesis. Most of us cherish some story about having escaped from danger or having been rescued by someone.

Myths then deal with matters of life and death, rescue and danger. They are invoked when danger is perceived either consciously or unconsciously, and they activate measures for dealing with the danger. Such measures may include autoplastic changes (changes in one's own thinking or conduct), for example denial, or alloplastic changes (attempts to change the outside world), for example, attacks upon others.

Myths serve other purposes as well. They provide reassurance against potential danger even when it is not present. They offer hope. At a moment of despair, Aeneas told his men "Perhaps one day it will be helpful to remember this" (*Aeneid*, book I, lines 283-4). He suggests assigning a mythic quality to the current misfortune, so that it can be used to sustain hope on another occasion. Of course, his intention is to encourage hope at this moment.

We ordinarily use the term myth to designate those accounts that are shared by a group. It is seldom used for the mythic accounts of individuals, though analysts do not hesitate to speak of individual myths. The myth helps to bind the group together, to encourage loyalty, as well as to support group morale. Sharing the myth signals membership in the group.

## Mythic Themes

Before reviewing the myths that are commonly circulated about Jews, let us survey some of the mythic themes that are almost universal.

## Myths of Origin

How does it happen that, for all of the differences in culture, climate, history, and habitat, myths in their basic structure, are virtually identical worldwide? I can think of three possible explanations. First, the readiness to orient oneself about a small number of simple, interpersonal themes may be hardwired into the nervous system and therefore transmitted genetically. Second, given that the experience of growing from infancy to young childhood in the company of parents and siblings is basically identical regardless of time, place, and circumstances, if we assume that myths represent elaborations of the memories of those experiences that become indelible but not retrievable, it would follow that the myths reflect the identity of experience. The third possibility would be a combination of the first two. The brain is hardwired by genetic transmission to accept early experiences as paradigmatic memories and to elaborate them into myths. This seems to me the most likely explanation.

## Myths of Birth

As we noted just above, myths concerning birth and origins are encountered in perhaps every culture and in many individuals. Obviously no one remembers his birth. Yet people who report "out of the body" or "life after death" phenomena, that is, the experience of feeling that one is about to die or be destroyed, speak of the sensation of traveling through a tunnel toward a light at the far end. Knowledge of the process of birth is combined with the universal association of the rebirth experience with illumination to create the fantasy.

Small children are curious about how they came to be born and that interest soon becomes generalized into curiosity about origins in general. Nunberg (1961) in a splendid monograph about neurotic curiosity, observes that small children are curious about three things, birth and origins, the difference between the sexes, and the sexual life of the parent. Probably every culture has it's creation myths.

## Mother and Child

Another set of myths are concerned with themes of being fed, nurtured, and protected by mother or of occupying a maternal claustrum.

Such myths vary from accounts of mothers who destroy their children
to mothers who rescue their children. In other words, the myths tap
some of the mother's ambivalence to her children, visible in infanticide,
abandonment of infants, and abuse of one kind or other. Oedipus has
given his name to a universal mythic complex characterized by rivalry
between the child and the parent of the same sex for the love of the
parent of the other sex.

*Individual and Group Mythology*

At this point let me interpose an explanatory parenthetical statement.
Since the personal myths of which I have been speaking are derived
from and reflect veridical or false memories and fantasies of childhood
experiences, and since, in mental illness, these same memories shape
symptoms and fantasies, we can expect to find a good deal of congruence between personal myths and the manifestations of mental illness
where it exists. Further, these same memories and their derivative fantasies form the raw material of dreams, and therefore we find congruence
between dreams, whether latent or manifest content, and the myths that
we have been discussing. If we concede now that group myths are created and elaborated in the psyches of individuals and are probably derived from individual myths, we shall not be surprised to find congruence
between group myths and individual fantasies and dreams. Psychoanalysis is basically a technique for discovering these individual fantasies or
myths, ascertaining how much veridical basis they have in the
individual's past, and confronting them with a recollected or recon-
structed reality. In those cases of mental illness engendered by the
individual's response to traumatic childhood experience, this demythologizing alone may exert a significant therapeutic effect. When an illness
is induced by a disequilibrium of another kind, for example, an inherited or constitutional lability of affect, the primary defect can usually be
treated chemically but analysis is needed to remove the secondary, myth-
based fantasies, pathologic ideas, and symptoms.

## Oedipus Complex

To return to the Oedipus complex, this phase of normal development
becomes prominent around the third and fourth year of childhood and is

largely resolved by the fifth or sixth year, to be followed by a psycho-sexual "latency" period. The complex comprises two separate elements, sexual desire for the parent of the other sex and rivalry with the parent of the same sex. When we speak of the phenomenon of latency, we mean that between five or six, and ten to twelve, these strivings lose their urgency and are obscured by the child's readiness to join groups of contemporaries, at school and in the playground, and to learn more about the world in which he lives. With the genital maturation of puberty, the Oedipus complex is reactivated. Since it is never really completely over-come, fantasies and myths derived from it will become visible on those occasions when rivalry with a parental or filial figure, or sexual desire for a forbidden sexual partner, becomes salient.

What I have been saying up to this point about the various mythic images and complexes, is fairly well known and accepted. The accounts are straightforward and, I believe, not debatable. However, at this point I should like to introduce some original observations. These deal with a particular variant of the Oedipus complex, namely the child's wish fan-tasy that he can return to his prenatal abode within mother's body, to encounter there father or his intruding penis. Here is a dream of an eight-year-old girl, reported by Berta Bornstein (1953), a distinguished child analyst. I have discussed this dream previously (Ostow, 1991).

> I saw a crocodile or alligator and I was in a small sort of cabin. The crocodile stuck his head between the bars and that looked funny. And the crocodile kept on moving from side to side and I kept on jumping from side to side too. And finally he got me. And instead of biting a chunk out of me, a sort of tooth stuck in me. And I tried to pull it out and I did not succeed. Then we went to supper and then I woke up.

On the day before the dream, Sunday, the child's parents had with-drawn into their bedroom, shutting out both the child and her little sis-ter. She always struggled to get into her parents' bed, to the dismay of her father who objected vigorously. Later that day, our little patient flirted coquettishly with her father and when he pursued her affectionately, she threw herself to the ground and grabbed his leg. (Another portion of the dream and associations dealt with her envy of her sister, but that is irrel-evant to this argument.) Given the history of her efforts to place herself between her parents in bed and her father's regarding her as an unwel-come intruder, it became fairly evident that the little log cabin repre-sents the maternal claustrum and the alligator's snout, a symbol of the intruding father with whom, in the dream, she conducts a flirtatious little dance. In a subsequent session she mentioned Pinocchio, who "met his daddy in the whale's stomach."

Poe's dramatic story, "The Pit and the Pendulum," can be understood as the horrible consequence of realizing this fantasy, being trapped between the pit filled with ugly, horrid monsters, and the knife-edged pendulum that threatened to slice him as it steadily moved lower and lower.

A pre-Kabbalistic form of Jewish mysticism is based upon the fantasy of seeking to encounter God as he is ensconced inside a claustrum that I believe symbolizes mother. In my recent essay (Ostow, 1995), I describe this complex in some detail. The early form of this mystical enterprise is called *Merkavah*, or chariot mysticism, since it is based upon Ezekiel's vision of God seated in his chariot (chapter 1). Twenty-one verses of that chapter describe the chariot, four beasts supporting a platform on which a throne rests, and the last three verses describe the image of God who occupies the throne. In my essay I cite material from the Kabbalah indicating that the throne has been interpreted as symbolic of a woman. In *Merkavah* mysticism, the throne and the vehicle are considered essential to the effort to see God—in the place where he is to be found. These mystical writers begin to appear perhaps during the second century B.C.E. After two centuries of the common era, Merkavah mysticism was succeeded by a variant called *Hekhaloth* mysticism, based upon the idea that God is to be found in a palace, but that access to him is blocked by various angels or other guards. Only the most pious and deferential, prepared by acquiring passes or seals or passwords, are granted access to God. Others are not only turned back but may be killed in their Promethean quest. Here again I infer that the *hekhal* represents mother, as does the throne on which God sits in the palace. The labyrinth may be regarded as a special kind of maternal claustrum that compels the intruder to confront the murderous father, and prevents his escape. These *Hekhaloth* fantasies lend themselves to the child's expectations that he or she will encounter dangerous obstacles in its attempts to return to mother—the murderous father and/or deadly sibling rivals.

## Sacrifice

It is probably the Oedipus complex that determines much or most of intergenerational rivalry. One unfortunate consequence of intergenerational rivalry is filicide in any of its forms. Infants were exposed or abandoned in the ancient world. Myths of infanticide were doubtless based upon real events or cultic practices. Child sacrifice is the subject of many myths, of which perhaps the best known in the Western world is the *akedah* or binding of Isaac in preparation for sacrifice[2], which was of course aborted. The story is told in Genesis, 22. It seems so inconsistent with the views promoted in the Jewish Bible interdicting the spilling of human blood and constraining the spilling of animal blood within ritually determined boundaries, that it has created a large library of commentary.

Martin Bergmann, a distinguished psychoanalyst and scholar who was a member of our study group, was moved by the discussion that arose there to study child sacrifice and its influence upon Judaism and Christianity. His book, *In the Shadow of Moloch* (1992), details the myths dealing with child sacrifice, the reality upon which the myths were based, and the consequences for religious development and especially for antisemitism. As some psychoanalysts understand human sacrifice, it represented an effort to appease a mythical god, the adult equivalent of the young child's parent. By sacrificing living children, one limits one's own personal loss, and acquires the opportunity to eliminate a potential or actual enemy. Child sacrifice, an attested ancient pagan practice was interdicted by the Jewish religion and was replaced by animal sacrifice. Centuries later, the residual impulse to sacrifice children combined with the dim memory from the remote past to create an active myth as well as fantasies and dream representations. Bergmann sees martyrdom—witnessing to the authenticity of the Jewish and Christian God—as a replacement for human sacrifice. He contends further that the *akedah* and the crucifixion, became central organizing events for the Jewish and Christian communities respectively, because they served to defuse the filicidal tension between fathers and sons. They both left residues, the *akedah* finding symbolic expression in circumcision, and the crucifixion finding symbolic expression in the Eucharist.[3] Striking a covenant with Abraham, God promised him fertility and vigorous and flourishing progeny in return for his having demonstrated his willingness to sacrifice his favorite son and for accepting the rite of circumcision. God changes his name from Abram, meaning exalted father, to Abraham which is explained (Genesis, 17:5) as meaning father of a multitude. In other words, God accepts circumcision as a symbolic substitute for child sacrifice and promises not only to spare, but actually to strengthen Abraham's progeny.

In fact, the *akedah* story is the second of two biblical accounts of aborted filicide. In the first, (Genesis, 21) Abraham banishes Ishmael and his mother, Hagar, who was Abraham's concubine, into the desert where they would have died had it not been for the last minute intervention of God, reminiscent of his last minute intervention to save Isaac. In both instances, after first having encouraged it, God rejects filicide as a form of worship.

Bergmann contends that despite these mythic events and the current symbolic representation of them, the filicidal impulse has not been completely overcome. It finds representation even now not only in the various forms of child abuse that persist in the contemporary world, but also in various forms of intergenerational conflict and the guilt to which it gives rise.

Contemplating the stories of the exposure of Ishmael and the *akedah* of Isaac, and the practice of circumcision in Judaism and Islam as well as in many other cultures, it has seemed to me that the filicide that is threatened but withdrawn, the aborted danger, the "pulled punch," acts to reinforce the bond between father and son. Pubertal initiation rites can be interpreted in different ways, for example, symbolic sacrifice, but they are also limited and circumscribed threats. If my conjecture is correct, it may contribute to an understanding of the remarkable cohesion of the Jewish as well as Islamic communities despite much outside oppression and internal divisiveness. And it also contributes to an understanding of the continued importance to the Jews of the *b'rith milah,* the ritual circumcision, in a largely secular world.

We should consider here the ritual significance of blood. The Pentateuch lays down many regulations restricting the ways in which blood may be spilled. Blood of either animal or man is not to be spilled irresponsibly, but only under rigorously controlled circumstances. The exhibition of blood has an apotropaic, protective value, as it did when smeared on the lintels of the doors of Jews on the first Passover night, and as it did when Zipporah circumcised her son and touched his father, Moses with the bloody foreskin. The exhibition of blood seems to say "I have fulfilled my obligation to God and I am therefore entitled to his protection." On a more biologic level, the exhibition of blood might also serve to invoke the archaic, instinctual inhibition against intraspecific killing. The power of the exhibition of blood would explain why the expression of at least one drop of blood is required to establish the validity of a ritual circumcision. That would explain too the centrality of the symbols of blood and flesh for the Eucharist, which in addition, seems to allude to a reference to a long-repressed and archaic cannibalistic tendency. It is because of its apotropaic power that temple ritual required that blood be smeared and sprinkled. The liturgy of the annual Yom Kippur service contains a section, *'Eleh 'Ezkerah,* that describes the suffering of martyrs tortured and murdered by the Romans. The protective power of martyrdom is expressed in the following verses that appear in some versions of that liturgy:

> Lord of Mercy remember
> These righteous and their murder.
> May their merit and the merit of their fathers
> Protect your children in time of need.

> (Goldschmidt, 1970)

But blood belongs only to God and the observant Jew must cleanse meat of its blood before the meat can be consumed.

If Bergmann is correct in his contention that primitive infanticidal cannibalism has not yet been put to rest, then the rituals and rules that we have discussed can be interpreted as part of the effort to keep the archaic impulses repressed, to prevent the consumption of meat that has not been drained of blood, but yet to make the symbolic exhibition of blood effective in propitiating the Divinity.[4]

This subject gives me an opportunity to illustrate the convergence of unconscious fantasy, group and individual myth, neurotic symptoms and dreams. A young man, a refugee from Germany, came to see me shortly after World War II, early in September. He reported that during the preceding few weeks, he had been experiencing episodes of anxiety, each lasting several minutes and recurring in response to no stimulus that he could recognize. He told of his escape from Germany and his finding a livelihood here as a cutter in the fur industry, his marriage, and his having a small child, a daughter. His father, who was dead, had been a Jewish religious functionary in the small town in which they had lived, a cantor, a ritual slaughterer (schohet), and a ritual circumciser (mohel), and he vividly remembered his father's long slaughtering knife and his circumcision instruments. He recollected with particular fondness attending synagogue with his father when the latter officiated.

At his session just a few days before the celebration of Rosh Hashanah, the Jewish new year, on the first day of which the account of Ishmael's banishment into the desert is read aloud in the synagogue, and on the second day of which the account of the *akedah* of Isaac is read aloud, he recollected that his father used to sing a song about the *akedah* at the Rosh Hashanah services, a song that always engaged him. At that point I asked him what his Hebrew name was. He replied Yitzhak (Isaac) and promptly began trembling with anxiety. He now understood the basis for his anxiety, namely, that he identified himself with the legendary Isaac and his father with Abraham. It was as though, having escaped from the Holocaust, he felt that he owed a debt to God and might be called upon to repay it. During the course of the brief psychotherapy that followed, he reported dreams in which children were being cut by their fathers. He saw that his own occupation in the fur industry complied with his fantasy of identifying with his cutting father, and he saw too the possibility that he might unconsciously identify with his father and harbor hostile feelings toward his daughter. Such a dramatic convergence of the manifestations of the various derivatives of unconscious fantasies is not often encountered clinically. Usually these congruences must be ascertained by psychoanalytic exploration. The case illustrates that individual and group myths both tap the motivating power of unconscious fantasies and thereby acquire that power.

## Sibling Rivalry

One might object: sibling rivalry is not a myth, it is real. It certainly is, but myths deal with reality as well as with fantasy. In fact, the more the myth is based on reality, the more difficult it becomes to discredit it in treatment. What is unconscious is the intensity of the rivalry, the murderous impulses to which it gives rise, and the objects of and occasions for contention. Sibling rivalry occupies an important place in the mythologies of most people. The Book of Genesis focuses on sibling rivalry as it appears in a polygamous society: Cain and Abel, Isaac and Ishmael, Jacob and Esau, Rachel and Leah, Jacob's sons who are the progenitors of the twelve tribes, and especially the rivalry between Joseph and his brothers.

Analysts point out that the Oedipus complex involves conflict between the generations for access to and for the love of a third person. But sibling rivalry can also focus on a third person. Defining rivalry, Peter Neubauer (1982), observes that:

> Psychoanalysts can easily link the meaning of *rivalry* to the original root of the term, namely, "one dwelling by or using the same stream as another," or "the fighting for the access to the river," or "one who is in pursuit of the same object as another" (The New Century Dictionary). The struggle is for the basic supply of water for survival or, in our terms, for the mother's supply to satisfy basic needs. Rivalry, the striving for the exclusive access to the source, implies an assertive, aggressive struggle against the rival. Only later, in favorable circumstances, does it lead to sharing of the source, the mother, to coexistence with the rival, a mutuality of interest, thereby preparing the conditions which later contribute to the solution of the oedipus complex. Rivalry is an act, based on the wish not to lose the object to the rival. Thus, in rivalry, the contact with the object is maintained.

Although some developmentally phasic behaviors are resolved and succeeded by others, sibling rivalry persists into adult life. As the child enters into the social life of childhood during latency the tendency toward rivalry continues. It prevails now with respect not only to the child's actual siblings but also with his contemporaries. Children at this point seem to be concerned with fairness and sharing equally. Moreover, latency children, as we noted above, (p. 33) tend to form groups that exclude others. Being included and excluded are experienced as rivalry.

During adolescence rivalry becomes even more prominent, in competition for favor with the other sex and in athletic and academic competition. In adult life competition extends to economic matters and social status. And the rivalry with siblings continues.

In many instances, rivalry alternates with conciliation and cooperation, or it is sublimated in play and may find expression in activities that avoid confrontation with the rival. Under sufficient pressure, however, it may provoke social tension, struggle, and even war.

In the Bible myths, the brothers compete not only for the birthright, but also for the father's favor. It will be relevant to our interest to note that in each biblical account the younger finds favor over the older, Isaac over Ishmael, Jacob over Esau, Rachel over Leah, and Joseph over his older brothers. Since the principals in the Genesis stories became the ancestors of various nations and tribes, these accounts suggest to us that these sibling rivalries anticipated wars among neighboring peoples, and even the ultimate separation of the original twelve tribes of Israel into two kingdoms.

## Intermediaries

In most cultures that revere gods or a leader with divine qualities, intermediaries are postulated. These are generally not considered essentially divine but possess characteristics of both the divine and the mortal, or rather, something less than the divine but more than the mortal. Being less than divine, they can converse and traffic with mortals. However, being more than human, they can intercede with the highest gods for the benefit or to the detriment of mortals. Several different varieties are familiar to us in the Jewish and Christian tradition.

The term *angelos* in Greek, roughly equivalent to the Hebrew *malakh*, means messenger. The word *malakh* is used in Scripture ambiguously for human and divine messengers or intermediaries between man and God. Angelology was elaborated in post-Biblical religion. Angels came to be thought of not merely as intermediaries but also as a host of ministering creatures, as guardians, or as servants. Angels of evil are also described, who seek to injure humans. Satan is the best known angel of evil.

The idea of angels has been challenged by some Jewish scholars. Maimonides tried to rationalize the concept by identifying the angels with Aristotle's "intelligences." Nevertheless, the craving for an intermediary who makes possible communication with God and the opportunity to influence Him, is so strong that belief in angels persists among many elements of the Jewish and Christian population. Angels play a prominent role in *Hekhalot* mysticism. They constantly sing praises before God and they guard Him against the intrusion of humans who attempt to ascend and enter the divine claustrum to get a glimpse of Him.

In mythology and in fairy tales, animals may possess supernatural powers and act to help or hinder humans in trouble. Romulus and Remus were nurtured by a wolf. Myths relate to actual animals or to fantasy animals, that is animals that are thought of as composites of the features of other animals. Some of the angels are thought of as chimerical beasts, for example, the bearers of Ezekiel's chariot, each of which combines the facial features of lion, eagle, ox, and human. We are familiar with chimeras, centaurs, minotaurs, basilisks, satyrs. Closer to the human are creatures like elves, trolls, fairies, giants, mythological dwarfs, goblins, and witches. Some of these creatures are exclusively malign, such as the basilisk. Many can be either helpful or hurtful. The gargoyles on cathedrals can, I believe, be interpreted as symbolic guardians of the seat of the Bishop, or the *hekhal* or residence of God.

Strangers appear in myths and in fiction, who, in the course of events, reveal that they possess some supernatural qualities and bring good news or bad, or intervene in human affairs, either helpfully or maliciously. When God appeared to Abraham to announce Sarah's forthcoming pregnancy with Isaac, He was represented by "three men." In the episode immediately following in which Lot is saved from the destruction visited on Sodom by being escorted out of the city, the Bible tells us that it is the same angels who had brought the good news to Abraham, but Lot knows them only as human strangers. The Pied Piper of Hamelin was a stranger who presented himself to the townspeople of Hamelin as a rescuer who would solve their problems with rat infestation. When they refused to reward him for his successful efforts, he turned against them and in a macabre revenge, led their children away. The story may be based upon the tragic events of the Children's Crusade. A stranger may possess potential for both good and evil. His behavior in myth usually accords with how well he is treated by his host. We shall see below that the Jew often appears to the Christian as a hostile intermediary.

While sometimes the intermediary of the myth appears in the singular, as in the case of the Pied Piper, in many dreams or myths, we hear of a multitude. In the angel stories of the Bible, it may be a single angel who delivers the message, or a group, as in the case of the Abraham story, and also in Jacob's ladder dream. In the mystical literature too, one reads of individual angels referred to by name, as well as enormous cohorts of angels. Devils or demons too can appear in myths individually or in groups. In general, small or weak creatures are likely to appear in large numbers whereas strong or huge creatures appear individually or in smaller numbers. That generalization however does not always hold.

Given that the creatures to which I am referring may function as friends or enemies, and that they may be of any size and appear in large numbers, we may speculate that they symbolize the siblings of the child as they appear to him. They may also symbolize groups of other children, the first social groups of latency with which the child may feel either comfortable or uncomfortable.

It is interesting that the word *host* signifies: a large number, an army, an enemy, a stranger, a friend, a sacrificial victim, and in Christian usage, the wafer of the Eucharist. All of these concepts are relevant to our subject. The Hebrew word, *tsava,* which we translate as host in English, refers to host in the sense of army, and to groups performing obligatory service or corvee, to the assignment of a service group, to the period of service, to plenitude or fullness, to power, to the angels, to the celestial bodies, to the population of heaven and earth.

## Apocalypse

To this point, in our comments about myths and the fantasies underlying them, we have focused on the themes. I should like to introduce here another dimension, namely affective charge. Some of the classical myths turn out to be accounts of unequivocal achievements or triumphs or gratifications, for example, the creation of the world. Others are unrelieved tragedies, the death of a hero for example, or a military defeat. Most myths however, combine elements of danger or destruction with elements of achievement or victory. The combination may take any of several forms. One may follow the other. The myth of Oedipus for example describes the triumph of Oedipus: he killed his father, became king in his place and married his mother, only to be punished for his sins. In the typical birth-of-the-hero myth, the hero is endangered in infancy but rescued, and survives to elude or destroy his enemies. In the Oedipal myth we find that sequence but it is followed by the protagonist's downfall. One event may be conditional upon the other. In Genesis, God makes covenants with man. Man is to make some sacrifice and God rewards him with a blessing and promise. In some myths, while the action may go in one direction, it may do so against a background opposite in affective significance. For example, the account of the creation of the world given in Genesis, starts with the statement that the earth was in a state of chaos and darkness. The creation undoes this initial state.

When we encounter such combinations of affective charge in clinically presented dreams or fantasies, we may speak of death fantasies and rebirth fantasies. Death fantasies relate to images of death, destruction, defeat, deprivation, any misfortune that causes grief, despair, or loss. Rebirth fantasies relate to recovery from that misfortune and a new start, a triumph or gratification. Occasionally it is a literal birth, or a resurrection, or pregnancy. It is accompanied by an expression of relief or pleasure.

In different myths, the sequence of death and rebirth components varies. In the Oedipus myth the triumphs of Oedipus are followed by his ultimate downfall. On the other hand, having been exposed and abandoned by his father as an infant, he survives and prospers. Isaac is placed in jeopardy by his father's intention to sacrifice him, but he is rescued, as is his half-brother Ishmael in the tale immediately preceding.

In dreams that are concerned with the regulation of affect, the initial episode of the dream usually reflects the current affective state of the dreamer. The dream then displays attempts to overcome or correct the affect, to restore the affective state to neutral. Usually the last episode of the dream returns to the affect of the initial episode. Here is a dream of a woman with a propensity for mood swings somewhat more prominent than usual.

> The world was being flooded. The water was reddish and grayish. It was turbulent with white crests. I saw rocks and houses. People were drowning. We were on a high level where there were white houses. I was on a boat, a nice boat, large with blond wood lacquer floors. There was a kitchen on the boat. I became concerned that it would capsize. We landed at a house on some land. We brought things onto the boat, glasses, no, plastic cups for fear that they might break, and food.
>
> What's the point of living if you're going to drown? I thought of suicide and became calmer. No, I said, there is always hope. If you die now you eliminate hope.
>
> I saw some people drowning, some with hands raised, some protesting, some peacefully.

The dream starts on a depressive note, a flood, people drowning. The dreamer finds security on a boat, but her depressive tendency threatens her with the possibility of capsizing. She has the boat reach land, where she replenishes the food supply. But then the depressive mood reasserts itself in thoughts of suicide. She comforts herself with hope but sees others drowning. The dream reproduces an ancient myth, one version of which is expressed in the Noah's Ark story. The latter ends, not as this dream ends, but with signs of rebirth, the dove's finding food and refuge, the actual landing of the Ark and God's promise that He will never again attempt to destroy the world, and His instructions to man to produce progeny. He designates the rainbow as the eternal promise of rebirth.

We have been discussing the thematic content of myths and dreams, but the thematic content is important primarily because it implies an attitude and/or an intention. When the narrative tells us that the individual in the story with whom the subject identifies suffers misfortune, the reader or hearer feels some form of unhappiness or distress. When that individual succeeds and is gratified, the subject's mood resonates with his. It is not simply that the myth or dream creates the mood; it gives expression to an existing mood and it makes it seem appropriate, and it may influence it to a certain degree. When the myth is presented from the outside, it mobilizes whatever appropriate affect is ready to find expression. When a myth circulates in a group—and we shall discuss group myths below—it synchronizes and coordinates the mood of the members.

The mood contributes to the decision to act or to refrain from action. An experience of frustration, if it does not lead to the paralysis of demoralization, may create anger and a determination to fight. We shall see how this relates to our topic. On the other hand, an experience of gratification or unusual success may lead to a determination to pursue a current or planned course of action. For example, in the case of the woman who reported the dream, she responded to her anticipation of calamity by reinforcing her philanthropic activities which were devoted always to rescuing people in trouble.

Let me remind the reader here of the discussion of the affect correcting mechanism and the problems that it creates (see above, p. 81). When an individual starts to move in a depressive direction, whether spontaneously or as a result of equilibratory processes, he unconsciously looks for the source of his misery in the outside world. If he feels bad, some one must be responsible for that feeling. These corrective processes are unconscious and we do not acknowledge that they arise from within. The individual must find a scapegoat, and he usually blames whoever is closest to him emotionally, the current representation of a punitive mother or father, as if that person were responsible for his unhappiness. This point is dramatically demonstrated in the case of some marriages in which the partners bitterly blame each other for their unhappiness. Although neither of them is clinically depressed, the state of mind may be considered a partially compensated depression, so that the administration of antidepression medication, in many instances, suffices to restore marital harmony.

We shall of course revert to the scapegoat theme in our discussion below of the mechanism of antisemitism.

The spontaneous tendency to regulate affect by replacing pronounced excursion in one direction by movement in the opposite direction, was exploited in a mode of writing and thinking that appeared in the Middle East during the second century before the common era, namely, the apocalypse. The paradigmatic example of the apocalypse is the Revelation of St. John the Divine which is said to comprise fragments written some time during or close to the first century C.E. The book contains extravagant threats of destruction followed by promises of salvation.

And I saw when the Lamb opened one of the seals, and I heard, as it were the noise of thunder, one of the four beasts saying, Come and see.

And I saw, and behold a white horse: and he that sat on him had a bow; and a crown was given unto him: and he went forth conquering, and to conquer.

And when he had opened the second seal, I heard the second beast say, Come and see.

And there went another horse that was red: and the power was given to him that sat thereon to take peace from the earth, and that they should kill one another: and there was given unto him a great sword.

And when he had opened the third seal, I heard the third beast say, Come and see. And I beheld, and lo a black horse; and he that sat on him had a pair of balances in his hand.

And I heard a voice in the midst of the four beasts say, A measure of wheat for a penny, and three measures of barley for a penny; and see thou hurt not the oil and the wine.

And when he had opened the fourth seal, I heard the voice of the fourth beast say, Come and see.

And I looked, and behold a pale horse: and his name that sat on him was Death, and Hell followed with him. And power was given unto them over the fourth part of the earth, to kill with sword, and with hunger, and with death, and with the beasts of the earth. (6:18)

And I saw a new heaven and a new earth: for the first heaven and the first earth were passed away; and there was no more sea.

And I John saw the holy city, new Jerusalem, coming down from God out of heaven, prepared as a bride adorned for her husband.

And I heard a great voice out of heaven saying, Behold, the tabernacle of God is with men, and he will dwell with them, and they shall be his people, and God himself shall be with them, and be their God.

And God shall wipe away all tears from their eyes; and there shall be no more death, neither sorrow, nor crying, neither shall there be any more pain: for the former things are passed away.

> And he that sat upon the throne said, Behold, I make all things new. And he said unto me, Write: for these words are true and faithful.
>
> And he said unto me, It is done. I am Alpha and Omega, the beginning and the end. I will give unto him that is athirst of the fountain of the water of life freely.
>
> He that overcometh shall inherit all things; and I will be his God, and he shall be my son. (21:1-7)

Revelation includes references to angels, beasts, devils as intermediaries between man and God.

But we should take note of some properties specific to apocalypses that may but do not necessarily appear in other myths. The name of the book is The Revelation of St. John the Divine and revelation is a consistent feature of the apocalypse.

> The Revelation of Jesus Christ, which God gave unto him, to show unto his servants things which must shortly come to pass; and he sent and signified it by his angel unto his servant John:
>
> Who bare record of the word of God, and of the testimony of Jesus Christ, and of all things that he saw.
>
> Blessed is he that readeth, and they that hear the words of this prophecy, and keep those things which are written therein: for the time is at hand. (1:1-3)

The apocalypse reveals to its recipient a vision of the future. The troubled (or too untroubled) receiver of the revelation is offered information that is intended to influence his behavior as well as to satisfy his curiosity.

The ancient world had few modes of transmitting information and the typical individual had no way of knowing what was going on about him in the present, much less to anticipate the future. The thirst for information gave rise to the phenomena of prophecy, divination, oracles, and revelation. Even today, people who do not tolerate either the uncertainty or the certainty of reality, seek comfort from purveyors of magical sources of information, astrologists, "channelers," fortune-telling media.

A doctrine that was presented as a revelation from supernatural sources was eagerly accepted by most and it carried great authority and cogency.

Most apocalypses speak of an individual, usually a supernatural creature, an intermediary, or even of God Himself as a savior who will rescue the recipient from the catastrophe that the apocalypse promises.

And I saw a heaven opened, and behold a white horse; and he that sat upon him was called Faithful and True, and in righteousness he doth judge and make war.

His eyes were as a flame of fire, and on his head were many crowns; and he had a name written, that no man knew, but he himself.

And he was clothed with a vesture dipped in blood: and his name is called The Word of God. And the armies which were in heaven followed upon white horses, clothed in fine linen, white and clean.

And out of his mouth goeth a sharp sword, that with it he should smite the nations; and he shall rule them with a rod of iron: and he treadeth the wine-press of the fierceness and wrath of Almighty God.

And he hath on his vesture and on his thigh a name written, King of Kings, and Lord of Lords. (19:11-16)

This element corresponds to the wish of the infant to be rescued from hunger and discomfort and the anxiety of being left alone, by a parent, usually mother. No matter how old we may be, this archaic wish persists and seeks gratification in one way or another. In time of trouble we look to a close family member for rescue or to a friend if necessary. As a member of a community we look for a new leader. Because of the unconscious source of our quest, we are not always reasonable or logical in our choice, often seeking a more charismatic rather than a more appropriate leader.

This quest for rescue by a parental figure lies behind the religious impulse for many individuals. The high gods of most religions are endowed with transparently parental characteristics. Other gods remind us of siblings.

The quest for rescue also gives rise to messianic hopes. Messianism has brought with it both good and evil and has incurred protest as well as eager receptiveness. Its history in Judaism is long and complex. For our purposes it is not necessary to review that history. I am here merely calling attention to the yearning for messianic salvation that, at times of despair, becomes intense. Messianism occurs not only as an accompaniment of apocalypse, but it is usually set in an apocalyptic background, and almost all apocalypses include hope for an eschatologic savior.

It would be helpful at this point to distinguish between classic apocalyptic and what I should like to call apocalyptic thinking or the apocalytic complex. The succession of the expectation or wish for death and destruction by the hope for rescue and rebirth, I consider the apocalyptic pattern of thinking characteristic of the apocalyptic complex. I find that in the dreams and fantasies of individuals who experience fluctuations of affect whether in normal life or mental illness. We also find it in many Prophetic Scriptures. Often Prophetic predictions of catastrophe are followed by the promise of restoration or messianic redemption. At the end of chapter 10, Isaiah announces with an arboreal metaphor, the destruction of Assyria for its deadly harassment of Israel. The forest will be cut down. Continuing with that metaphor in chapter 11, he promises that Israel will be reborn, that "a shoot will grow out of the stump of Jesse," the father of King David, and "a branch from its stock." A messianic rescuer will appear who will destroy the enemy and initiate a utopian age.

Such Prophetic passages usually refer to specific, local events. They do not deal with cosmic predictions nor eschatologic revelations. Classical apocalypse on the other hand complies with a fairly rigid pattern. As we have seen it in the case of Revelation, cosmic events and ineluctable patterns of history are described. The revelation is formally announced. The predictions are expressed in symbolic language that requires interpretation. There is no room for altering the outcome by repentance. The destruction leads directly to the *eschaton* that will mark the preternatural rebirth.

Not all apocalypses are religious. Many current apocalyptic writings are secular. Many of the religious apocalypses see the destruction as punishment for evil in the universe and the rebirth as reward for the righteous minority. However this moralistic concern does not apply to all apocalypses, nor even to all religious apocalypses. Not all individual apocalyptic fantasies and dreams contain concepts of punishment and reward.

Some scholars see the *eschaton* as an essential feature of all apocalypses. The *eschaton* is the hypothetical end of time, the last days. Most apocalypses not only envision death and rebirth but predict that these will occur when the current historical epoch will end, usually fairly abruptly. Time will come to a standstill and nature will be altered. This fantasy tells us that reality and the natural processes of the real world will be abrogated, so that what we fear can be avoided and what we wish can be gratified without the resistance of reality and nature. The old world has been destroyed and a new one has been born. The strange and unnatural elicit fear and awe, but simultaneously usher in the rebirth.

Most of us can entertain that idea as a myth or as a hope or as a
religious belief. At the onset of a psychotic episode, the patient may
believe that the world has changed, that there has been an abrupt dis-
continuity. In essence this idea signifies the death of the patient's reality, which symbolizes himself, and the new world represents his rebirth.
Here is a classical description of an apocalyptic, psychotic delusion,
given by Freud in his discussion of the illness of Schreber (Freud,
1911). (Schreber was a lawyer and judge in late nineteenth-century
Germany who became psychotic and described his experiences in a
published memoir.)

> At the climax of his illness, under the influences of visions which were "partly of a
> terrifying character, but partly, too, of an indescribable grandeur", Schreber be-
> came convinced of the imminence of a great catastrophe, of the end of the world.
> Voices told him that the work of the past 14,000 years had now come to nothing,
> and that the earth's allotted span was only 212 years more; and during the last part
> of his stay in Flechsig's clinic he believed that the period had already elapsed. He
> himself was "the only real man left alive" and the few human shapes that he still
> saw—the doctor, the attendants, the other patients—he explained as being "miracled
> up, cursorily improvised men". Occasionally the converse current of feeling also
> made itself apparent: a newspaper was put into his hands in which there was a
> report of his own death; he himself existed in a second, inferior shape, and in this
> second shape he one day quietly passed away. But the form of his delusion in which
> his ego was retained and the world sacrificed proved itself by far the more power-
> ful. He had various theories of the cause of the catastrophe. At one time he had in
> mind a process of glaciation owing to the withdrawal of the sun; at another it was to
> be destruction by an earthquake, in the occurrence of which he, in his capacity of
> "seer of spirits", was to act a leading part, just as another seer was alleged to have
> done in the Lisbon earthquake of 1755. Or again, Flechsig [his psychiatrist—M.O.]
> was the culprit, since through his magic arts he had sown fear and terror among
> men, had wrecked the foundations of religion, and spread abroad general nervous
> disorders and immorality, so that the devastating pestilences had descended upon
> mankind. In any case the end of the world was the consequence of the conflict
> which had broken out between him and Flechsig, or, according to the aetiology
> adopted in the second phase of his delusion, of the indissoluble bond which had
> been formed between him and God; it was, in fact, the inevitable result of his
> illness. Years afterwards, when Dr. Schreber had returned to human society, and
> could find no trace in the books, the musical scores, or the other articles of daily
> use which fell into his hands once more, of anything to bear out his theory that
> there had been a gap of vast duration in the history of mankind, he admitted that his
> view was no longer tenable: "...I can no longer avoid recognizing that, externally
> considered, everything is as it used to be. Whether, nevertheless, there may not
> have been a profound internal change is a question to which I shall recur later." He
> could not bring himself to doubt that during his illness the world had come to an
> end and that, in spite of everything, the one that he now saw before him was a
> different one.

The text makes clear that Schreber's delusional fantasies dealt with the conflict between his wish to be dead and his wish to be reborn. The death of the world replaced his own death, just as in the dream of the flood that we considered, the patient overcame her wish for suicide by seeing other people drowning. Despite Schreber's attempt to displace his wish to be dead onto the world, derivatives of the wish nevertheless appear in his delusional ideas that he had in fact died. Yet the new world represents an attempt at rebirth, though not a successful one.

The unconscious ideas that lie behind myths and dreams, do not recognize reality. The myth tries to reconcile them with reality. However apocalyptic myths explicitly reject reality. The readiness of so many individuals to accept them tells us just how much of a burden reality is to most, and how hard we try to ignore it and reject it if and when our efforts cannot overcome it.

Apocalypses, though they seem so bizarre to most adults in the West, actually easily find resonance in the current issues of the day. The advent of the turn of the millenium, the possibility of nuclear war, of environmental strangulation, of earthquake, of inner-city riots, of genetically altered plant or animal life, all encourage apocalyptic thinking. Apocalypse, as I observed, can be thought of as a specific variant of the affect regulating mechanism. Clinically we encounter it in at least the following three circumstances.

The flood dream tells us that the dreamer invokes the apocalyptic mechanism in an to attempt to overcome her depression. The dream fails but it does indicate that she is able, to a certain extent, to deal with her depression and suicidal tendencies by identifying with the rescuer, the philanthropist. Apocalypses that arise out of despair often include messianic wishes, the hope to be rescued by an intermediary with supernatural powers. This messianism is expectant rather than activist.

The second type of apocalypse is exemplified by the Biblical story of the Flood, as a punishment for misbehavior. The Book of Revelation similarly threatens punishment for sinful conduct. The Evil Empire, Rome, will be punished for its degeneracy while the Christians will be saved. The same apocalypse will punish the Romans (second type) but rescue the Christians (first type). In each of these two apocalypses, the righteous remnant survives. Here is an example of an individual apocalypse appearing in a dream and basing itself upon Revelation. This material is kindly provided by Dr. Jacob A. Arlow, one of the participants in our study.

The patient has put his apartment up for sale. He is hoping to get enough money to enable him to leave his law practice and go to Hollywood to pursue a career in film. He intends either to write about film, to write scenarios, or perhaps even to produce. The patient has no experience or training in this field. To him, however, going to Hollywood means throwing off the shackles of inhibition and especially the proscriptions of the church regarding sexuality. In previous months, the patient has produced a great deal of material of a frankly incestuous nature, coupled with thoughts of castration and damnation for sexual wishes, together with fear of authority figures. This material, however, has come out in an extremely isolated form. The patient repeats what he has learned as if it were a catechism. His insight is reduced to a formula which is repudiated as such. The patient is most isolated in his productions. He gives hardly any details of day-to-day activities, conversations with other individuals, or fleeting fantasies, unless a specific inquiry is made about such items.

Over the past weekend, preceding the Independence Day holiday, the patient had as a weekend guest his only close friend. This is a man whom he has known from college days. Both are Catholic and lawyers with serious sexual problems. Both are dissatisfied with the practice of law and would like to leave it. The friend, Adolph, however, has two children and a wife and feels trapped. During their earlier years, the two would share sexual fantasies and giggle about "exploits" they had with girls. Although this is the patient's closest friend, he sees him perhaps once or twice a year. Adolph's wife is extremely withdrawn as is their older child. It is clear from the description that the patient and Adolph, who shared sexual fantasies and thoughts both suffer the same kinds of inhibitions. Over the weekend they went for a walk together and discussed their sexual inhibitions and the role of the Catholic Church in frightening them with eternal damnation for sexual transgression.

After his friend Adolph, Adolph's wife Sylvia and the two children left, the patient spent a quiet Fourth of July holiday reading a book which was essentially an interview with the Italian movie director, Fellini. On the night of July 5th to July 6th the patient had the following dream.

> My wife and I were somewhere up in the mountains in some small village. There were four people coming on horseback. They were knights like the Four Horsemen of the Apocalypse. They had stopped to tell us that there was going to be an earthquake and some of the area would be flooded. We were on a small island. They told us to move to a larger island, which we did. While we were there, the earth began to quake, fire began to flow and the small island where we had been was inundated with water. We were clinging close to the ground while the earth was shaking.

The patient stated that the dream must be traced to what he was reading in the Fellini interviews. Fellini spoke about the pervasive influence of the Catholic Church in Italian life. Its two thousand year old influence pervades every aspect of Italian thought. Most particularly, however, Fellini emphasized the role of the Apocalypse. The ultimate vision of the Apocalypse is in the background of every Italian person's thinking and, as such, it gives vibrancy to the lives of the Italians. Everything is lived against the background of the ultimate great struggle of the Judgment Day, when people will either be damned to eternal perdition or go to heaven with the angels, etc. Fellini felt, and the patient agreed, that it was the Church, not God, that introduced the idea of sexual pleasure as sin, making the apocalyptic vision one fraught with fear and trepidation.

Later in the session the patient quoted a further element from the Fellini interview. Fellini was questioned about the picture "8 1/2" and Anita Ekberg. Fellini said he had not known Anita Ekberg, but when he saw a picture of her in an American film magazine, in which she was dressed in a skimpy leopard skin, he exclaimed, "I hope to God I never run into her. I could never resist such temptation." In discussing this aspect of the material, the patient said, "There again is woman as the devil, woman as the temptress and seductress."

To which I added that Anita Ekberg was noted for her large, sensuous breasts. The patient agreed and I then reminded him of the sex play with his mother's "apples."

The patient had been in Italy ten years ago, he recalled, after the earthquake in southern Italy. He was at the Amalfi Drive and saw how the earth had just been torn apart by the quaking, how fragments of roads were separated from each other by dozens of yards as a result of the earthquake. He had also seen a mild eruption of a volcano in Sicily. The flowing lava connected with volcanic eruptions reminded him of visions of fire and brimstone in apocalyptic visions in the Bible in the Apocalypse of St. John.

The four knights in the dream the patient identified with the Four Horsemen of the Apocalypse. He could not, however, remember their names or exactly what they stood for but he knew that they represented portents of great danger and ultimate destruction. In the dream, however, he was struck by the fact that the four horsemen were actually saviors and helpers. While discussing the four horsemen, the patient kept fondling his tie reassuringly.

I called to the patient's attention that the four horsemen represented tremendous threats—conquest, war, famine and death. It was when I mentioned Death and the Pale Rider on the white horse that the patient recalled that aspect of the Fellini interview that dealt with Anita Ekberg.

This material was used to demonstrate to the patient how, in spite of his advanced thinking, he still clings to the fear instilled in him by that part of the Catholic teaching about sex (incest) being a mortal sin, punishable by eternal damnation. This in spite of the fact that earlier in the session he supported Fellini's view that God really takes the total balance of man's deeds, good and evil, over the course of the 70 or so year span and weighs man in the balance, but He would not condemn an individual just for one act of mortal sin, that it was the Church that introduced the idea of eternal perdition. In spite of all this, however, the patient, out of his own castration anxiety and guilt, still has to grapple with the fear of damnation (castration).

From our point of view, this case illustrates the second type of apocalypse, that is destruction in response to sin. The patient however is not punished with the wicked, but escapes with the aid of the Four Horsemen who, in the dream, abandon their classical role of portents of death and destruction, and become helpers and rescuers. The reason that the threat fails is that, because of his lifelong masochism and depressive character the patient had begun a program of antidepression drug therapy with me a year earlier. His response to all medication had been positive but only temporary. On 22 June, 20 milligrams of fluoxetine had been prescribed in addition to the 60 milligrams of methylphenidate per day, and 0.5 milligrams of lorazepam, three times a day that he had been taking. He had responded nicely to the fluoxetine. The dream, which occurred on 6 July, reflects the remedial effects of the latter in the patient's seeing himself as one of the saved rather than one of the doomed, and the Horsemen as friends rather than demons. This case illustrates the fact that mood influences the outcome of the mythic drama as it is played out.

The third variant of apocalypse represents the individual's attempts to overcome his depressive state by attacking some enemy. He will bring about the end of the world but he and his friends and family will survive. What he is actually doing is displacing his suicidal impulse outward. In contrast to the dreamer of the flood dream who merely focuses on the misery of the others so that she can be less miserable about herself, the apocalyptic of the third kind actually attacks the outside world that may or may not be the source of his misery. Because the others are attacked he is saved. Here is the dream of a man in his early fifties who came for treatment of depression. Antidepression medication alleviated his depression but made him more antagonistic toward his wife. They quarreled, especially over his increased appetite and pronounced weight gain.

> I live in the country. We heard that a plague of locusts was coming so I decided to create a gap, like one controls a fire, to stop the locusts. I would do it by burning the forest. So we started a fire but it got out of control and became a major forest fire. I opened a gate and let animals run out to escape, a rhinoceros. Before that I was sure all the windows and doors in the house were closed. A lion was loose and came up to the house. I'm not afraid. I gave him something to eat. Then I thought maybe he eats people. I got frightened so I took a large slab of meat. I'll throw it over him so I'll go into the house. I did throw it over him and then I woke up.

The locusts represent the patient himself since they eat everything they encounter. To control them, he sets a major forest fire. To undo that damage, he releases wild animals, who again represent himself. He feared the lion but he controlled it by offering it food. The antidepression medication did not fully alleviate his distress but did give him enough energy to retaliate against his wife whom he found too controlling. But he was afraid his anger would escape control, the locusts, the fire, the lion, so he attempts to control himself by appeasing himself with food, specifically meat, that is, food derived from killing another living creature. Is there an allusion here to cannibalism? He starts a major forest fire and looses wild animals, but he survives.

The case seems to run counter to the observations I made above to the effect that antidepression treatment can pacify an angry, depressed individual. In this case the antidepression treatment provoked a quiet, depressive man to activity and anger. The fact is that angry depressives may become tranquil with antidepression medication, while quiet, inert depressives may respond with appropriate anger to the same treatment.

## Summary

In our discussion of myths, dreams, and the unconscious fantasies that generate them we have found that: first, most of them deal primarily with ultimate concerns, life and death. Even when sexuality enters consideration, it becomes a source of rivalry and combat or guilt provoking Promethean aspirations. Second, in their conscious derivatives, these themes are associated with specific affects or moods. In dreams at least, the mood of the dream is not determined by the content of the dream, but rather the reverse: the content of the dream is determined by the mood. The mood determines how the dream starts and how it ends. Third, the mood determines whether or not the dreamer will take some action, but what action will be taken is represented or can be influenced by the content of the myth or dream.

The circulation of a myth in a community elicits an appropriate affective response when the affects are ready to seek expression. A circulated myth also acts to synchronize and coordinate the behavior of the members of the community.

The myth tells us that under certain circumstances man has little or no freedom of will. The drama acts itself out despite the efforts of the subject. Greek tragedy indeed focuses on the struggle between the protagonist and his announced fate. Man is destined to attempt to fulfill childhood wishes; he is destined to be punished if he succeeds too well, and to be depressed if he fails. Tranquility can be found only if one succeeds neither too much nor too little. The measure of what is too much and what is too little, varies from individual to individual but the same dynamic governs us all.

Of the various types of myth that we have considered, the apocalyptic myth carries the most extreme affects. The fantasy of the apocalyptic destruction of the real world symbolizes and replaces suicidal fantasies, so that when apocalyptic fantasies generate action, the action is paradoxically likely to be self-destruction, or indirectly and ultimately to lead to it. On the other hand, the fantasy of rescue that appears in the passive type of apocalypse encourages hope and reinforces morale.

We have taken the trouble to study myths because we have found that in our study of case histories, as well as the history of antisemitism, antisemitic behavior and frequently antisemitic sentiments too are given impulse, coordination, direction, and encouragement by myths that circulate in the ambient society. Let us turn now to the classical antisemitic myths.

## Notes

1. Histories, V, 5:3 quoted by M. Stern (1980) *Greek and Latin Authors on Jews and Judaism,* Israel Academy of Sciences and Humanities, vol. 2.
2. Approaching the subject from a study of classic Jewish texts, Liebes, 1993, pp. 58f., comes to the same conclusion.
3. The Oedipal implications of the *akedah* and crucifixion are treated psychoanalytically also by H.F. Stein (1977), and Trachtenberg (1989). Grunberger (1964) explores the influence of the Oedipal conflict on antisemitism.
4. *Shehitah* is the Jewish ritual for slaughtering animals for human consumption. The ritual was intended to prevent wanton slaughter and spilling of blood, in compliance with the biblical injunction against consuming meat torn off a living animal, or even animal blood. It was devised by the rabbis of the Rabbinic period so as to minimize the animal's pain and drain the blood lest it be consumed with the meat. After the animal is slaughtered in compliance with the ritual, it is *kashered* before it can be eaten. *Kashering* is a procedure for drawing off the blood remaining in the meat by exposing the meat to water and then to salt crystals and permitting the salty fluid to drain by gravity.

   Michal Bodemann has suggested that in the Middle Ages these ritual procedures for draining meat of its blood were perversely misinterpreted as a method of *obtaining* blood for ritual purposes. If red wine symbolizing blood is drunk at the Mass, why should Jews not harvest blood for their rituals? And if animal blood was acceptable, would not the blood of Christian children be even more acceptable for the ritual?

   Reverting to Bergmann's argument, the Jew has devised rituals to repress and prevent cannabalistic impulses-but the antisemite interprets these rituals as a method for indulging these impulses.

# 4

# Antisemitic Myths

Against the background of mythic themes in general, we are in a position now to consider antisemitic myths in order to detect the universals from which they obtain their power and authority. Clearly we cannot undertake here a history of antisemitism but we shall take up some of the more egregious themes that have appeared at various times and places. I shall compare them with the general mythic themes that we have considered. I shall also attempt, where I can, to specify the circumstances that gave them the form and content that they assumed at the time.

## Hostility to the Jews in the Bible

The earliest antisemitic expressions that we know are found in the Jewish Bible. In Exodus 1, verses 9 and 10, the new pharoah of Egypt tells his people "Look, the people of Israel are more numerous and powerful than we. Let us deal wisely with them, lest in the event of war, they ally themselves with our enemies and fight against us." There follows the well-known oppressive enslavement of Israel. We do not see here the same stereotyping of Jews that we encounter in subsequent antisemitic canards. The Israelites have not assimilated into Egyptian society. As an alien element, they are not to be trusted, and besides, they are a plentiful source of manpower.

The second account, from the Book of Esther, resembles the first. In chapter 3, verses 8 and 9, Haman says to King Ahasuerus, "There is a certain people scattered and dispersed among the others in all of the provinces of your kingdom, and their laws differ from the laws of every other people and they do not observe the King's laws and it is not appropriate for the King to tolerate them. If it pleases the King, let it be recorded that they are to be eradicated and I shall count out ten thousand

talents of silver to be turned over to the stewards of the royal treasury."
Here the situation is a little more complex. Haman is antagonized because the Jew, Mordecai, will not show him proper obeisance. He is so
angry that he responds with a plan to murder all the Jews in the empire.
It is not the separateness of the Jews, but their idiosyncrasies, especially
in withholding the respect that he feels is due to him. Moreover, there is
some historical baggage. The struggle between Mordecai and Haman
becomes a current edition of, and metaphor for the historical struggle
between Israel and Amalek, Israel's traditional enemy from the time of
the exodus. In both stories, Israel is attacked and mistrusted as an alien
people, even though the Persian Empire was composed of many peoples,
each retaining its own identity and language. Haman says that they do
not observe the King's laws and in that way differ from all other people
in the empire.

We must infer that the alienness of the Jews makes them subject to
special feelings, negative as we see here, but also positive. We observed
in chapters 1 and 2 that antisemitism often alternates with philosemitism.[1]
The two historic exiles of the Jewish people, by Babylonia in 587 B.C.E.[1]
and by Rome in 70 and 135 C.E., contributed heavily to the Diaspora,
but Jews traveled widely in the ancient world even when not under com-
pulsion and settled in most countries to which they had access, always
as recognizable minorities. After a generation or two they were no longer
strangers, but they continued to be regarded as alien. We discussed
stranger anxiety in chapter 2. We asked, does the tendency to reject the
Jew reflect stranger anxiety? To say that the Jew is not a stranger because he may have lived in the community for generations does not
really address the issue. The Jew may not be a stranger after living in
the same community for years or generations, but he remains an alien
and his alienness will be communicated to non-Jewish children by their
non-Jewish parents. Even today in the United States, after a Jewish presence dating back more than a century before the American Revolution,
and a major presence for about a century, non-Jewish Americans recognize Jewish names, occupations, speech patterns, and some modes of
behavior as distinctive. That distinctiveness carries a positive or negative sign or both, or first one and then the other.

Each developmental phase may contribute its characteristic images
and fantasies to antisemitic myths. With respect to the child's earliest
attachments to its mother, the Jew reminds one of the father or other

caretaker who may be experienced as someone trying to seduce the child away from its mother. In the phase of separation-individuation (ages one to three), the Jew represents the stranger who is the rival of the father. Subsequently in latency, the child who is seen as distinctive because he is Jewish, helps to define fraternal group boundaries. The adolescent must deal with his antagonistic impulses, that is, his resistance to committing himself to group membership and his resistance to complying with superego imperatives, imperatives imposed by the community and his parents. He can do that by attributing the individualistic, noncompliant tendencies to Jews who maintain their distinctiveness. Or he may be attracted to Jews because of their distinctiveness, and then, when his mood changes, turn against them for having seduced him away from his natural allegiances.

## Pre-Christian Antisemitism

Jews were well represented in the Roman Empire during the early centuries of the Common Era, and are estimated to have comprised 5 to 12 percent of the population. Although some were quite successful and a few even became Roman knights, most were poor and some even scrounged a living by begging or by questionable practices such as telling fortunes. The Roman government treated them well and did not discriminate against them, except for a few years after the Bar Kokhba revolt when the practice and teaching of the Jewish religion were prohibited. In fact, the Roman government granted the Jews special privileges so as to make it possible for them to observe religious obligations without being held responsible for conflicting civic obligations. Nevertheless most of the references to Jews in the works of Roman writers that we have are unfavorable. But again, it was the distinctiveness of their customs that seems to have troubled these observers who interpreted what they saw to the detriment of the Jews. They were critical too of others with different and distinctive customs, for example, Germans and Gauls. Tacitus, considered by scholars to have been among the greatest of Roman historians, had a good deal to say about Jews. He wrote about them during the first decade of the second century of the Common Era. Apparently he attempted to give an accurate account of then current theories about their history but he permitted his personal feelings fairly free expression. The Jews permit what Romans abhor, they regard as profane what Romans hold sacred. Jews are base, abominable, and depraved. They do not tolerate infanticide.

What we see here is once more, discomfort in the presence of difference and distinctiveness. The writer criticizes Jews for their religious customs and personal behavior, finding fault essentially with their separateness. But we hear no calls for attacking them or driving them away. There were violent conflicts between Greeks and Jews in Alexandria, but these had more to do with conflict of interests, economic and political, rather than ideological prejudice.

## Antisemitism of the Christian Scriptures and the Church Fathers

In the Christian scriptures we find at least three issues, each of which has since inspired anti-Jewish sentiments. The first of these is an issue that sounds strangely contemporary, namely, who is Jew? The issue has become current because many Jews who, having lapsed from ritual observance either because of individual option or government repression, desire now to be recognized as Jews for the purpose of acquiring eligibility for citizenship in Israel, or as marriage partners or parents of potential marriage partners to more observant Jews. Recent immigrations to Israel that have included many individuals with no Jewish ancestry, have exacerbated the problem. In Israel a self-designated set of supreme religious authorities have claimed the right to determine who qualifies as a Jew. They have aroused the antagonism of many ardent but nonobservant Jews who have, to this point, successfully resisted that kind of authoritarian and arbitrary control over their lives and destinies.

In the first century, the question of who is a Jew arose not over returnees or secular Jews, but over sectarian deviants who, despite the consensus of Jewish practice and belief then prevailing in Jerusalem, insisted upon being recognized as legitimate Jews, namely the Jewish Christians. The problem was complicated when these Jewish Christians proselytized among the gentiles and brought into their religious community many who converted to their religion but without accepting circumcision, which is required by Jewish ritual. It was the irreconcilibility of the two positions that established for all time the antipathy between Jews and Christian gentiles and led to the establishment of a separate church toward the end of the first century (Parkes, 1981).

The dissidents, who later were called Christians, had evolved a new system of beliefs that they saw as an improvement over the old, and a new set of observances. The validity of either, precluded the validity of the other, so it became necessary to affirm one's own legitimacy vigorously. Both Matthew (1:1-17) and Luke (3:23-38) offer mythical and somewhat different genealogies of Jesus so as to establish his legitimacy as the expected Messiah. Much of the Christian Bible, and especially Paul's writings, deal with the Christian dispute with the Jews about who is a Jew. Should we consider the rivalry between the Jews and the early Christians an instance of sibling rivalry or Oedipal rivalry? Do the two contestants see each other as brothers quarreling over a birthright, or as father and son? At this point at least, it seems to me that the two are quarreling about who is the legitimate son to the Father, who will be loved and protected by the Father, who has access to the Father. In the following passage, Jesus affirms that the father of the Jews is not God but the devil:

> Then said they to him, We be not base born; we have one Father, even God.
>
> Jesus said unto them, if God were your Father, ye would love me: for I proceeded forth and came from God; neither came I of myself, but he sent me.
>
> Why do ye not understand my speech? even because ye cannot hear my word.
>
> Ye are of your father the devil, and the lusts of your father ye will do: he was a murderer from the beginning, and abode not in the truth, because there is no truth in him. When he speaketh a lie, he speaketh of his own: for he is a liar, and the father of it.
>
> And because I tell you the truth, ye believe me not.
>
> Which of you convinceth me of sin? And if I say the truth, why do ye not believe me?
>
> He that is of God heareth God's words: ye therefore hear them not, because ye are not of God. (John 8:41-47)

We could speculate that the authors of the Christian Scriptures had some question about their own position, otherwise they might not have found it necessary to be so contentious. However, they were preaching and writing to convert others and so their vehemence was intended for that purpose. Nevertheless, since the Jews have never accepted the legitimacy of the Christian argument, Christian conviction could not be complete.

What is involved here is not simply who has the correct approach to God, but how do we guarantee access to Him. For the Jews it was by observing the laws of the Torah and the values and rituals of the evolving rabbinic religion. For the dissidents, it was by the intervention of the Messiah, Jesus, an intermediary who guaranteed access to the Father. It seems evident that the struggle involves not merely a difference of opinion, a cognitive choice, but an affirmation or denial of a deeply held conviction, one that arises from unconscious sources and is based upon earliest needs. The discomfirmation of one's belief leaves one disoriented and at loose ends and therefore induces anxiety. To the extent that religious belief is central to his life, and to the extent that he sees the Jews still disconfirming his beliefs, the Christian must feel threatened—even today. To the extent that the messiahship of Jesus is necessary to one's confidence in one's position in the universe, Jewish "obstinacy" is a threat.

> It is indeed impossible for a group based upon an ideology not to be proselytising and not to seek to destroy not only its enemies, not only the objects of projection mentioned earlier, but also all those who remain outside it. Since they do not enter into the game of those who uphold the illusion, they represent a fault in the illusion itself. Since they do not abandon reality testing to the incense-bearers of Illusion, this is ipso facto thrown into question ('those who are not with us are against us'). It is thus essential to reduce those who are indifferent (and the sceptics) and to oblige them to cede to the "believers" the function of reality. (Chasseguet-Smirgel, 1985)

Since even the thought that belief might be conditional might itself threaten one's composure, the whole conflict can become unconscious and contribute heavily to the unconscious sources of antisemitism.

I would consider the verbal abuse directed against the Jews in some sections of the Christian Scriptures, a second source of anti-Jewish sentiment.

> Woe unto you, scribes and Pharisees, hypocrites! for ye devour widows' houses, and for a pretense make long prayer: therefore ye shall receive the greater damnation.
>
> Woe unto you, scribes and Pharisees, hypocrites! for ye compass sea and land to make one proselyte; and when he is made, ye make him twofold more the child of hell than yourselves.
>
> Woe unto you, ye blind guides, which say, Whosoever shall swear by the temple, it is nothing; but whosoever shall swear by the gold of the temple, he is a debtor! (Matthew 23:14–16)
>
> Woe unto you, scribes and Pharisees, hypocrites! for ye make clean the outside of the cup and of the platter, but within they are full of extortion and excess.
>
> Thou blind Pharisee, cleanse first that which is within the cup and platter, that the outside of them may be clean also.

Woe unto you, scribes and Pharisees, hypocrites! for ye are like unto whited sepulchres, which indeed appear beautiful outward, but are within full of dead men's bones, and of all uncleanness.

Even so ye also outwardly appear righteous unto men, but within ye are full of hypocrisy and iniquity. (Matthew 23:25-28)

Ye serpents, ye generation of vipers, how can ye escape the damnation of hell? (Matthew: 23:33)

To those who consider Jesus a model for behavior, this type of excoriation of the Jews by Jesus establishes a precedent and invites projection of one's own faults upon Jews, as well as rejection of Jewish morality and religion as hypocritical. Again, this readiness to castigate Jews based upon models given in Christian Scriptures, may remain conscious or become unconscious in which event it can exert an even more profound influence.

No less fateful for Jewish destiny was the introduction of the theme of blood into the Christian Scriptures, the third of the three enduring prejudicial issues. Matthew introduces the theme of the murder of Prophets:

Wherefore, behold, I send unto you prophets, and wise men, and scribes: and some of them ye shall kill and crucify; and some of them ye shall scourge in your synagogues, and persecute them from city to city.

That upon you may come all the righteous blood shed upon the earth, from the blood of the righteous Abel unto the blood of Zacharias son of Barachias, whom ye slew between the temple and the altar.[2] (Matthew 23:34-35)

We have taken note of the importance of blood earlier. On the one hand, as an evidence of sacrifice, it exerts an apotropiac, protective effect. On the other hand, the spilling of human blood is the greatest source of guilt. With the statement in chapter 27, verse 25, "His blood be on us and on our children," Matthew manages to impute blood guilt to the Jewish people and their descendants forever, and at the same time to obtain for the followers of Jesus the grace and forgiveness that human sacrifice commands. Even the *akedah* of Isaac was an aborted sacrifice, and the circumcision is a token, and the sacrifices of the temple were of animals not humans, and performed under ritual restraint. Here we have a regression back to the experience of human sacrifice, and it is blamed on the Jews!

In fact we are dealing here not merely with human sacrifice but with cannibalism.

Verily, verily, I say unto you, He that believeth in me hath everlasting life.

I am that bread of life.

Your fathers did eat manna in the wilderness, and are dead.

This is the bread which cometh down from heaven, that a man may eat thereof, and not die.

I am the living bread which came down from heaven: if any man eat of this bread, he shall live for ever: and the bread that I will give is my flesh, which I will give for the life of the world.

The Jews therefore strove among themselves, saying, How can this man give us his flesh to eat?

Then Jesus said unto them, Verily, verily, I say unto you, Except ye eat the flesh of the Son of man, and drink his blood, ye have no life in you.

Whosoever eateth my flesh, and drinketh my blood, hath eternal life; and I will raise him up at the last day.

For my flesh is meat indeed, and my blood is drink indeed.

He that eateth my flesh, and drinketh my blood, dwelleth in me, and I in him.

As the living Father hath sent me, and I live by the Father; so he that eateth me, even he shall live by me. (John 6:47-57)

Every analyst knows that Catholic children participating in the mass are strongly affected by the impression that they are indeed biting, chewing, and swallowing human flesh and blood. Here is a section of a poem entitled "The Property of Hunger," written by a woman in her effort to deal with her orality.

On Saturdays, I gave confession, counting
each lie, each stolen thing on rosary beads;
my Priest granted me communion:
a tasteless wafer of bloodless flesh
and pseudo-blood sipped from the chalice.
I wanted to wrench it from his hands
and drink it down;
I went away with a wicked thirst.

**Who eats my flesh and drinks my blood
lives in me and I in him.**
I hold the Eucharist beneath my tongue
in a slow dissolving. I feed on this
ecstasy, on the flesh and wine that
seeps through my thirsty lips and
the warm liquid-spirit that penetrates
me. I keep confusing who is wounded
and who is fed. I squeeze the milky

beads of my rosary too hard, as if
mercy might ooze from my faithful
fingering, a Holy water that

bathes the sick soul of me,
purging the sin that wants to be
set loose from every cell of my skin.
I feel this Lord enter me;
I tell no one of this possession.

(Smith, 1993)

Cannibalistic fantasies prevail probably universally early in life. Children imagine both being consumed by their parents as suggested by Little Red Riding Hood, Jack and the Beanstalk, and Hansel and Gretel, and consuming their parents. Such fantasies make their appearance in nightmares, phobias, and fairy tales. Jesus offers his flesh and blood as symbols of his having been sacrificed, so that his followers will be saved thereby. The flesh of some of the animal sacrifices of the Temple were normally consumed. But cannibalistic fantasies themselves create guilt that becomes easier to expiate if one remembers, "His blood be on us and on our children." Other stimuli of cannibalistic fantasies, for example, hunger due to famine or poverty can also arouse blood guilt that is unconscious and displaced onto Jews.

If we recall now our earlier discussion of myth as both a device for celebrating rebirth and escape from destruction, and also as a means of binding a community together in that celebration, then we can understand the message in the Christian Scriptures. The new religion that centers on the messiahship of Jesus, it is affirmed, was almost destroyed at birth by the Jews. Jesus was killed. However, since Jesus was the Messiah, he had the power to overcome the murderous schemes of the Jews and he was indeed "reborn." In this way belief in Jesus is vindicated and the Jews are revealed as his enemies. The death of Jesus is a human sacrifice the benefit of which accrues to the Christian, while the guilt and punishment accrue to the Jew. This lesson is passed on explicitly to Christians of subsequent generations, but the myth of resurrection gives the story an unconscious cogency, it creates a readiness to believe. Denouncing the Jews is a way of acting out the myth.

The Church fathers continued their efforts to distinguish the Christians from the Jews and to discourage their contact. To this end they indulged in vituperative denunciation. John Chrysostom (which means golden mouth) spoke of the synagogue as a theater and a brothel, a home for robbers, wild and filthy beasts, and demons.

The Church fathers moreover made an effort to appropriate the Jewish Scriptures, to disinherit the Jews. All the heroes of the Jewish Bible were claimed to be Christians even before Christ.

I pointed out above that Matthew exploited the crucifixion by appropriating its saving, sacrificial influence for the Christians and by attaching the guilt for murder to the Jews. Many of the Church fathers extended the technique of dissociating allusions in reinterpreting the Prophetic writings of Jewish Scriptures. Typically, the prophets address the sins of the people of Israel, warn them of the dire consequences of sinning, that is, rejection and punishment, and then proceed to a message of comfort and the promise of reconciliation between Israel and God. The Church fathers read into this formula a statement of the reprobation of Israel but the elevation of the Christians! The two components of the prophecy are separated: the negative aspect applies to the Jews and the positive aspect to the Christians.

Yosef Yerushalmi, speculating about whether the rivalry between Christianity and Judaism is Oedipal rivalry or sibling rivalry, asks who is the object of the rivalry. Who is the mother? He answers: "The Torah, the teaching, the revelation, the Torah which in Hebrew is grammatically feminine and which is Midrashically compared to a bride."

Rivalry is also forwarded by a series of contrasts, for example, between siblings: Cain and Abel, Isaac and Ishmael, Jacob and Esau. The younger of the two brothers represents Christianity while the older, the Jew. The Church has superseded the Jews as the elect of God.

Of all the practices of the Jews that trouble these Christian writers, the one most commonly mentioned is circumcision. Historically, it was circumcision that distinguished Jewish Christians from gentile Christians. But its salience hints at the importance of circumcision as a symbol of blood sacrifice, a subject that excited great ambivalence among these people.

At this point another adverse note is struck that is later developed into one of the major antisemitic themes, namely, the existence of a Jewish conspiracy. Parkes (102f.) quotes a number of sources that contend that the Jews really knew that Jesus was the Messiah but would not admit it out of shame and guilt. In some versions of the story, they convert. Allegations of a Jewish conspiracy to do one or another dastardly thing became more common subsequently. But the accusation demonstrates a mechanism for reconciling what is felt because of unconscious ideas or fears on the one hand, and what is plainly visible on the other. Ordinarily we try to reconcile incompatibilities between what we see and what we wish by any of a number of defenses such as denial, minimizing, or isolation. Creating a conspiracy theory accomplishes the same thing by invoking projection and creating a paranoid system. If the Christian harbors some doubts with regard to his beliefs, then the Jew can be held responsible, for example, for creating an illusion that challenges belief and for coming between the believer and his God. In this case, it is held that the Jews know that the accounts of the Christian Scriptures are true, but they deliberately discredit them in order to mislead Christians.

### Antisemitism After Constantine

With the achievement of political authority in Rome during the fourth century, the Church continued its policy of degrading the Jews, but now with governmental power. The Jews were still disparaged as nonbelievers. They were not permitted to build new synagogues or repair their old ones, by contrast with the churches which became ever grander. Christians were repeatedly warned by the Church against fraternizing with Jews as they had apparently tended to do. Jews were compelled to attend Christian sermons intended to persuade them to convert.

But why did the Church not attempt to eradicate the Jews as Christian mobs were ready to do in many places and at many times? Three reasons are given: the fact that the presence and appearance of the Jews would serve as witnesses of the truth of the Christian Bible; the hope that they would convert, thereby confirming the truth of Christianity; and their status as the people of the "Old Testament." In addition the Jews were identified with Cain who murdered his younger brother and whose life was to be spared, but who is to wander homeless forever, recognizable by the "mark of Cain" which was how the circumcision was to be regarded. That mythic attribution would fail if the Jews were now killed.[3]

However, we must wonder what the "real" reason might have been for permitting the Jews to survive. Perhaps it has been guilt that has been the inhibitory factor. The model would be the sparing of Joseph by his brothers who hated him because he was his father's favorite, his "chosen." Second, given any system of belief prevailing within a society, inevitably doubts arise in the minds of some. Under those circumstances, it is helpful to have a foil available to whom one can attribute inciting the disbelief. One can attribute one's own doubts to an external malicious influence and so be spared having to deal with one's own conflicts. Third, humiliating and degrading the Jews served to buttress the belief in Christianity, to demonstrate that they were being punished because of their perverse rejection of Christ.

## Antisemitism in the Middle Ages

During the Middle Ages antisemitism varied considerably from time to time and place to place. The seventh century saw a number of expulsions and forced conversions, but thereafter, except for sporadic and locally confined attacks, Jews did not fare too badly in Western Europe until the end of the eleventh century, that is, until the First Crusade. Some Jews had acquired wealth and some had achieved great influence with kings and princes. The Crusade of 1096 started a new era. The crusaders destroyed Jewish communities in the Rhineland. Starting in the twelfth century, mobs attacked Jews in response to blood libels. Norman Cohn (1970) gives examples of murders by bands of millenarians. We shall discuss the problem of the pogrom mentality in chapter 5.

The reasons for this intensification of antisemitic violence are not self-evident. We shall consider here some of the psychologic issues dealing with specific kinds of antisemitic accusations and canards.

During and after the eleventh century, the regular and deliberate degradation of the Jews resumed. More restrictions were imposed and life was made more difficult. Intense pressure to convert persisted. With the passing of the civil structure of the Roman Empire, Jews became, in law, "serfs of the Royal Chamber." As such they were not really slaves, but rather proteges of the king. Their privileges were circumscribed but not eliminated. Their residence in many places was contingent on the favor of the local prince. They were excluded from all but very few occupations. By the thirteenth century they were effectively excluded from agriculture. Many were impoverished. Others managed to achieve a status equivalent to burghers. Only moneylenders retained the possibility of living in any comfort, and their earnings were highly taxed. Jews were socially ostracized. The Jewish badge goes back to the fourth

Lateran Council of 1215, and the first ghetto was established in Venice in 1516. These restrictions were imposed to demonstrate the perpetual servitude and reprobation of the Jew.

It is important to emphasize that not all Christians in the Middle Ages were antisemites. Had vicious antisemitism been universal, the Jews would not have survived. I discussed just above possible reasons for sparing the Jews. We must infer a dynamic interplay between destructively antisemitic and philosemitic tendencies. In those times, philosemitic views could be expressed only by modulating the degree of one's antisemitism. We know of definite differences between the attitudes of the aristocracy and the mob, and between the popes and the friars. The elite have usually though not always been more friendly to the Jews and the populace more intolerant.

Starting in the twelfth century and extending until modern times, a series of accusations against Jews have dealt specifically with blood. Ritual murder accusations have resulted in Jewish loss of life, especially during the twelfth and thirteenth centuries. Jews were accused of crucifying or torturing or mutilating or drawing the blood of little Christian boys, generally for the purposes of their religious rituals.

Let us first establish that these accusations had been made previously against Jews and others. Apion, an Alexandrian Greek anti-Jewish propagandist reported that King Antiochus Epiphanes had found an intended Greek victim in the Jewish temple, who was being fattened for sacrifice. In the second century, Tertullian, a Church father, complained that Christians were being accused of ritual cannibalism. In the Middle Ages, some heretical Christian sects were also objects of such accusations. In Byzantine Europe, starting during the eighth century, in a series of canards, Jews were reported to have stabbed icons or crucifixes (Parkes, 1976, *passim;* Poliakov, 1974, vol. 2, *passim*). These religious objects made the crime known by miraculously gushing blood. In the end of the story, the Jew is usually converted.

By contrast, a less happy outcome followed a series of accusations that the Jews tortured Christ by assaulting the consecrated host (Poliakov, 1974, vol. 2; Parkes, 1976). The host emitted cries and blood, calling attention to the Jewish perpetrators. Blood was the evidence of a crime— as it was even in the case of Cain. Thousands of Jews were slaughtered. Even more egregiously, Jews were accused of ritual cannibalism. In 1235 the Jews of Fulda in Germany and in 1247 the Jews of Valreas on the French boundary of the Empire, were accused of taking the blood of Christian children for ritual purposes (Langmuir, 1990, p. 265). Related to these canards, is the belief that by poisoning wells, the Jews were responsible for the Black Death, that is, the plague. Between 1348 and 1350, thousands of Jews were massacred and hundreds of Jewish communities destroyed. Some reports allege that the Jews were working under the orders of a conspiratorial network which also murdered Christian children (Ziegler, 1991).

We can look for the causes of these attacks in two directions. First in the real world. Why should the issue of murdered children have become active in Western Europe during the thirteenth century? A reliable answer to that question would require full knowledge of social, economic, cultural and political conditions. However, one is not surprised to learn that in Western Europe during the thirteenth century, the population was rapidly outstripping the food supply. Population growth itself was attributable to an improvement in living conditions during the previous two centuries, that is, following the First Crusade in 1096. But the limitation of available food put an end to that growth. Western Europe suffered disastrous harvests and recurrent famines in the thirteenth century. "Cannibalism was a commonplace; the poor ate dogs, wrote one chronicler, cats, the dung of doves, even their own children." (Ziegler, 1991). Duby (1988) reports that infanticide and abandonment of children were not rare in the Middle Ages. By today's standards, infant mortality was extremely high. However limited abandonment of children and infanticide might have been, it would be reasonable to expect that it was an impulse that had to be controlled in some way even by those who themselves would not indulge. Accusing others of menacing one's own children would have alleviated the guilt for harboring such a thought even unconsciously.

The following pieces of information taken together support my argument that economic issues among others create reality problems, the imagined solution of which must be repressed—not admitted to consciousness. The repression is complemented and reinforced by the attribution of the same impulses to others, namely the Jews.

In 1212 groups of children set out from Europe to the Holy Land. One group was led by a French shepherd boy. A second was led by a ten-year-old child from Cologne, called Nicholas. It is estimated that he attracted 20,000 children from the Rhineland. Many of the children died and others were enslaved. What might we infer from the fact that so many children of such tender age were eager to leave their homes, and that their parents permitted them to do so? (*Encyclopaedia Britannica*, 15th ed., s.v. "children's crusade").

In 1235 thirty-four Jews were murdered in Fulda on the charge of having killed three Christian children on Christmas Day in order to obtain their blood for ritual purposes (Langmuir, 1990).

In 1284 many or most of the children disappeared from the town of Hamlin in northwestern Germany, a market center dependent upon the Abbey of Fulda. A legend links the departure of these children with the guile of a rat catcher, the Pied Piper, who is said to have led the children away in revenge for not having been paid for ridding the city of its rats (*Encyclopaedia Britannica*, 15th ed., s.v. "Hamlin").

Cologne, Fulda, and Hamlin lie at the vertices of an equilateral triangle about 125 miles on each side.

I am not proposing an exclusively economic explanation for the murderous attacks on Jews. However, the economic problem is a reality challenge that must be managed within the religious Weltanschauung of the local population. Langmuir (pp.307f.) demonstrates that there was much concern at that time with the literality of the transubstantiation of the wine and wafer to blood and flesh. He calls attention to the then contemporary concern with the extirpation of heresies that were associated with magic rituals and diabolic fantasies. We may guess that if the Jew is responsible for doing away with Christian children, while utilizing their blood for magic ritual purposes, for mocking the Eucharist, then he certainly can be recognized as the principle of evil, as the obstacle between the Christian and his God.

Hsia (1988) adduces cases in the fifteenth and sixteenth century in which fathers are known to have murdered their own sons and then accused the Jews. Like Langmuir, he relates the accusations against the Jews to the importance of blood superstition and magical belief.

Second, the realm of unconscious conflict adds to our understanding of this phenomenon. We have already discussed the religious significance of blood. On the one hand, it seems to protect against misfortune, signifying a propitiating sacrifice. On the other, obtaining the blood incurs guilt. Whereas rabbinic Judaism has restricted concern with human blood to the one time act of ritual circumcision, Christianity encourages its worshippers to imagine consuming Christ's blood and flesh at every Eucharist. While the intention is clearly to reinforce belief in the saving power of these symbols of Christ, the accompanying guilt may not be completely overcome. That particular issue may have become problematic especially during the period that we are considering. Christians, says Langmuir (p. 307), had long debated whether and how Christ's body and blood were present in the consecrated bread and wine of the Eucharist. In 1215, the Fourth Lateran Council promulgated the dogma of transubstantiation, and the cult of the body of Christ, of the consecrated host, was developed. It was at that time that Jews were accused of torturing Christ by assaulting the consecrated host. (It was at the same Council that the Jewish badge was officially instituted and that Jewish sacred texts were condemned.)

That participating in the Eucharist generated cannibalistic fantasies is suggested by the following quotation.

> Friar Berthold...explained that communicants don't see the holy child in the wafer because "who would like to bite off a baby's head, or hand or foot?" (*Encyclopaedia Judaica*, s.v. "blood libel")

Here again the guilt for cannibalism is projected out onto the Jews. The Christian obtains the protection while the Jew is held responsible for the spilling of the blood.

Baron (1957) acknowledges that the role of "widespread failure of crops and mass starvation" as well as "spiritual" motives contributed to mass participation in the First Crusade. However, he attributes the subsequent bitterness to the Christian belief that Jews hated Christians and would retaliate vindictively for the slaughter perpetrated by the Crusades. In fact, the Crusade experience itself, he asserts, poisoned the relations between Jews and Christians in Western Europe for centuries. (pp. 89ff.) His theory is strengthened by the fact that many Germans today fear retaliation by Jews for the Holocaust.

Accusations of Jewish ritual murder usually though not always center about incidents associated with Passover or Easter. The Jews, they say, require the blood of Christian children for making the Passover matzot, the classic blood libel. One of my patients, a Polish Catholic remembers having been told that by his mother when he was a child. She threatened to turn him over to the Jews for that purpose if he did not behave properly.

Passover is thought of as the occasion that marks the historical killing of the Egyptian first born, possibly in retaliation for the attempt to kill all Israelite male infants. The association with the crucifixion and the resurrection of Jesus also marks this period as especially appropriate for anti-Jewish calumnies and massacres. What is ironic though is that it is the Christian who in the Eucharist combines wafer (matzah) and wine as flesh and blood.

The fact that the Christian is accusing the Jew of offenses that no one has seen, that are not reasonable, and that have been rejected by reliable Christian authority including several of the Popes, is dealt with by assuming the existence of an invisible conspiracy. The Christian attaches destructive power to the *idea* of the Jew. The gap between idea and reality is bridged by the myth of the invisible conspiracy. This conspiratorial theme is carried through many antisemitic accusations.

In Visigothic Spain, Sisebut, a seventh-century king, was encouraged to eliminate the Jews from his domain by rumors that a world Jewish conspiracy had betrayed the Byzantines to Persia (Baron, 1957, vol. 3, p.38) In Toledo, 1499, attacks against conversos (marranos, Jewish converts to Catholicism) were accompanied by propaganda including the publication of forged letters between the leader of the Jewish community of Toledo and the leader of the Jewish community of Constantinople concerning a plot to destroy Christianity. (Beinart, 1972).

The Jew was accused of conspiring to extract blood from Christian children, to cause the plague by poisoning wells, to contaminate the race, to take over the world and its economy. The invisibility of this malign Jewish influence is attributed to the magical power of the Jew. Religious ritual is consciously thought of as a way of influencing God. To assume that it has magical power to affect mortal affairs would be a natural extension. In ancient times people did believe in the efficacy of magic even more than moderns do, in the absence of scientific knowledge and knowledge of events beyond their immediate horizon. The concept of influence at a distance and by invisible means bridged the attribution of malignant influence to Jews and the lack of visible evidence of their involvement. Even in the prescientific age it was widely appreciated that illness, and especially epidemics could be induced by poisoning or by direct contagion. Since the outbreak of illness followed the contact by an appreciable time interval, one could again assume Jewish invisible influence. The fantasy of Jewish physicians who killed Christian patients was complemented by its obverse, the Jewish physician who could magically cure them. In the Middle Ages, Jewish physicians were venerated and granted special privileges, but if a royal patient did badly, the physician was likely to lose his life as well.

As we saw in chapter 1, we know of two sources of psychic pain, the frustrations and disappointments of the real world, and the inner mechanism that deters excessive gratification and pleasure. In each instance, we feel serious distress, but the feeling is the same whether the influence arises from the inside or the outside. So it is easy and in a sense natural to confuse the two. If the distress arises internally, we can do nothing about it. But if we imagine that the cause is external, we can create the illusion that we are doing something to help ourselves by attacking an apparent source, a virtual reality. In the medieval world, encouraged by centuries of Church propaganda, Christians chose the Jews to play the role of external cause of internal misery, even when it was some obviously adverse external circumstance that brought about the unhappiness. For example, famine or plague, to the extent that it could not be controlled, it could be interpreted as the consequence of the malign intervention of the Jews. Jews in some way interfered with Divine protection.

As a result of the operation of this mechanism, the Jew was literally demonized. Medieval literature and woodcuts delineate the Jew as a form of demon, as an ally of Satan, diabolic in many ways (Trachtenberg, 1983). The Jew and his demonic allies were also often identified with the Antichrist, a mystical pseudomessianic figure who was expected to appear as a savior among the Jews but who had struggled to defeat the saving power of Christ. The image of the Jew in picture, story, and popular theatrical performance is that of deformity, usually with a grotesquely enlarged nose, frequently with clawed feet and other bestial structural characteristics. The Jew-badge and conical hat that Jews were obligated to wear were meant to reinforce the visibility of the Jew, the stigma attached to him, and the general impression of degradation, strangeness, and unnaturalness.

We spoke above of the concept of intermediaries between man and God. The intermediaries are thought of as though they are siblings in the family. This symbolic equivalence becomes evident in dream interpretation. They might be helpers, allies in the child's approach to the parent, or enemies, obstacles. Sometimes they play a quasi-parental role, as did the wolf for Romulus and Remus. They may function as older or younger siblings. Usually as in the case of angels, they answer to the same master or authority as the human who imagines them. Within the family, a favorite animal is often thought of by the child as a potential protector or adversary.

Religion knows a host of such intermediaries, of which, the most familiar are angels. Angels are generally thought of as benign. The concept of a destroying angel became more familiar as angelology became more developed. The monotheistic religions had difficulty in accounting for the existence of unfairness, injustice, and evil in the world. The polytheistic religions would often posit an evil deity and imagine a conflict between that and the benign deity. The assumption of angels with evil natures, that is, demons, under God's control, but with a certain amount of freedom, helps to resolve the discrepancy between the assumption of a beneficent god and the existence of visible evil. As we saw above, the intermediaries could be helpful or harmful or even alternate in their qualities.

The subject is relevant to our concerns here because in the medieval Christian world Jews were seen primarily as malign intermediaries. For example, as the deicides of the Christian Scriptures, the Jews threatened to abort the Christian religion. As the beneficiaries of the Antichrist, they could be seen as opponents of and threats to the true Christ. By their refusal to believe in Christian doctrine, that is, as infidels, they threatened the belief of true Christians. As allies and agents of the devil, they impeded the Christian's communication with Christ. It is Jews who were held responsible for the disowned infanticidal and cannibalistic impulses of starving Christians. Norman Cohn (1970) quotes French miracle plays to the effect that Jews were thought of as "demons of destruction whose one object was the ruin of Christians and Christendom" (pp. 7f.). "Jewry and clergy," he wrote, "together formed the foul black host of the enemy which stood opposite the clean white army of the Saints" (p. 87).

In a thoughtful and fascinating essay, Jacob Arlow (1991) has related Christian antisemitism to the usual angry rejection of the new baby by the older sibling. The newborn is seen as a rival for the mother's limited resources of food and affection.

While in terms of religious history, the Jews actually antecede the Christians, the Church fathers, as we observed above, preempted the Jewish Bible claiming that even the Patriarch Abraham was already Christian and that Christianity had superseded Judaism, just as in the stories of Genesis, the younger brother superseded the older, becoming the father's favorite or usurping the birthright. Having succeeded to the privileges of older sibling, the Christian now resented the Jew, seeing him as an interloper preempting the love of the parent, and as the hostile intermediary. The hostility led to the desire to get rid of the Jew, as Cain did to Abel, or as the older brothers tried to do to Joseph. The theme of cannibalism appears there in the fabrication that a wild animal had consumed him.

If Jews are alternately welcomed and resented as brothers, the alternation of philosemitism and antisemitism can be related to family romance. The von Rezzori stories, summarized in chapter 2 illustrate the intrusiveness of Jews, separating the Christian from his parent or preventing him from attaining some ideal or goal, and we took notice of the relation between this phenomenon and the family romance. In the first story, as a thirteen year old, he was disturbed and antagonized when a Jewish boy whom he had befriended seemed to have replaced him in his aunt's affection, inasmuch as the boy was an accomplished pianist. In the second story, it was the Jewish gatekeeper, the clerk of a seedy hotel, who prevented his consummation of a sexual liaison. The dragon guarding the virgin is signaled here as a motif, but it is not clear to me whether the rivalry is Oedipal rivalry. In the same story, he angrily breaks away from a Jewish lover because she would not give up her Jewish characteristics to become his ideal. In the third story, he violated the trust of a Jewish woman who had befriended him in order to win the admiration of a Christian friend. The fourth story deals with the conflict between his affection for his Jewish friends and his loyalty to family antisemitic "ideals." Finally, in the last story, he looks back sadly upon an unsuccessful life, his professional failures, his failed marriages, and his inability to rid himself of his antisemitism. He attributes the antisemitism to "a sick jealousy" and loyalty to his parents. His son by his Jewish second wife had died at five, preventing him from realizing his ambivalent fantasy of what he would be like if reincarnated as a Jew. Just as his Jewish lover in the second story refused to remake herself to comply with his fantasies about her, so had his Jewish wife refused to tolerate his remaking himself to comply with his own fantasies about himself. His child who would have made it possible to realize his identity as a Jew, was dead, and he had strong and ambivalent feelings about that. The stories clearly tell us that by attracting the author, the enlightened scion of antisemites, Jews create resentment inasmuch as they help to weaken or break his bond to his parents.

We have certainly seen family romance in the patients whose cases we discussed. In almost every instance antisemitic sentiments had been preceded at some time during the individual's life by philosemitic sentiments. Usually some reason was given for the shift in attitude, a disappointment, a rejection (for example, in the case of a gentile woman rejected by her Jewish lover, or a black lawyer rejected by his Jewish colleagues), guilt aroused by conflicting loyalties (as in the case of von Rezzori's allegiance to his antisemitic forebears), envy of Jewish success, or jealousy of a successful Jewish rival for the love of a woman. Historically we have documents from several periods in which Church authorities discouraged and forebade fraternization between gentile and Jew and we must infer from that, that fraternization did commonly occur. Both parental and religious authority interpret fraternization with Jews as literal betrayal of the biologic and religious family and respond by portraying the Jew as unwholesome, dangerous, disease ridden, degraded, and inhuman. In addition, Jews are further stigmatized by having to wear special clothing so that they can be avoided more easily. Their monstrous character is suggested in myths that they have horns and tails. That particular fantasy relates the image of the Jew to the image of the devil. For the Christians, the ultimate rejection and reprobation is expulsion, which has the additional advantage of enabling them to appropriate Jewish property.

## The Merchant of Venice

The true antisemitic burden of *The Merchant of Venice*, I believe, is the idea that the Jew represents the capriciousness and cruelty of fate. Benjamin Nelson and Joshua Starr (1944), in a fascinating historical review entitled "The Legend of the Divine Surety and the Jewish Moneylender" trace the antisemitic elements of the plot to the combination of two separate but related themes.

The first appears in a Midrashic legend of unknown origin, that Rashi[4] associated with a cryptic comment about Rabbi Akiba[5] in the Babylonian Talmud (Nedarim 50a). In it, God and the sea are designated as surety for a loan to Rabbi Akiba and when he is unable to repay the loan on time because of illness, the sea carries to the creditor a treasure that repays the loan. This theme appears not long afterward in a seventh-century Byzantine tale in which Theodore, a Christian shipmaster of Constantinople, is generously financed by a magnanimous Jew, Abraham, even after Theodore has lost two cargoes to the sea, and his request for financing has been rejected by his Christian friends. The only surety that Theodore can offer Abraham is a legendary icon of Christ. Theodore discharges his debt by committing gold pieces to the sea in a chest, which the sea then floats rapidly to Abraham. When Abraham denies having received the payment in an effort to understand how the surety worked, the icon miraculously reveals that he has. Abraham is impressed and he and his family convert to Christianity.

In fact, The Theodore-Abraham story seems to be based upon an incident in the life of St. John of Alexandria, called the Almoner. The character of the Jew is modeled after that of the saintly Christian patriarch. Greek and Slavic variants of this story appeared subsequently.

What is the message implicit in the story? It deals with the problem of the capriciousness of fate and with the need to confront hazard and risk, and with the attempt to find in religious faith a means for overcoming uncertainty and ensuring that things will go well. The sea is the source of danger, but under the influence of Jesus, it becomes the avenue to successful trade, and a miraculous channel for repaying the indebtedness incurred in arranging the voyage. Note that the antisemitism here is muted: the Jew is called friend and brother, and the money is lent without expectation of interest or profit, merely out of love and respect. That the Jew converts testifies that he has been persuaded that Jesus does indeed protect against danger. Christian faith is justified.

The second theme appears in variants of the Theodore-Abraham story that appeared in the West toward the end of the eleventh century. These diffused widely and in the course of the diffusion, drastic alterations were made.

Some of the earlier Western versions retain the benign image of the Jew. Others, however, add noxious features. In one story, in addition to offering Christ as surety, the Christian merchant promises that, in case of default, he will become the Jew's slave. In another variant, the Christian hero offers his son as surety. Although the sea, as in the earlier Eastern stories, returned the loan to the Jew, he denied having received it and demanded the son as chattel. Here the villainous idea of human security for the loan overshadows the issue of religious protection and miraculous, divine intervention.

In the later Western variants, the element of the timeliness of the re-payment becomes salient although it had been subdued in the earlier versions or absent from them.

By the twelfth century when antisemitism had become more malignant, the stories demonstrated the openhanded generosity of the noble and enter-prising Christian merchant, as opposed to the cunning and chicanery of the vindictive Jewish moneylender. They accompanied campaigns against the use of Christian servants and slaves by Jews, and against Jewish money-lenders. The campaigns, of course, followed the First Crusade and were accompanied by ritual murder charges, pogroms, and expulsions.

In a later set of stories, including the *Il Pecorone* story of Giovanni Fiorentino, money borrowed from a creditor must be returned by a cer-tain day or the debtor pays with his flesh. In many of them, the debtor forgets his obligation until it is too late. The sea is not called upon to speed his repayment as it did in the Theodore-Abraham stories.

The message of these stories seems to be that self-indulgence and hubris may deliver the Christian into the hands of the venal and blood-thirsty Jewish moneylender, who now represents the harshness of fate. If Christian faith fails to protect the Christian against catastrophe, it is because of the malevolence and vindictiveness of the Jew, who, as the devil, can thwart, or almost thwart the protection of Christ. In the earlier stories, the Jew protects the Christian against danger; in the later sto-ries, he personifies the cruelty of the real world.

But let us now return to *The Merchant of Venice*. The dangers of the real world are again represented by the hazards of sea travel and the role of chance is represented by that, as well as by Portia's risk in having to accept as a husband a man chosen by chance. Freud (1913) suggests that the three caskets represent the three fates and the need to choose, man's inexorable confrontation with destiny.

In the play, faith is no longer invoked as protection against harsh reality. Rejecting even the prudence of maritime insurance, which had been available since early in the fourteenth century (Nelson and Starr), and in a display of hubristic self-confidence, Antonio tempts fate by offering his own life as surety. Antonio is ultimately rescued from his foolishness, not by a religious miracle, but by a quibbling lawyer who tricks the Duke and her husband, and outtricks the Jewish trickster.

There is more concern here with the devil than with Jesus. The mes-sage is no longer a religious one. It is that the cruelty of reality, now represented by the Jew, can be defeated by avoiding Jews or beating them at their own game, trickery.

But the Jew represents not only reality. He is the target onto whom are projected the viciousness of Antonio and Portia, the treachery and covetousness of Lorenzo and Jessica, and the greediness of Bassanio. Even in the utopia of Belmont, wives trick and humiliate their husbands.

The Oedipal theme appears here in the struggle of the daughters, Portia and Jessica, to escape from the efforts of their fathers to restrict their choice of lover. And it is the daughter, Portia, who bests the father Shylock. Ironically, after all the turmoil about choosing one's lover freely, each woman marries a feckless parasite.

But why did these matters become an issue for Shakespeare at the end of the sixteenth century in England?

From a practical point of view, *The Merchant of Venice* was produced five years after Marlowe's *The Jew of Malta* was received enthusiastically and profitably by English audiences, and it may well be that the success of Marlowe's play inspired Shakespeare to write his.

From an ideological point of view, it may be relevant that controversy about the legitimacy of usury prevailed during medieval times and continued unabated during the sixteenth century. It contrasted Deuteronomy 23:20–21, permitting the taking of interest from strangers, with Luke 6:35, prohibiting the taking of interest from anyone.

Finally, although officially no Jews dwelled in England after 1290, unofficially one found in London many Marranos or New Christians, Jewish tradespeople from Holland and other countries, and Jewish diplomats. Moreover xenophobia prevailed in Elizabethan England as the populace rejected not only the New Christians but other aliens as well. Anti-alien riots occurred in 1588, 1593, and 1595.

Rodridgo Lopez, a Marrano, who is alluded to in *The Merchant of Venice* ("thy currish spirit governed a wolf" [lobo]), served not only as the Queen's physician, but also as an international diplomat who tried to effect peace between England and Spain. It was in the wake of the failure of his endeavours that the militarists secured his downfall, which was followed by widespread Jew baiting and a host of anti-Jewish plays, among them, *The Merchant of Venice*.

During the fifty years between the creation of Shylock and the suppression of the theater by the Puritans (1642–56), at least nine plays with prominent anti-Jewish roles were produced. Evidently they were responding, not merely to the Lopez affair, but to the reappearance of the Jew in commerce and in diplomacy, which resulted in the pressure that led Cromwell to propose to Parliament in 1655 the formal readmission of the Jews to England.

The resurgent antisemitism was not only the response to the potential economic rivalry, it also projected onto the Jews the malice that gave rise to the Jew baiting and the xenophobic riots.

The Jew who challenges the Christian's belief in the saving power Christ, says Shakespeare, is the same Jew who lusts after Christian flesh and blood. The Jew is the principle of evil.

## The Deists

Considering the dissents of the deists from the traditional mysteries, myths, and orthodoxies of the official Church, and their emphasis upon reason and tolerance one would have expected them to discard antisemitism as well. In fact, deism as a philosophy includes no generally agreed upon attitude toward Jews, neither antisemitic nor philosemitic. However, although a few of the better known among the deists repudiate antisemitism vigorously (for example, John Toland, de La Brede, Marie Huber, Ange Goudar, Espiard de la Cour and Abbé Coyer), many or perhaps most gave voice consistently to both criticism and contempt for Jews. And others expressed derogatory and appreciative views of Jews alternatingly (Montesquieu, Pierre Bale, Marquis Jean-Baptiste d'Argens. Antisemitism was not a preoccupation as it had been with the Church fathers and the lower clergy of the Middle Ages, but it was there (see Poliakov, 1975, vol. 3, part 1).

However, in contrast to the antisemitism of the Middle Ages, the antisemitism of individual deists did not constitute a movement. Even though from a deist point of view, Judaism was considered an archaic, authoritarian rather than reasonable religion, the antisemitic sentiments that were expressed in deist writings reflected individual rather than uniform views. The myths were classical and traditional but they differed from one writer to the other.

Poliakov reprints some of the antisemitic statements favored among deist writers (pp. 63ff.). If given an opportunity, Jews would attempt to convert Christians. God may reject Christians if they accept Jews. The Jews claim to possess "the sole uncorrupted Scripture." The local Jews are savage and Christian "bloodbaths and crimes" could be "justified by Biblical precedent" (Matthew Tindal). The Jews' religion is "national and temporal" (Thomas Morgan). Jews are noisy, stinking, odious, and abominable (Pastor Woolston). The wretchedness of the Jewish people proves that God is angry with them (Jacques Basnage).

I find no consistent theme among these accusations. They allude to the corrupting power of the Jews, to their viciousness, to the narrowness of their religion, to their general inferiority, and to their wickedness. Clearly these views express no common concern and suggest no common background of antisemitic psychology. They give expression to the general prejudice that, whatever kind of scapegoat an individual needs, he can find it in the Jew.

Among the antisemitic deists, Voltaire holds perhaps the best-known and most hostile position. His antisemitism was considered extreme even by his friends. He accuses the Jews of immorality, going back to the Bible to cite examples. He seems preoccupied with Jewish sexuality and with circumcision. Jews, he says, are unspiritual. They are ignorant, barbarous, greedy, superstitious, hateful, and ungrateful. They sacrifice human victims. They abuse the sacred host. Jews are calculating rather than thoughtful. Jews are plagiarists. Like Negroes, Jews are "an inferior species of man."

In his splendid history of French Jewry of the period of the Enlightenment, Hertzberg (1968) grapples with the issue of Voltaire's unusually harsh antisemitism. He believes that we do not possess enough information to discern the psychologic basis for it, but he does argue that in Voltaire's mind, it grew out his favoring the pagan civilization of Greece and Rome over ancient Jewish civilization. Hertzberg argues that Voltaire repeats the anti-Jewish comments found in classic Greek and Roman sources, rather than the usual antisemitic cliches of the medieval Christian world. It should be noted though that Voltaire harps on Jewish usury and Jewish abuse of the sacred Host, both nonissues in the pagan world. In fact, however, Voltaire's identification with the anti-Jewish pagans can easily be interpreted as a self-serving conceit masking ordinary Christian antisemitism. We have no reason to accept his public position at face value.

Voltaire accuses the Jews of aggressiveness, self-indulgence, and lack of self-control, sexual and financial. One is tempted to speculate that his antisemitism might be an expression of the projection outward of inner weakness, of his difficulty in living up to his own standards and in controlling his own impulses, as well as the fear of Jewish malevolence that arises from inner anxiety. One is not surprised therefore to read (Poliakov, 1975, p. 91) that he was sexually inhibited and frustrated, that he was excessively fearful of death, that he was anxious, hostile, and angry, that he hated his older brother's "ferocious habits," that alone among the Biblical patriarchs, Joseph, found his favor. Voltaire invokes the traditional antisemitic myth that the Jew is unscrupulous, vicious, and immoral, perhaps (but only perhaps) in order to contain his own self-doubts and self-criticism.

We noted above that when an individual suffers from the threat of distress imposed either from the outside or the inside, he tends to attribute the threat to an external, malignant influence, in Western civilization the demonized Jews, and he responds with vicious antisemitism. Voltaire's concern with the blood libel and his conviction that Jews attack the Host may well represent the same fear that appears in his hypochondria and obsessive fear of death. His continuing anger and hostility responds to his fear of destruction, a fear arising internally but attributed to the threat of the Jew. As I observed in chapter 2, the most viciously antisemitic of the patients whom we considered were the most angry.

## The Protocols of the Elders of Zion

The history of this notorious antisemitic document has been elucidated in recent years by the historian, Norman Cohn who has published enlightening studies of two other irrational plagues, the medieval millenarian excesses (1970) and the subsequent witchcraft mania (1975). Cohn's history of the *Protocols* (1981) gives us an extensive account of how a specific antisemitic canard has been used by many people and groups in Europe and elsewhere to promote their political purposes. We do not possess such detailed and reliable accounts of the history of previous antisemitic accusations. During the Middle Ages, "confessions" of Jewish conspiracies, for example, to murder Christian children for ritual purposes, were extracted from prominent Jews under torture, and were used to justify murderous attacks on the Jewish community. In most instances, the pogrom, while satisfying whatever conscious or unconscious psychic need of the instigators, also served some more practical purpose, such as robbing Jews of their possessions or avoiding repayment of debt, or embarrassing the local sponsor of the Jews, nobility or higher clergy. In a series of books, articles, and letters culminating in the *Protocols*, the refinement of getting a word-of-mouth statement from a Jew has been eliminated. The *Protocols* completes a series of fabrications concerning, not the local misdeeds of a specific Jewish community, but of a conspiracy to dominate the whole world, to topple all national governments and to seize all gold and money. Cohn gives accounts of a series of such fabrications, their named targets and the political purposes that were intended. He starts with a 1797 account by a French cleric, Abbé Barrud, of a conspiracy which Barrud dates back to the fourteenth century that culminated in the French Revolution, led by the Freemasons and the Illuminati. He added the Jews to the conspiracy under the influence of a letter from an unknown Italian who claimed to be an army officer and who said that he had tricked some local Jews into revealing the dimensions of a world conspiracy to destroy Christendom. The letter had appeared in 1846 and Cohn reasons that its intent was to arouse opposition to Napoleon's policy of social reorganization and liberalization, from which the Jews had benefited. Similar false accounts of a Judeo-Masonic conspiracy had begun to appear around the middle of the nineteenth century in Germany as a weapon of the German right against the growing forces of nationalism, liberalism, democracy, and secularism. Shortly thereafter a German writing under an assumed British name, published a novel containing a fictional account of a mystical Jewish cabal that planned to dispossess the rest of the world and to enslave all other nations. Cohn suggests that the story represented an effort to oppose the emancipation of the Jews in Germany. This fiction was picked up by Russians, French, and Czechs, elaborated and presented as a veridical report and entitled "The Rabbi's Speech." A book written by a French lawyer, Maurice Joly, *Dialogue aux Enfers Entre Montesquieu et Machiavel,* intended as a disguised criticism of the regime of Napoleon III, was associated with "The Rabbi's Speech" and the two became the basis for the elaborate concoction that became known as *The Protocols of the Elders of Zion.* The latter comprises twenty-four chapters, about one hundred pages altogether, and according to Cohn, refers to three main themes, a critique of liberalism, an analysis of the methods by which world domination is to be achieved by the Jews, and a description of the world state that is to be established. Cohn surmises that the whole was cobbled together in France during the height of the

agitation over the Dreyfus affair, probably by, or under the guidance of
P. R. Rachkovsky, the head of the foreign branch of the Okhrana, the
tsarist secret police. Rachkovsky used forgeries skillfully and freely in
his sinister activities.

Early in this century, the *Protocols* were used to defend the Tsar and
his regime against revolutionary forces by associating the antigovern-
ment forces with the malevolent schemes of the Jews. After the Russian
Revolution, they were used to obtain sympathy for the defeated White
Russians by associating the Bolsheviks with the Jews. Simultaneously,
the *Protocols* were used in Germany again to oppose the forces of liberalism and democracy, especially during the Weimar Republic. Subsequently,
that, and Hitler's *Mein Kampf* and Alfred Rosenberg's *Myth of the Twentieth Century*, became the central scriptures of the Nazi party. Obviously
the same antisemitic canard can be used to further many different causes.

The Protocols is the prototypic conspiracy theory. It pretends to reconcile the discrepancy between the benign, visible aspect of the neighboring
Jews and the malevolent intentions and behavior attributed to them. But
the idea of secrecy has implications other than the practical, namely mystical and magical. (See the discussion of curiosity—Ostow, 1995)

Do the people who promote such material really take them seriously?
Cohn adduces evidence that some clearly believe in their authenticity
while others cynically foist them on others, to obtain the effect they
desire, generally hostility to the Jews and to the social, political, and
economic forces that they link to the Jews. The question for us is why
were—and are—so many people so ready to credit these absolutely bizarre fantasies despite their obvious inconsistency with observed facts.
It is as though we possess two psychic mechanisms for dealing with
frustration or gratification. The more archaic one, which Freud called
the primary process, seems to prevail during infancy and early childhood. It deals with absolutes, good and bad, favorable and unfavorable.
It doesn't know of inner motivation or inner conflict. All experience is
imposed from outside at the pleasure of a good or bad parent, or a benign or malevolent sibling, or an intruder or stranger, or beast. Animate
objects are assumed to have human intentions and inanimate objects are
endowed with feelings and responses. Primary process is associated with
good or bad feelings, cries for help, wishes to destroy, and displays of
anger. Fate can be controlled or influenced by crying, appealing, appeasing, or defying. Primary process is not simply irrational thought. It

is a nonrational but nevertheless deterministic procedure for generating fantasies, wishes, and impulses in order to gratify instinctual desires and resolve problems and the anxieties that they arouse.

The psychic mechanism that Freud called secondary process becomes effective later in development and gradually replaces the earlier one. It recognizes and attempts logically to manipulate and accommodate to the real world. It knows realistic cause and effect, real and imaginary, animate and inanimate, right and wrong, responsibility and negligence, but also ambiguity, indeterminancy, and ambivalence. While in the course of ordinary adult life, secondary process prevails, nevertheless, primary process does break through at times. It breaks through for most of us on occasions that elicit emotional responses, situations of gratification or frustration, pleasure or anguish, and more frequently for those of us whose emotions are poorly regulated. To return to the question, simplistic blaming operations reflect primary process. People whose secondary process was never developed as a result of limited education and experience, or whose emotional control is faulty, or whose living conditions are threatened, or who are confronted with starvation, illness, or pain, are governed by primary rather than secondary process. When a charismatic leader or community consensus declares that something or someone is responsible for distress or danger, the individual welcomes that statement and responds to it as he is instructed by the leader or by the community. Since religion taps and influences primary process, it acquires its power to motivate people to acts of great generosity or acts of destruction. Under the influence of primary process, individuals will credit and respond to a canard blaming a particular individual or group for one's current distress or for some approaching danger.

*The Protocols of the Elders of Zion* and its nineteenth-century antecedents appeal to primary process because: they offer a clearcut explanation for unhappiness and anxiety; they are sponsored by religious, governmental, or charismatic authority; and they appeal to prejudices inculcated in childhood, that is opinions that were accepted from caregivers or contemporaries without secondary process evaluation.

## Current Antisemitism

Antisemitism has never become a concerted or strong movement in the United States. Social discrimination against Jews, once quite prevalent and vigorous, continues to prevail in many circles today though more muted and limited. In the 1920s, Jews had to fight for Jewish immigration, against a *numerus clausus* in the universities and against discrimination in employment. In 1902, New York saw an antisemitic riot with the police on the side of the antisemites. In 1913, a Jew, Leo Frank, was lynched in Atlanta. In the 1920s the *Protocols* were exported to the United States and disseminated with the strong support of Henry Ford. Populist preachers, George Winrod, Gerald L. K. Smith, and Father Charles Coughlin attracted some following in the twenties and thirties. During the first decades after World War II, under the pressure of a general horror at the Holocaust and with postwar prosperity and increased immigration into the United States, the ethic of pluralism in the United States was reinforced and antisemitism declined.

On the positive side, especially since the end of World War II, both as individuals and as a community, American Jews have attained great successes: in the economic level of the overall Jewish community; in philanthropic support for the State of Israel and for Jews in the former Soviet Union and Ethiopia; in contributions to the universities, hospitals, and general philanthropies of the United States; in individual achievements in business, finance, science, medicine, law, and academia. Jewish studies have flourished both within the Jewish academies and in non-Jewish universities as well. Postwar America has truly made possible one of the major "golden ages" of Jewish history by virtue of the absence of major and consistent persecution, oppression, discrimination, and prejudice. For this opportunity we have to thank the Fathers of the American Revolution who made the deliberate decision to found an enduring democracy and who refused to countenance the import of the hatreds of the Old World, and while providing for the freedom of religious observance, insisted upon the separation of Church and State. In the well-known words of George Washington which echo those of Moses Seixas, warden of the Hebrew Congregation of Newport, Rhode Island, "the government of the United States gives to bigotry no sanction, to persecution no assistance."

What else has contributed to keeping the United States so relatively immune to the virus of militant antisemitism? One can speculate that Americans, by contrast with their European ancestors, have been spared the devastation of conquest, of famine, of disease, and, the Civil War notwithstanding, the bitter internecine struggles among small principalities. American Jews have not had to live in a monolithic society dominated by a single church that wielded governmental authority and prescribed what was taught to children and what prejudices were forced upon adults. That having been said, we must remind ourselves that all previous Jewish "golden ages" have each come to a bitter end, and while America has so far been relatively immune to antisemitism, we have so far also not had to suffer long periods of widespread famine, widespread unemployment, or the demoralization of military defeat.

To return to the present, the past two decades have seen the recrudescence of antisemitic sentiment in the United States. I am not referring to black antisemitism upon which I shall comment in this chapter, but the antisemitism that presents itself as criticism of the State of Israel which I mentioned in chapter 2. As I noted there, critics of Israel point out that all criticism of Israel cannot be interpreted as antisemitism, and that is certainly correct. I contend that a criticism of Israel does betray antisemitism if the critic voices only criticism and never appreciation of Israel; if Israel is held to standards applied to no other country; and if the data proffered to support the criticism are incorrect or misleading.[6]

Such criticism is spearheaded by some church leaders but it is not limited to them. It focuses on Israel's continuing war with its Arab neighbors, on its continuing occupation of territories seized when it was attacked in 1967, on its active, responsive, and preemptive war with Arab terrorists, and on the Lebanon campaign. These anti-Israel churches identify with the political program of the Arabs, which fortuitously and, for them, felicitously complies with age-old Christian antisemitism, while Arabs sponsor and disseminate traditional Christian antisemitic myths to support their political programs.

I don't know to what extent these Christian critics see their views as antisemitic. In chapter 2 I gave the example of a Christian clergyman who responded to a request for a small increase in fee with an antisemitic dream in which the Jewish analyst permitted a gold Cross pen to become soiled by having been dropped into a privy. The association of Jews, gold, the Cross, and excrement reproduces medieval Christian fantasies and iconography. I am persuaded that the gentleman was certainly free of any conscious antisemitic prejudice, but the request was received by a primary process readiness to see Jews as materialistic and filthy despoilers of the Cross, reinforced by his own conflict with his father about business as an occupation.

What has caused this current resurgence of antisemitic feeling can only be guessed. I presume that for America's Christians, the Jews have exhausted their capital of guilt. With the rise of the Jewish state, the Jews have lost their wretched, underdog condition and no longer warrant sympathy. Moreover they no longer demonstrate by their wretchedness the virtue of Christianity over Judaism. They are less inclined than ever to demonstrate the truth of Christianity by converting. Nor should we ignore the less spiritual identification of American oil interests with their Arab associates.

As we noted in chapter 2, the antisemitic comments that we heard from our patients did not fall into any consistent pattern. There were complaints that Jews threatened gentiles in various ways; that Jews were too exclusive, thinking of themselves as the chosen people; and that Jews were dirty, smelly, materialistic, and immoral. In other words, there was no consistent general complaint, no generally credited libel or canard, merely a diffuse, low level antisemitic sentiment.

We have had the opportunity to hear the experience of our analytic colleagues in Germany and Austria. The analytic situation there is complicated, especially when either the analyst or the patient is Jewish and the other is not. The non-Jewish member of the pair tends to protect the Jewish member by inhibiting expressions of criticism or anger, with a resultant increase in guilt or hostility. Tensions develop between Jewish analysts and their non-Jewish colleagues when discussion of antisemitism arise in conferences and meetings.

One issue that arises frequently in analysis in Germany and Austria is the Christian patient's conflict about his feelings toward his parents. Were they Nazis? If so, how active? Were there extenuating circumstances? If the patient sympathizes with his Nazi parents, or even non-Nazi but nonprotesting parents, then he feels guilty by postwar standards. If he condemns his parents and sympathizes with the Jews, he then feels guilty toward his parents. In this situation, the Jew almost literally seems to come between the child and the parent. I cited this mechanism above in discussing medieval tendencies to see Jews as malignant intermediaries between the Christian and God, as devils, Satan, Antichrist, or demons. In addition, Christians fear the retaliatory anger of the Jews and become appeasing, suspicious, or hostile accordingly.[7] In the analytic community itself, controversies have arisen about who collaborated with the Nazis and who resisted them. Probably another generation will have to pass before these particular conflicts are resolved. Outside the analytic community, growing factions of radical left and radical right have both become noisily antisemitic, once again appealing to the latent or overt antisemitism of their neighbors in order to draw support for their political position.

## "Racial" Antisemitism

I enclose the word racial in quotations marks because there is no such thing as racial antisemitism. Jews cannot be considered racially separate because we know of no biologic features that reliably distinguish between Jew and gentile, and because by virtue of intermarriages over the centuries, present-day Jews incorporate significant genetic contributions from the many peoples among whom they have resided.

Early in the Christian era and in the Middle Ages, antisemitic rejection could be overcome by conversion. Conversion of the Jew was desired by the Church and many Jews died to avoid baptism. In the eyes of the Church, Jewish disadvantage was overcome by conversion.

However, we know two situations in which by conversion the Jew gained little or nothing, namely fifteenth- to seventeenth-century Spain and twentieth-century Germany. To prevent the Jews from escaping their inferior status, they were declared undesirable and were rejected on the basis of genealogical criteria—falsely called biological in Germany. More precisely, having converted in large numbers, the Jews of Spain found themselves still considered outsiders by Spanish Catholic society and were denied the promised benefits of conversion by applying to them a new criterion, *limpieza de sangre*, purity of blood. The Germans, on the other hand, never made religion a touchstone for acceptability. Conversion would not be an escape route for Jews. Regardless of religious profession, the existence of "Jewish blood" of specified dilution, condemned the individual to the status of the "subhuman" Jew.

What psychologic advantage is obtained by this maneuver? As in the case of the other antisemitic campaigns, one can adduce some real conflict of interest between the Jews and the non-Jewish elements of the locality in which they lived, business and professional rivalries for example. However, Jews were never attacked as rivals, but as Jews whose Jewishness was reason enough for their being subject to humiliation. Let us note that Spanish and German situations differ from each other in many respects. One difference that relates to our problem is that the Nazis but not the Spanish formed a well-disciplined movement, a dedicated homogeneous group for which homogeneity and exclusion of alien elements were essential features. We shall have more to say about this in chapter 5. In each instance, the Jews had been highly integrated into the society, had become prominent in it, and many had tried to assimilate. The society, in each case, after a phase of philosemitism, was reacting into active antisemitism. This phenomenon, which we have encountered also in the case of the antisemitism of individuals, can be thought of as the negative, withdrawal phase of the family romance.

The concept of the Jews as a race, was promoted in the United States with the campaigns against immigration in the late nineteenth and early twentieth centuries. W.Z. Ripley in 1899 wrote *The Races of Europe: A Sociological Study,* in which he divided Europeans into three distinct races. Although he did not label the Jews as biologically distinct, he did speak of them as physically degenerate. Madison Grant promoted the idea of "mongrelization" as a danger to the nation in his 1916 book, *The Passing of the Great Race: Or, the Racial Basis of European History,* and he focused especially on the Jew as a danger to the "stock of the nation" (Singerman, 1986).

The concept of purity deserves some consideration. Let me elaborate the discussion given in chapter 1 (pp. 37–38). It is found in Biblical religion, and I suspect, in all other religions.

> Who shall ascend the mountain of the Lord and who shall stand in his holy place? He who is clean of hands and pure of heart, Who has not taken oaths by My life dishonestly, nor sworn deceitfully. (Psalm 24)

The psalmist here uses cleanliness and purity as metaphors for honesty and rectitude. Cleanliness and purity acquire their metaphoric power by virtue of their religious importance. Biblical ritual concerned itself with cultivating purity and avoiding contamination or undoing it: "Cleanliness is next to godliness."

Purity can be considered an archaic concept relating to the anal phase. Once he has achieved bowel control, the child may not appear before the parent in a soiled state. Deliberate soiling expresses defiance, and keeping oneself clean, acquiescence. One patient, every time he spoke of his anger toward his father, recalled a children's rhyme that told of an infant's defiant determination to defecate on his father. Religious purification can be achieved by suffering a period of isolation, by ritual cleansing with water or fire, or by sacrificing. But even outside the realm of religious ritual, we naturally turn to similar devices when we feel ourselves to be in some state of physical or spiritual contamination. The individual who finds himself in distress may think of himself as distant from his God and may attribute that distance to contamination. We have seen that at other times, people attributed that remoteness to the intrusion of the Jew or the devil. Here the metaphor changes. The Jew is no longer the obstruction to the radiation of God's grace. Here he is designated as the source of contamination, and relief is sought by distancing oneself from him or cleansing oneself from him by burning him (in both Spain and Germany), or offering him as a sacrifice, whether or not it is named a sacrifice. The reader will recall that two of our patients grew up in homes with strong fecal odors and with mothers who were very much occupied with feces. The patients would at times speak of their parents' foulness, but at other times they attributed the fecal quality to the Jewish analyst and to Jews in general, in the one case figuratively, in the other literally. Rationalizing this behavior creates the fiction of "racial purity." The religious criterion had become obsolete in Spain because the Jews had already converted, and in Nazi Germany because it was a largely secular society. The impurity criterion was invoked to explain why the Jew was still the source of evil.

But purity need not be seen as only a failure of anal development. In essence it refers to anomaly and to the notion that things are out of place (Douglas, 1966). From this broader point of view, we can recognize impurity also in the context of other phases of development, where reliability and regularity are central. Douglas speaks of wholeness, completeness, and physical perfection and tells us that in primitive societies their absence creates danger. Hybrids are especially dangerous. Nazi laws prohibited sexual contact between Jews and gentiles, and Nazis persecuted individuals with even small titres of "Jewish blood," as did the Spanish.

### Antisemitic Mythology in our Clinical Sample

Let us see whether we can recognize these mythic themes in the antisemitic comments that were made by the patients whom we studied. A review of all case reports yielded more than twenty different accusations:

Jews are excessively concerned with acquiring money. This statement occurred at least nine times in our universe, the most common of these comments. We heard too that Jews are aggressive but physically cowardly. Uncomfortable allusions to circumcision were heard twice. Jewish appearance was commented upon. Jews have long noses, Jews are ugly, Jews are dirty. Their names and language are idiosyncratic, and the *yarmulke* (the skullcap worn by observant Jews) was singled out in a pejorative context. Jews seek power by monopolizing professional positions of authority. They consider themselves "chosen," expressing presumably inappropriate self-confidence to the point of arrogance. Jews don't mix with other people; they keep themselves apart and won't intermarry. They are all prosperous and successful. (This is not said in an admiring context.) Jews are "oversexed." They are greedy bloodsuckers. They are oriented materially rather than spiritually. They are untrustworthy and will stab you in the back. Jews expect gentiles to feel guilty for the Holocaust. The Jewish state behaves like the Nazis. One individual, identifying with Jesus, felt persecuted by Jews. Jews are inferior, bad, degraded, and they smell. They are radical politically.

Clearly none of these stands out as primary and egregious and shocking as were the canards of the well-known pogroms of history, the blood libels, the major conspiracy theories such as the *Protocols*, the accusations of racial poisoning. Their diversity and their *relative* mildness indicate not any major, univocal campaign, but rather a fairly prevalent, low-level, diffuse antisemitism. These various accusations can be accumulated into a small number of groups, which in turn can be accumulated into an even smaller number of more inclusive categories.

The bloodthirstiness, the greed, the pursuit of power all suggest that the image of the Jew is basically evil in intent. The accusations that Jews are communists and untrustworthy belong to a category that might be called the Jew as dangerous. The categories of evil and danger can be combined with the accusation that the Jews threaten to punish the gentile because of the Holocaust. All three constitute an overall category in which the Jew is seen as the source of active danger, a primary personification of the principle of evil.

The idea of the unnaturalness of the Jew includes the accusation that the Jew is ugly, as well as the gentile's experience of distress at the thought of circumcision. The image of the Jew as degraded and shameful, as indicated by various flaws such as aggressiveness, cowardliness, being oversexed, and the accusation that Jews are materially rather than spiritually oriented, combine to form the second category in which the Jew is seen as alien in the sense of being undesirable and a source of discomfort.

The attribution of success to the Jews and the resentment of their self-confidence, their chosenness, both emphasize their separateness, but also imply envy of these qualities, the third category. Envy and rivalry of course suggest that Jews are seen as siblings, specifically hostile and disruptive siblings. Envy and rivalry contribute to antisemitism in two ways. First, it is often a conflict of interests that provides realistic basis for competitiveness and hostility. But more important, it is the image of the Jew as the prototypic, archaic, dangerous sibling of early childhood fantasy, often associated with murderous impulses, as the story of Cain and Abel suggests, that unconsciously creates the mythic antisemitic hostility that prevails through the ages. As we observed above, the Church fathers thought of the Jews as the older brothers, now to be superseded by the younger brothers who inherit the birthright. In fact, they often speak of the Jews metaphorically as Cain. In this spirit, they preempted the Jewish Scriptures and usurped the image of the favorite sons; they are the newly chosen people. The accusation of deicide adds the attribution of murderousness to the other foul qualities of the despised sibling, the mythical Jew. The confluence of the Jew as the real rival and the archaic rival creates a particularly powerful source of antisemitic animosity.

In our discussion of sibling rivalry in chapter 3, we observed that the various benign and hostile intermediaries between man and his deities symbolize the siblings. The Jews are seen as hostile intermediaries, rivalrous and dangerous siblings, who fancy themselves the first born and chosen, and usurp the Christian's rightful place. If misfortune accrues to the Christian, the fault lies with the Jew who intervenes between the Christian and his god. Even when the Christian is attacked by a third party, he believes that he has two enemies, the real enemy and the Jew who has caused the misfortune to come about. In fact, he reverses their meaning: he considers the mythical enemy real and the real enemy accidental. Hitler weakened his war efforts against his actual enemies by diverting his resources to his "War against the Jews," the felicitous title that Lucy Dawidowicz chose for her landmark book on the Holocaust (1975).

The admiring comments about Jews, their success, achievements, and distinctions, are often intended as expressions of envy, as if the Jews have appropriated what was properly the gentiles'.

We observed in chapter 2 that in many instances antisemitism and philosemitism alternate. The patients' comments that I quoted above, were made by individuals, many or most of whom at other times expressed affection and true admiration for Jews. This alternation often involves ultimately entering and withdrawing from a family romance fantasy. A Catholic German from Bavaria sometimes pretended to himself that his family was really Jewish but had become Catholic to escape the Nazis. A woman whose parents had attacked Jews in Eastern Europe, once she arrived in the United States, attached herself to Jewish friends and associates.

In sum, the mythology behind the mild to moderate antisemitism of our modern Western patients, although it includes references to Jews as dangerous and alien, seems mainly to originate from the set of sibling myths that were salient early in Christian history and prevailed thereafter, though sometimes obscured by more murderous fantasies.

## Nonreligious Antisemitism

We have already observed the basic difference between the antisemitism of medieval Europe and of *The Merchant of Venice*.

In Shakespeare we find little concern with churches or quarrels with the Jews, no reference to deicide, to ritual murder of Christian children, no desecration of sacred objects. The Jew is reviled for his avarice, his malice, his separateness.

The antisemitism is social and reinforced by economic rivalry. The only religious references are to not being a believing Christian. The Jew in the play retains his state of degradation which was established earlier in Christian history, but his fault or vice is no longer a religious one.

In the case of the Spanish persecution of the fifteenth and sixteenth centuries, the fact that Jews converted to Christianity brought them scant respite from abuse. Here too, economic and social rivalry made use of the previously established designation of the Jews as the enemy of Christian society and refused to give up that designation even after the Jew acceded to demands to convert. The religious difference was revealed as a sham, an excuse to conceal a more material, less spiritual sentiment. The Jew, they said, became the source of danger by introducing impurity into the blood of the Spanish people.

Among the writings of the deists, one finds many comments about Jews, some favorable, some unfavorable. Some compare Jews and Judaism unfavorably to Christians and Christianity. Some find fault with Judaism precisely because it was the predecessor of Christianity. The Jews have a base character. In many instances it is rivalry, financial or other, that is manifestly the root of the hostility. While religious arguments abound, it is the person and behavior of the Jew that seems to be the source of the writers' distress.

In the case of *The Protocols of the Elders of Zion*, the context is clearly religious, but the Jewish schemes involve mostly secular matters, money and power.

The literature of the Nazis attacked Jews as a pseudobiologic entity. Again their character was denigrated, their behavior disparaged, their appearance mocked, but no distinction was made between the religiously observant and nonobservant, between identified Jews and assimilated Jews. Conversion offered no escape. The Jew was the source of impurity and disease. This could not be eradicated.

Again current African-American antisemites, both Christian and Muslim, cooperate to condemn Jews for their behavior rather than for their beliefs. They are accused of having engaged in slave trade in the past, of persecuting Palestinians, of exploiting African-Americans.

Whatever antisemitism is being stirred up nowadays in Japan certainly has no religious basis. Economic power is cited as the threat from the Jews.

Among our patients too, we heard little about religion and much about the character and behavior of the Jews, their untrustworthiness, their readiness to take advantage of Christians financially, sexually, socially. It is primarily among some fundamentalist religious groups that one hears echoes of medieval accusations.

In most of the instances I have cited, it seems as if the religious issue is invoked to justify victimization that is based upon other considerations. The obvious source of contention is competition for resources, for status, for power. However as I have noted above, the Jews seldom realistically or seriously threaten the interests of their attackers in whatever area of contention. There were few Jews in Shakespeare's England. *The Protocols* and Hitler's propaganda grotesquely exaggerated the power of the Jews. Hitler's obsession with the Jews can be understood only as the attribution to them of cosmic power to destroy him, as an ultimate principle of evil that could be overcome only by eradicating every living Jew. All of these enemies of the Jews accept the designation by the early Church of Jews as the source of cosmic catastrophe. They accept this designation not necessarily because they are committed to Church doctrine, but because they need a recognizable, visible demon and Christian Scriptures and the Church Fathers seem to confer an aura of reality to that designation, confirmed now by the tradition of the ages.

It is ironic that even though most of the West lives in a largely secular world, rivals of the Jews have invoked the antisemitic mythology of the Christian Church and its designation of the Jews as the principle of evil.

## Conclusions

It becomes clear that in every antisemitic campaign, we find at least two sets of motivations: one real and practical, whether competitive rivalry, antagonism to the Jews because of their role as tax farmers for the princes, or for their role as moneylenders; and second, a mythic fantasy, the Jew interferes in the connection between the Christian and his God, or he murders Christian children, or he is conspiring to control the whole world. We also find that no single fantasy or myth controls all the antisemitic campaigns that we have considered. The Jew as demon, or "subhuman," or as the poisoner of wells, or the ritual murderer of Christian children, or the tempter to immorality, or the demon who impedes access to God, or the communist-capitalist conspirator, or the source of infection or contamination. all of these have, at one time or another, shaped antisemitic crusades, but none of them is essential.

What is essential then? What is constant in all of these antisemitic campaigns in so many different countries and at so many different times? In each case some person or persons are blamed for current distress, whether or not there is a real reason for that blame. In each case the Jew or the Jewish community is selected for that role and a myth is created that explains how the Jew brings about Christian suffering.[8] That, I would suggest is the essence of antisemitism, the readiness to select the Jew as the responsible agent. I would attribute that readiness to the continuing influence of Christian authority, both ecclesiastic and lay, preachers and parents, in so stigmatizing the Jews since the composition of the Christian Scriptures. Even the Nazis who had no great respect for Christianity, had each absorbed in childhood the message of Jewish culpability. In every case, the Jew is the principle of evil.

Having described above the contrasting features of primary and secondary process and their complementary roles in the antisemitic endeavour, let us focus on the paradoxes that their interplay creates. Everyone who looks at the phenomenon of antisemitism is struck by these paradoxes. Jews are accused of transgressions of which they are not guilty, murdering Christian children, poisoning wells, deliberately transmitting illness, conspiring to obtain control of the world and destroy Christendom. Yet these accusations are credited by antisemites. Often the accusations are mutually inconsistent, for example, the concurrent accusations that the Jews foist capitalism on Christians and that they conspire to undermine capitalism in the interest of the communists.

William Styron in *Sophie's Choice* very clearly describes the Christian's puzzlement about Jewish behavior. In the workaday world they go about their business, functioning as merchants, professionals, bourgeois of various occupations, "warmly, thoroughly assimilated," he says, "unexceptional participants." But then they would disappear "into their domestic quarantine and the seclusion of their sinister Asiatic worship—with its cloudy suspicion of incense and rams' horns and sacrificial offerings." He continues that as a child in his home town in Virginia, he gazed upon the synagogue with "deep suspicion, along with a kind of indefinable dread. God, what unspeakable things went on in that heathen sanctum." Among the "savage rites" he imagines, "circumcising goats, burning oxen, disemboweling newborn lambs." Although it is dramatically presented and from the point of view of an eleven-year-old, small-town, Southern boy, the description probably reflects the images, conscious or unconscious, of many American Christians who are not on close terms with Jewish friends.

The archaic fantasy that Styron has described, represents in conscious imagery a primary process impression, archaic, filled with affect, and with prejudice. It maintains its integrity and affect charge despite time and incontrovertible evidence to the contrary. It cannot be corrected. Styron expresses his dual image of the Jew even more dramatically in the person of Nathan, his chief male character. In the first part of the novel, Nathan is presented as an intellectual, generous, loving young man. At the end, he is revealed as a psychotic drug addict who poisons his Christian lover and himself.[9]

Because the reality of the Jew and the fantasy contrast so strikingly, myths are created to reconcile the two. Jews maintain an *invisible* conspiracy. They *secretly* poison Christians with chemicals and disease causing agents. They foment revolution and *secret* cabals.

The presence of antisemitism where there are no Jews is often cited as a paradox. Following our argument to its logical conclusion, antisemitism doesn't require Jews. The Jew of the antisemitic myths is a myth. The real Jew is an inconvenient evidence to the contrary. For the antisemite, the caricature of the Jew in theater, passion play, and propaganda supersedes the image of the Jew encountered in the real world. Both images are registered mentally, but for antisemites, the primary process Jew prevails.

Christians who deal with real Jews in their regular activities, or who mingle with them as neighbors, will often distinguish between the individual Jew who is their friend and the stereotype whom they devalue. The individual is the actual Jew, the stereotype is the primary process image. The individual Jew is usually spoken of in the singular but the stereotype is generally given in the plural: "You can't trust them."

Certain other consequences flow from the primary process of the antisemitic myth. Primary process imagery and "thinking" carry strong feelings. In fact, one may say that while secondary process modulates feelings, they arise in the transactions of primary process. I contend that affects are governed by a regulatory system. When as a result of external gratification or internal dynamics, the ego becomes supercharged with libidinal energy that is perceived as ebullience and euphoria, a corrective influence is invoked that turns the affect excursion around and moves it toward a more normal, center range. Conversely when the ego is depleted of energy, a corrective influence returns the energy level and the accompanying affect to the normal range. For most people these adjustments are carried out sensitively and almost imperceptibly. Most of us have moods and up and down days, but by and large we maintain a fairly even disposition. Others, on the other hand, regulate their moods inefficiently or not at all so that extremes of mood often follow each other in quick succession. When these affect fluctuations control overt behavior or fantasy life, or when they are detected in dreams, we see a succession of death and rebirth fantasies that resemble those that we encounter in the religious genre called apocalypse. As we observed above, the classical apocalypse anticipates widespread death and destruction out of which a new world will be born. The Book of Revelation, which is generally considered the prototypical apocalypse, is mostly concerned with threats of punitive destruction, and the promise of rebirth comes at the end. (Note the apocalyptic final sentence in the Loewenstein letter quoted on page 46)

We encounter apocalypse in at least three circumstances. The depressed patient may be obsessed with suicidal thoughts, expecting or promoting his own death. Dreams that are reported when a person is in that state usually reveal hopes of rebirth that usually fail until the patient is ready to recover. When the patient is religious he looks for religious salvation. The patient who is too "high," that is too ebullient, self-confident, too presumptuous, may experience intimations of coming disaster that may be interpreted as punishment. In extreme situations, for example, schizoaffective disease, the fantasy may be implemented by self-damaging acts associated with the illusion of rebirth. That scenario, too, lends itself to a classical religious interpretation and punishment for presumption. The punitive agent may also be seen as the demonic Jew who envies and wishes to destroy the triumphant Christian. The third situation that favors apocalyptic thinking is the depressive tendency that is fought by mobilizing aggression and anger, a common situation among those with labile affective dispositions. The individual hopes to achieve rebirth and overcome the depressive pull by fighting. Since he cannot fight an internal dynamic, he must select an external enemy who seems to him to be the threatening agent. This is the mythical role assigned to the Jew. Even where there is an actual enemy, it remains important to fight the mythical enemy as well, as Hitler demonstrated. The real enemy may be a human antagonist, but the Jew, by coming between the gentile and his God, is responsible for his destiny. As I pointed out in chapter 2, the more antagonistic antisemites were people who were more aggressive in general. Although I have only a small sample to go by, I believe that this generalization holds.

Let us note that it is primary process affect regulation—its concern with death and rebirth—that causes individuals with defective affect regulation to see things in dualistic terms: Jew versus gentile, black versus white, God versus the Devil, Christ versus the Anti-Christ, right versus wrong. The word apocalypse means revelation. Each apocalypse characteristically begins with a revelation. The receiver of the revelation, the announcer of the apocalypse, is told some secret relating to death and rebirth, how and when it will come about, who will die, and who will be saved. In antisemitic apocalyptic mythology, the secret that is revealed is that it is the Jew who is at fault for the suffering and who must be destroyed. The antisemitic myth is the apocalyptic revelation.

The simultaneous presence of primary and secondary process in the image of the Jew can be seen in most of the case studies that we encountered. Patients who reported contempt for Jews, did go to Jewish analysts for treatment. The alternation of philosemitism and antisemitism represents not the parallel images of primary and secondary process, but alternating primary process images. Let's look again at the letter of Loewenstein's patient. He despises the Jew as his parents did, "an undercurrent of antisemitism, which as we know came from way back." Rezzori similarly inherits the antisemitism of his parents. Loewenstein's patient idealizes the Jew under other circumstances in identification with his grandmother. (Since the Jews are doing so well, he no longer has to feel guilty.) "I didn't have to feel sorry for the Jews any longer. I could feel with them. I know how my grandmother would have felt. And I do too. 'We stand at Armageddon and we battle for the Lord.'" The secondary process view of the Jew governs his selection of a Jewish analyst and his civil and friendly relations with his Jewish neighbors and co-workers. "Einstein or Freud or any of those overtalented individuals don't remind me much of the people I know any more than those martyrs [that is of the ghettos and concentration camps—M.O.] or the little greaser behind the counter. The fact of course that I do know a lot of Jews is beside the point. They were just friends and my antisemitism, except in very veiled form, was usually felt or directed against the Jews I didn't know." Here we have a clear distinction between secondary process on the one hand and both favorable and unfavorable primary process on the other.

Let us try to frame our conclusions in another way. We all experience unhappiness, more or less intensely, more or less frequently. We speak of anxiety, anguish, despair, melancholy. The experience of unhappiness may be induced by events in the real world, a loss, a disappointment, a frustration, disease, pain. Some of these occur fortuitously: in the state of our present knowledge, by chance. Others are brought about by the direct hostile intentions of other individuals, as a result of rivalry with us, or because we might have disappointed or frustrated another, or because of envy. Sometimes people find themselves living in a society that cannot provide the physical necessities of life, or any degree of comfort, or any sense of structure and constancy or security against enemy attack. In the case of some of us, unhappiness of any of the varieties that I mentioned can also appear without external influence, merely as a result of inner affective dysregulation; we may respond to a relatively minor stress with an excessive lapse into depression, or we overcompensate an elevation of mood by a similar depressive decline.

Whatever the source of unhappiness, we respond in either or both of two ways. On a realistic, rational plane, we try to ascertain what is the veridical cause and what can we do about it. Is there a protective action that we can take, a remedial action, appeasement of an adversary, or attack? However we also respond in a consciously or unconsciously more archaic, nonrational way. We think of ourselves as having been abandoned by a parent, or separated from his or her benign influence, subjected to a principle of evil that prevails in the universe, that impinges on the life of any of us at unpredictable times. "Why me?" we ask, as though we did not know that misfortune strikes at random. Whatever the cause, the automatic response, when we are not depressed, is to blame someone around us. Children and adolescents blame their parents, adults blame their partners or spouses. The more invisible or incomprehensible the source of the distress, the greater the temptation to attribute it to an unnatural, malignant source, often an agent with religious or magical powers. The culture in which we grew up and in which we live, usually provides us with a persona with which to label the principle of evil which we dimly apprehend but which we experience as the source of our misery. The polytheistic religions accommodate this need easily, offering both benign and malignant gods. The monotheistic religions have a greater problem with it. The monotheistic god is postulated to be both omnipotent and benign. How can he permit us to be plagued by evil? This problem, the problem of theodicy, has occupied theologians seemingly from the beginning (Russell, 1981).

Although tempted to assign evil to independent agents like Satan, the canonizers of the Jewish Bible and the scholars of the Talmud and

Midrash tend to adhere fairly closely to strict monotheism. In the Pentateuch, God has no worthy divine challengers. God warns us that future suffering will come about only as punishment for individual or communal misbehavior. Assyria has defeated Israel only because of Israel's wickedness, says Isaiah (10:5). "Assyria is the rod of my anger, a staff in the hand of my fury." Israel has not been overcome by an independent principle of evil, but only as a result of its own guilt. The same God who protected, now punishes.

The Book of Job deals specifically with the issue of the source of evil. God permits himself to be teased into yielding to Satan the freedom to harass Job. Satan deprives Job of his wealth and children and afflicts him with a painful illness. Since Job was a person of extraordinary virtue, his misfortune violated the expectation that prevailed among Jews that virtue is to be rewarded and sin to be punished. Job is indignant that he has been dealt with unjustly and would like to remonstrate with God. Job's three friends on the other hand, in accordance with their conviction regarding reward and punishment, try to account for Job's downfall by assuming that he merited it by misbehavior. In the end, God admonishes Job not to question his ways; human understanding is limited. Job accepts the admonition and God restores him to favor and prosperity.

The story tells us what happens when the power to do evil is even temporarily and experimentally ceded to another authority. The principle of reward and punishment breaks down and man loses the comfort of believing that he lives in an orderly universe. God assures us that what is defective is man's capacity to understand his ways. The principle of reward and punishment, he implies, remains intact. But if man cannot understand how that principle applies, then it is of limited use to him as a guide to behavior and as reassurance of the orderliness of the universe. A believing Jew is then left with the need to live by two different views: behavior will be dealt with by reward or punishment, whichever is appropriate; but on the other hand, as a practical matter, we live in a capricious world. At times the discrepancy between fate and justice is so overwhelming that philosophic and religious rationalizations utterly fail, as the problem of the theology of the Holocaust demonstrates. In any case the religious Jew may not believe in an independent principle of evil.

An instructive set of anecdotes is given in the Babylonian Talmud (B.T. Gittin, 55b–58a) relating to the Roman triumph over Israel. The causes are given variously as immorality, bad judgment, internecine quarreling, the cruelty of the Romans. The text also includes protest against God's failure to protect his people. No external principle of evil is invoked.

The continuing tension between monotheism and dualism is expressed in the Talmud (B.T. Hagigah, 15a; T.Y. Hagigah 2:1) in the legends surrounding a second-century scholar, Elisha ben Abuya. Upon observing the murder of distinguished scholars and the death of a man immediately after he had performed a virtuous act, he is reported to have renounced Judaism and to have speculated that there are indeed two divine domains.

Yet for all the occasional references to Satan in Talmudic literature, the tradition adheres firmly to the position that there is no independent principle of evil. One attributes to God two modes: his *middath hadin,* the mode of strict, punitive judgement, and *middath harahamin,* the mode of merciful love. The liturgy for the second *amidah*[10] of the three pilgrim festivals declares in unmistakable terms: "It is because of our sins that we were exiled from our land."

Jeffrey Burton Russell in a series of books, *The Devil,* (1977), *Satan* (1981), and *Lucifer* (1984), presents classical Christian views of the existence of a principle of evil independent of God. While in general, early Christianity continued Jewish resistance to dualism, Russell contends that the Christian Bible sees that the Kingdom of God is challenged by the Kingdom of the Devil who represents what the author saw as the "immediacy of evil." *Satan* reports the opinions of the Church fathers and *Lucifer* the views of the medieval scholars about the principle of evil. Russell makes it clear that the problem found no easy resolution. The Gnostic Manichaean and Marcionite heresies represented extremes of duality. Some of the Christian authorities came out clearly for the dualistic view. Evil in the world is attributable to the action of a principle of evil which is independent of God and often works in opposition to Him. Others contend that Satan serves as an instrument of God, tempting and punishing only in response to God's judgment or to human weakness. Many tried to find a middle ground. Satan can trap and punish only those humans who are prepared to sin.

We see here a struggle between the wish to remain classically monotheistic in order to avoid the temptation to worship a power of evil, presumably in evil ways, and the need to assign responsibility for misfortune in a consistent and useful way, that is, a way that does not require that one acknowledge that good and evil fortune are neither predictable nor controllable. This latter position seems to be the more "natural" position whereas the former implies a mental outlook and behavior discipline more difficult to achieve.

While the scholars debated these issues, it seems likely that the common people took the easy way out. It is my impression that the accounts available to us of behavior during the Middle Ages, disclose common belief in the devil, or Satan, or Lucifer. Most people did not trouble themselves overmuch about whether Satan was truly independent or limited in his actions. Satan would ensnare them. Their best chance of resisting damage, disease, injury, misfortune, lay not only in virtuous behavior, but also in cultivating tactics for resisting the devil. The current practice of "knocking on wood" when speaking of good fortune, and of crossing one's fingers when faced with danger, attest to the persistence among modern, sophisticated people, of not merely notions, but compelling convictions that magical gestures to defeat the devil who is believed to be paralyzed in the presence of the cross, can protect one against misfortune.

The devil, or Satan, or Lucifer lacks one quality that would make him more appropriate as the proximal cause of evil, the quality of visibility, of immediacy. Also, these demonic creatures are designated as the essence of opposition to Christ, and they share this quality with the Jews. As a result, in antisemitic Christian mythology, the devil and the Jew are usually closely associated. In medieval iconography, the devil is often drawn with stereotyped features of the Jew and the Jew with stereotyped features of the devil (see Trachtenberg). To the Christian who is struggling to maintain the conviction of an orderly universe in which reward and punishment are assigned with justice, where chance plays little role in determining one's fate, where cosmos prevails over chaos, assigning to the Jews the role of the principle of evil seems not only reasonable but necessary. The Jew could and can easily be seen as the source of disease, of poverty, of war, of misfortune of every kind, the poisoner of wells, the practitioner of sorcery, the usurer, the kidnapper of presumably neglected children, the physician who murders his patients. Christian antisemitism may be seen as a disguised form of religious dualism.

Bernard Lewis (1993) observes that, like Judaism and Christianity, Islam, also a monotheistic religion, has at various stages been influenced by dualism, usually of Iranian origin, "a cosmic clash between good and evil, light and darkness, order and chaos, truth and falsehood, God and the adversary, variously known as the devil, Iblis, Satan and other names." This cosmic struggle easily acquired political and military dimensions. In the view of the Muslim world, the archetypal enemy of God, Satan, says Lewis, is currently seated in Western and especially American culture. But even more focused is the association of Satan with Jews and Israel.

Let us look more closely at antisemitism in Islam.

## Muslim Antisemitism

None of our group had ever treated a Muslim patient, nor had any of us ever come into contact with Muslim antisemitism. Therefore our project has made no effort to contribute to that subject. Yet Muslim antisemitism is rapidly becoming a more serious problem than Christian antisemitism and so it would not be inappropriate to comment on what I have learned and inferred from what I consider to be reliable sources (Lewis, 1984, 1986; Stillman, 1979) and to relate it to our arguments.

Muhammad at the start of his career as prophet, encountered the animosity of the Jewish tribes resident in Medina to which he had migrated in order to escape persecution in Mecca where he had been born and lived. Many historians believe that he had hoped to be welcomed by the Jews of Medina and when he was rejected, that is, when they refused to convert to his religion, he turned against them. However the conflict between Muhammad and his followers on the one hand, and the Jews on the other, differed from that between the Christians and the Jews in important ways. Jesus was crucified, but Muhammad was triumphant. Muhammad never claimed to be divine or to be a messiah. Jewish opposition to the new religion was central to Church history but of relatively minor significance in Islamic history. The Muslims did not present themselves as the new Israel as had the Christians and did not see the survival of the old Israel as a challenge to their beliefs. In short, the religion of Islam did not require the Jews as witnesses or as rivals.

From the outset, both Jews and Christians were considered *dhimmis,* that is, protected, non-Muslim subjects of a Muslim state. They were tolerated but subject to constant humiliation. The humiliation involved behavior and clothing—visible indications of lower status. They were subject to special taxes. The degree of tolerance and the degree of humiliation varied widely among different times and different places. Outright persecution, murder, forced conversion were sporadic, not frequent.

In Christendom, Jews were often tolerated and sometimes welcomed. However, in Islam, mutual separatism and social and religious disdain not withstanding, in many places and over relatively long periods of time, Jews and Muslims lived in a degree of cooperation that Goitein calls an Arab-Jewish symbiosis (1974). It was not necessary for Muslims to emphasize differences in religious doctrine and practice from Jews to the degree that Christians did. Indications of mutual influences in religious writings and religious practice are not difficult to find. That the Arab and Hebrew languages are cognate favored a reciprocal interest in cultural development that reached its high point in a genre of Hebrew poetry in the Middle Ages. Jews often played an important role in finance, trade, and government administration within the broader Arab empire. The Turks welcomed them when they fled the expulsions and persecutions of Western Europe. Yet the difference of the status of the Jews in Christendom versus Islam was only relative. Goitein (p.88) quotes the great Hebrew philosopher and poet, Yehudah Halevi (d.1141), who had lived both in Christian and in Muslim Spain, that one was as bad as the other.

However, the Christian type of persecution of the Jews started to appear in Islam in the Middle Ages, under the influence of the Christians in the Moslem community, both Christian converts to Islam and the Christian population of Constantinople that had been conquered by the Moslems in the fifteenth century. Blood libels had been circulating there for some time.

By the nineteenth century, Islam had come into closer contact with the Christian countries of the West and during that century, under the influence of Christians who lived among them, blood libel persecutions of Jews became common. One of the earliest of that century occurred in Damascus in 1840. A Capuchin monk had disappeared. His fellow monks, instigated and encouraged by the French Consul, declared that he had been killed by the Jews for ritual purposes. Jews were tortured to confess. International pressure, led by the British, brought about the termination of the affair.

Lewis (1984) lists more than thirty such instances of blood libel in the Moslem world in the nineteenth century. He calls attention to four elements: the libel, he says, almost always originated in the Christian population and was promoted by the Christian press. Second, the accusations were supported by diplomatic representatives of the European powers. Third, the Ottoman authorities, on the other hand, tried to discourage these assaults and to protect the Jews. Fourth, the Greek and French figured among the instigators, and the British and sometimes the Prussian and Austrian authorities provided support for the victims.

The twentieth century has seen a remarkable proliferation of antisemitic propaganda initiated and promoted by Islamic governments as well as Islamic religious and educational authorities and the press. The propaganda includes derogatory remarks about the Jews as individuals, about the Jewish religion and the Talmud. The Jew has been depicted as a ritual murderer, and as a conspirator against the entire world. *The Protocols of the Elders of Zion,* having been effectively discredited in much of the West, has enjoyed a vigorous revival among the Arabs. It has had numerous translations into Arabic, and has been promoted and taught vigorously under the highest auspices. During World War II, the Arabs favored the Nazi cause and welcomed Nazi assistance in their own war against the Jews. Of course, Zionist resettlement in Palestine and the establishment of the State of Israel created the reality basis upon which the antagonism was anchored. To this day, many in the West believe that were the State of Israel to disappear, unrest in Islam would disappear too. They ignore the fact that violence and terror within Islam kills more Arabs than Jews.

Let us look a little more closely at the content of Muslim antisemitism. In the early centuries of Muslim-Jewish interaction, Jews as well as all other non-Moslem subjects of Moslem governments were, as a matter of policy, to be humiliated and degraded. The Jew was an infidel and to be treated abusively, but he was not regarded as a danger to the true faith. The exposure to Christian antisemitism has resulted in the transfer of the classical Christian myths into the Muslim universe. I have noted that the blood libel associating Jews with the murder of Christian children in order to obtain blood for ritual purposes was imported in the Middle Ages from Christian nuclei and especially from Byzantine Christianity. The transfer was accelerated in the nineteenth century with the greater exposure of Islam to the West. To what extent these accusations merely provided another pretext for pursuing rivalries that were based upon economic and social matters on the one hand and to what extent they found a special resonance among the Muslims, perhaps because of their own ambivalence to their children, on the other, is not clear from the data that I have. Blood does not possess the same ritual significance for Muslims that it has for Christians. Muslims, like Jews, ritually circumcise their male children.

With progressive secularization of the culture, religious motifs lost their salience in antisemitism both in the West and in the East, and the conspiracy theory embodied in the *Protocols* replaced them. The establishment and rapid growth of the State of Israel have provided the reality "confirmation" of the notion that the Jews are conspiring to take control of the entire world.

The Shiites, the more ritually oriented heterodox element of Islam, are concerned with purity and pollution. Pollution follows not only self-polluting activities such as contact with one's excreta, semen, or blood, but also contact with non-Muslims. Therefore any physical contact with them or their clothing must be avoided. We have seen that pollution and purity are fairly universal concerns. Although the issue is reflected in religion, it is not exclusively tied to religion so that it became an issue of great moment to Nazi secular antisemitism.

Having concluded that antisemitism among Christians may represent an effort to account for evil in the world by assigning to the Jews the role of the principle of evil, we must wonder whether the same is true in Islam. Islam, like Judaism and Christianity, is a monotheistic religion, and like them has difficulty in assigning responsibility for evil. Islam too invokes the figure of a devil, called Iblis, the obvious counterpart to Satan. Islamic theological literature deals with the question of how much independence Iblis has, and generally concludes that he functions only with the permission of God who uses him for testing and punishing humans. Reviewing Arabic writings about Jews of the past three centuries, Lewis (1986) concludes that the Jew is now seen as a "figure of cosmic evil." Here, as in Christendom, a material, visible, principle of evil replaces a hypothetical, invisible one.

We have so far not considered the contribution of Islamic fundamentalism. The obsessive, vicious antisemitism that has come to prevail in the world of Islam recently, is not exclusively the domain of the fundamentalists, but exists among "moderate" religious leaders and even in secularist states. We shall take up the issue of fundamentalism in chapter 5, but here let me note merely that the fundamentalist group is always organized in opposition to an enemy. While those in the enemy camp usually include members of the same religion that do not conform to the level of purity that the fundamentalists declare proper, it also includes secularists and members of other religions, "infidels" as well as "heretics." With the rise of the intensity of fundamentalist antisemitism, secular antisemitism has flourished as if to match it. Even if the secularists and moderates do not match the level of fundamentalist irrational hatred, they will not be outdone in making war on the enemy.

What conclusion can we draw from this brief excursion? Given the eager acceptance by Muslims of Jewish malice as the source of all evil in the universe, whether in the Christian context of the blood libel, or the secular context of *The Protocols of the Elders of Zion,* we may infer that the need for a cosmic principle of evil endures and persists, probably everywhere and at all times. When the Church and the Church fathers designated the Jews as that principle, the designation was easily accepted by Christians and subsequently renewed and refurbished whenever and wherever "evil" had to be confronted. Only in the aftermath of the Holocaust did it become evident to the world that the Jew was the victim while his persecutors were the true principles of evil. But the need continues. While the paranoid psychotic is confident in his own solipsistic recognition of the source of his persecution, most others will accept a delusion only if it is sanctioned by the entire community or some recognized authority. For whatever reasons which I am not competent to spell out, the Muslim world nowadays feels itself under some pressure to deal with stress, disappointment, perhaps humiliation and deprivation. The Christians believed and many still believe that they have identified the source of all distress in the degraded and contemptible, now aggressive and powerful Jew, and many Muslims now welcome that delusional idea. Antisemitism is exportable. It can easily invade a population that needs help in contending with distress and anguish but that is not overburdened with considerations of rationality, civility, or decency.

## Notes

1. Before the Common Era.
2. This last verse is puzzling. II Chronicles 24 records that Zacharias, son of Jehoiada, denounced the people for transgressions and by order of the king he was stoned in

the courtyard of the Temple. Zacharias, the son of Berechiah, was a prophet whose prophecies are recorded in a scriptural book designated by his name. There is no tradition that he was murdered. It would seem that Matthew confused the two individuals. (Zacharias is a Greek form of the Hebrew name that is more accurately rendered as Zechariah.)

3. Michel Bodemann says of these functions that the Jews perform *ideological labor* for the Church, by means of which they affirm the dominant values.

4. Rashi (Rabbi Solomon ben Isaac, 1040–1105, France) was a distinguished medieval scholar and commentator.

5. Rabbi Akiba was a leading rabbinic scholar of the early century, C.E.

6. It might be objected that Israel holds itself to higher standards of behavior than other states, and Jews outside of Israel also expect it to adhere to these higher standards. An outside observer might point out that a given action violates Israel's own standards, but he would not be justified in condemning it without referring to the standards of its neighbors and enemies.

7. This fear of retaliatory anger supports Baron's suggestion that fear of retaliatory anger intensified Christian antisemitism after the Crusades. (p. 110 above.)

8. Ginsberg (1993) describes many instances in which antisemitism was encouraged and exploited to promote political, social, or economic purposes.

9. In 1985, Styron suffered a debilitating and suicidal depression which he described in a book published in 1990, *Darkness Visible: A Memoir of Madness* (New York: Random House). In the book he acknowledges that depression had been a presence in his life for years. And he acknowledged too that that depression was reflected in *Sophie's Choice*. When the depressive process began he found that he had to give up alcohol which he had used as a self-medication. I think that one might infer that Nathan with his two aspects, civilized intellectual and suicidally disturbed mental patient, represents Styron himself in the same two aspects. Styron has projected his duality onto the Jew, the demon behind the intellectual facade. Styron believed that he recovered on his own; psychiatric treatment had not been helpful. The psychiatrist who, he felt, had been most unhelpful he designated with the pseudonym, Dr. Gold, suggesting thereby the stereotype of the money hungry, avaricious, incompetent Jewish physician.

10. The *amidah* is the centerpiece of each of the three daily services as well as of the supplementary morning service of the Sabbath and Holy Days.

# 5

# The Pogrom Mentality

The reports of our clinical experience and our discussion of mythology have dealt with the antisemitism of individuals, the antisemitism of prejudice and discrimination. However distressing as these may be, the really murderous antisemitism, the pogrom, is a group phenomenon. In this section I shall report and develop our discussion of group antisemitism. Actually we pursued the study of group antisemitism only to a limited extent because we considered it too far removed from our area of expertise. When we recognized that we were going to move in that direction, we invited Dr. John J. Hartman, a psychoanalyst with solid credentials in both psychoanalysis and sociology, to join us.

## The Nazi Phenomenon: *Triumph of the Will*

Dr. Hartman introduced us to the subject of group antisemitism by screening *Triumph of the Will,* a documentary motion picture account of the 1934 Nazi Party Congress in Nuremberg, directed by Leni Riefenstahl. As a propaganda film, it would not be expected to represent accurately the true state of affairs. Nevertheless it is obviously calculated to display what the Nazis considered an ideal image of their movement, how it wished to be seen by both outsiders and by the Nazis themselves.

The film begins by setting the Congress in the context of the German defeat in World War I, and the German "renaissance," that is, its renewal with Hitler as chancellor. The film goes on to show Hitler's flight to Nuremberg, the motorcade to the city, and his arrival at his hotel. In a second scene, Hitler reviews a band concert outside the hotel. The film then goes on to show Nuremberg as a sleeping city, and in it a tent city of soldiers and workers, all wholesome, healthy, vigorous, and in good spirits. The people parade and the troops are reviewed. The film then displays the Nazi Party Congress itself with comments by Nazi Party leaders. Then one sees a number of rallies: labor service, storm troopers, youth, and then a military and cavalry review. There follows a twilight rally, a tribute to war dead, a military parade, and finally the closing meeting. The film ends with a shot of impressive phalanxes of marching soldiers. The film runs for somewhat over one and a half hours. Antisemitism as a subject does not come up. However, at one point, Streicher comments "A nation that does not value its racial purity will perish."

The value of the film for our purposes lies in its explicit display of the themes that the party and the director of the film wish to communicate. Hartman made the following observations. *Triumph of the Will* is the utopian group fantasy seeking to create a complex myth about Hitler and the Nazi Party: Hitler is a hero, a savior, a god, the progenitor of a New Germany who, by demanding submission and loyalty from the group will render its members united, powerful, and immortal. The film attempts to involve participants and viewers in sharing this fantasy communally.

Specifically, Hitler is presented as a messiah and a god who descends from the skies to the accompaniment of music of the Wagnerian genre, suggesting German mythic themes. Scenes of breakfasting imply that Hitler can feed the people. He is photographed with the light radiating from a source behind him, thereby associating him with divinity. Mist and clouds reinforce that effect. (They suggest a dissolution of boundaries thereby promoting feelings of mystical union—M.O.) From a psychoanalytic point of view, one observes an "idealizing transference" and a family romance implying royal descent. (Transference is the attribution to a current individual of the qualities of an important person from the subject's childhood. We say that it is idealizing when the image projected is distorted so as to make it seem more ideal, the omnipotent, unstintingly generous parent whom we all crave.)

The film suggests a mythic unity. Both the Congress and the film seem to create the image of unity by blurring boundaries between the individual and the group; by showing marching and singing in unison; by displaying flags, banners, and uniforms; by employing verbal imagery suggesting the merging of the individual into the group, for example, "one nation, one leader"; and by stressing the need to unite against enemies. Hartman perceived in these qualities indications of the individual's merging with the mother by group cohesion.

The film by displaying appropriate symbols, suggests the myth of rebirth: the recurrent cycles of nature, the rising sun, the awakening city, and the recovery from the defeat of World War I. Hartman saw here the attempt to convey the impression of impregnation by the phallic potency of Hitler.

The film suggests the myth of immortality by references to a "thousand-year Reich" and by the fantasy of mixing the blood of the dead and the living in the flag ceremony of the tribute to the war dead. It also hints at revenge so as to consolidate the utopian order.

Dr. Jacob Arlow made a similar set of observations. The film displays, he noted, a heightening of expectations, an image of a divine messiah, the dawning of a new day associated with communal unity, an optimistic sense of well being based upon the impression of a united country, an ecstatic sense of group participation with loss of one's identity in the mass, fire as a stimulus for instinctual urgency as well as creating a dreamlike aura, submersion of the individual into a mass identity, a deliberate attempt to increase tension by delaying Hitler's appearance, hysterical adulation of Hitler, an intimidating effect exerted by the mass turnout and hysterical enthusiasm, the absence of women participants, the appeal of the activities displayed by the soldiers and workers to the level of a ten- or eleven-year-old child, Hitler's control of the crowd by his speeches, obliterating their individuality, the impression Hitler gives of not needing the crowd, and Hitler's appearing as the sole intermediary between the German people and the dead, in the War Memorial scene. Arlow reminded us of some of the ideas of Christine Olden. The movies utilized those psychologic qualities, he said, that we know cause individuals to make narcissistic object choices (to select the people they love on the basis of similarity to their own self-image), to fuse with their ego ideal (the see themselves as identical with their image of an ideal person), and to lose their sense of identity in the group that the ego ideal represents.

Let us review these impressions and themes in a different way. Two issues stand out, the nature of the group and its cohesiveness, and its apocalyptic quality. What is striking about the group phenomenon is the relatively abrupt cohesion of hitherto separate individuals from all parts of the country who had not known each other. Not only do they cohere, but they identify with each other. The identification is manifested overtly by similarity in appearance, in costume, by mutual assistance, by forgoing rivalry, and by obedience to the same leader. At one point in the labor service rally, workers from the most remote regions of Germany engage in a drama of unity including a unison declaration of their devotion to the country. This identification is manifested subjectively by mutual affection, by subscribing to common ideals, and by acknowledging that they have the same allies and the same enemies. Hitler's address to the Youth Rally demonstrates these issues:

> My German youth! After one year, I have an opportunity to welcome you here again. Those of you who stand here in this stadium are only a small segment of the masses who stand outside, *all over Germany.* We wish that you German boys and girls [there are virtually no girls evident in the film], absorb all that we expect of Germany in times to come. We want to be a *united nation,* and you, my youth, are to become this nation. In the future, *we do not wish to see classes and cliques,* and you must not allow them to develop among you. One day, we want to see *one nation,* and you must educate yourselves for it: we wish this people to be *obedient,* and you have to practice obedience: we wish this people to be peace-loving, but also brave, and you will have to be peace-loving. You must therefore be peace-loving and *courageous* at the same time. We do not want this nation to become soft: instead, it should be hard, and you will have to harden yourselves while you are young. You must learn to *accept deprivations* without ever collapsing. Regardless of whatever we create and do, we shall pass away, but in you, Germany will live on: and when nothing is left of us, you will have to hold the banner which some time ago we lifted out of nothingness. And I know it cannot be otherwise because you are *flesh of our flesh, blood of our blood,* and your young minds are filled with the *same spirit that dominates us.* You cannot be but *united* with us. And when the *great columns* of our movement *march* victoriously through Germany today, I know that you will *join* these columns. And we know that Germany is *before us, within us, and behind us.* (Italics added)

The apocalyptic quality of the group is manifest. The revelation here consists of the "party line," the principles of Nazi doctrine as enunciated in the speeches to the Congress, but also in Nazi literature, especially *Mein Kampf.* At this Congress, since it was staged not only to reinforce group ties, but also to impress the outside world, repulsive aspects of Nazi doctrine, including especially the antisemitism, were not expressed. However, messages of unity, loyalty, victory were clearly articulated.

The destructive element of the apocalyptic position was also minimized or denied. The military review is played down and occupies not more than one minute and twenty seconds of the entire film. In the speech quoted above, Hitler tells the young people that they must be "peace-loving." Throughout that period he contended elsewhere that it was the

Jews who were interested in war and who were determined to destroy
Germany and the rest of Europe.

The rebirth aspect of the apocalyptic scenario is represented here most
prominently: the emphasis on youth, the awakening of the sleeping city,
the rising sun, the self-confident projection into the future, massive pa-
rades by day and by night, and a portrayal of the Nazi movement as the
recovery from World War I.

The messianism of the apocalypse is salient. The film opens with
Hitler's descent by plane as if he were a semi-divine agent coming down
from the heavens. Throughout he is treated as a semi-divine messiah
who has come to rescue the German people.

## The Nazi Phenomenon: The Freikorps

A more veridical picture of the Nazi state of mind can be obtained by
a study of the Freikorps. The Freikorps were a group of largely autono-
mous armies, each commanded by its own charismatic leader and engaged by Chancellor Ebert to bring order to revolutionary Germany in
1918. Between 1918 and 1923 they fought Polish communists and nationalists, the Russian Red Army, Latvian and Estonian nationalists in
the Baltic region, and the German working class throughout Germany.
They fought because they were well paid, because they wished to take
revenge on the leftists who, they thought, had stabbed Germany in the
back, and because they devoted themselves to fighting. After 1933, they
became the core of Hitler's SA and some of them became key function-
aries in the Third Reich. Certainly they represent the same population
that subsequently became the essential Nazis.

Klaus Theweleit (1987), a West German writer, studied the writings
of some of the more articulate of the Freikorps, autobiographies, novels, eyewitness accounts by men in the Freikorps, and novels written
about them, and he has drawn inferences from these about their behavior and thinking.

Theweleit points out that for the Freikorps, women in this material
fall into one of three categories: women and fiancees who are left behind and relatively neglected in the memoirs of the men of the Freikorps;
the "white nurses," chaste, upper-class German women; and the "Red
women," vividly and aggressively sexual, whores, insulting the Freikorps
men or attacking them physically. The "white nurses" I would infer,

remind them of their chaste mothers, the madonnas. The wives and fiancees are relatively faceless people in these writings, in whom the men show relatively little interest. They are fertile but not sexual. The "Red women" are red for three reasons. First, blood is associated with their flagrant, unrestrained sexuality. They are obscene, disgusting, and dangerous monsters. Second, they are associated with the communist enemies, the "Reds," so that the enemy is associated with sexual demands. And third, the women are red because the Freikorps men are inclined to destroy them and leave them "a bleeding mess."

The Freikorps men, Theweleit demonstrates, were troubled by liquid movement, floods, that they apparently associated with female sexuality. The allusion seems to be to uncontrolled and uncontrollable disorganizing movements leading to chaos. They loved the German people and fatherland, the homeland soil, the uniform, their comrades, the community of blood among their fellow countrymen, weaponry, hunting and fighting, and friendly animals, especially horses. They associate the enemy with dirt, mire, morass, slime, pulp, excrement, and the concept of "behind," all of which they fear and which repel them. Not surprisingly, blood figures prominently in this material. It appears in three contexts. In a victorious mode, blood is spilled when the Freikorps man murders his enemy, male or female, and in the same mode, he can feel the excitement of contained blood within his blood vessels, pounding with excitement. In a defeated mode, he fears being engulfed by rivers of blood that are unleashed by war.

Theweleit creates a composite picture of the Freikorps man. He respects his mother and does his marital duty but fears sexual temptation. Sexuality must be contained. He enjoys fraternal comradeship with men who share his predilections and his aversion to sexuality. He enjoys the thrill of fighting and the accompanying excitement that reinforces his sense of phallic potency. Spilling blood creates excitement and gratification. However, when this excitement gives way to fear, the blood threatens, in retaliation, to overwhelm him.

We have spoken about blood in the context of antisemitism several times. In religious ritual, blood exerts, we have said an apotropiac effect. It protects the subject who exhibits it against danger. With respect to sacrifice, the ritually extracted blood of the victim protects the sacrificer. That holds true for ancient ritual animal sacrifice, for the sacrifice of the paschal lamb the blood of which was smeared on the doorposts of the Jewish houses in order to protect the first born from the Angel of Death. It also held true when Zipporah circumcised Moses' son and touched Moses with the bloody, detached foreskin. When the Christian partakes of the wine and wafer of the Eucharist, symbolically ingesting Christ's blood and flesh, he becomes identified with Christ and is saved by virtue of Christ's sacrifice.

When a person in a savage state of mind spills blood, he becomes more excited and unrestrained. His savagery feeds on itself and self-controlling or self-punitive measures, if there are any, are delayed until after the experience. One member of our group, Dr. George Wiedeman reported that he had been in contact with a civilian in Europe who had been obligated to house Nazi soldiers in his home during their active persecution of Jews. By day the Nazis exhibited no remorse or regret. At night, however, their sleep was disturbed by nightmares, insomnia, and calling out ("Macbeth does murder sleep" [*Macbeth* 2.2.33]). For the vicious murderer, the blood of the victim excites him. It is only in retrospect that he suffers remorse ("Out, damned spot! Out,I say!...yet who would have thought the old man to have so much blood in him" [*Macbeth* 5.2.35]

No Jewish victim of a pogrom, to my knowledge, was ever spared because of the persecutor's response to his blood. Theweleit describes no Freikorps murderer who was deterred or distressed by the sight of the victim's blood. For the apocalyptically minded individual, destruction is necessary and even blessed by whatever god authorizes the apocalyptic prophecy.

*Triumph of the Will* emphasized the fraternal nature of the Nazi movement by visual demonstration and in the speeches. The men of the Freikorps too formed a fraternity devoted to each other but potentially distractable by sexual women.

## The Fraternal Group

The phenomenon of the homogeneous group invites some consideration. Most analysts who have dealt with the subject agree that psychologically the individual members of such a group merge their identities into the mass (Freud, 1913, 1921).In merging identities, the individuals create the illusion of reunion with mother. "It is as if the group formation represented of itself the hallucinatory realization of the wish to take possession of the mother by the sibship, through a very regressive mode, that of primary fusion" (Chasseguet-Smirgel, 1985, p. 85). Each person's megalomania, says Chasseguet-Smirgel (p. 82) finds expression in his ego's being extended to the whole group. They lose their individuality, she continues, and begin to resemble ants or termites. The group thereby becomes homogeneous. Each individual identifies with the totality of the group, acquires an omnipotent ego, a colossal body. "These sports meetings of young people in totalitarian countries where, with the help of streamers or colored placards a group of individuals create immense slogans or gigantic portraits, is a manifestation of the fusion of the ego into the collectivity." The scenes of mass assembly in *Triumph of the Will* exemplify Chasseguet-Smirgel's thesis. In fact, the members of the group merge, not only with each other, but also with the leader, with their land, and with their ideals.

Scheidlinger (1974) has reviewed the concept of the "mother-group" as it has appeared in the literature of psychoanalytic group therapy. In an earlier paper, (1964), he had proposed that identification with the group entity entailed ascribing to the group an emotional meaning, an instrument for need satisfaction or a mother symbol, and a surrender of personal identity. He suggested too that the universal need to belong, to establish a state of psychological unity with others, represents a covert wish to restore an earlier state of unconflicted well-being, the infant's exclusive union with the mother, in order to counteract a fundamental fear of abandonment and aloneness.

Hostility to outsiders characterizes the group as well as unconditional love for the insiders. It almost seems as if the anger is primary. The anger does not take second place to the fraternal love in the Freikorps material, but it is deliberately suppressed in *Triumph of the Will* though hinted at very delicately. Neubauer (1982) observes that turning against the stranger strengthens the group bond. The Nazi ideology about racial purity, he says, "expressed the need to consolidate the familiar which is considered to be endangered," for which, "the destruction of the stranger was absolutely required." Within the group, each member surrenders his own personal morals, values, and standards to the group and to the leader. His own personal ideal is replaced by the group ideal. "To free oneself from the pressure of one's own conscience," writes Neubauer, "and thereby to achieve the acceptance of and belonging to others gives comfort, particularly when the conscience is appeased, when the group adheres to a new ideology which transcends the individual for the good of all." In fact, reality testing itself is ceded to the leader of the group. What is real is only what the leader says is real. (cf. Chasseguet-Smirgel, pp. 86ff.). Absent the guidance of reality testing and of one's ordinary moral standards, the group becomes capable of the most heinous behavior, and becomes unresponsive to normal inhibiting signals, such as the blood of the victim. With the repudiation of conventional morality, guilt does not appear. We hear nothing of guilt from the Nazis or Freikorps. Our colleague, Jacob Arlow reminded us of an observation by Hans Sachs, when everyone is guilty, no one is guilty.

The Nazis and Freikorps all had difficulty with sexuality. They were willing to perform conventional marital and paternal duties, to fulfill the male role in the life of the family and of the community. However, they were repelled by what they considered unbridled sexuality. The seductive, loose woman threatened them. The Freikorps condensed the images of the sexual woman and of the communist enemy so that each represented the other. The Nazis labeled the Jews as sexually immoral and warned that they, if unchecked, would infect the whole world with their immorality.

We are faced with the question: did these people join a fraternal group because they were fleeing sexuality, or did they flee sexuality because the group demanded that they do? It seems to me that the relationship is circular.

Theweleit's description of the preferences and aversions of the members of the Freikorps indicate that they had difficulty with chaos, with uncontrolled and unorganized forces. In his words, all fluids had to be dammed.

In these fraternal groups, homogeneity becomes essential. Small differences are ignored or denied. Large differences from the mass make the subject ineligible for membership. In the speeches of the Nuremberg Party Congress, one heard repeatedly that there could be no rank or caste. It was not that everyone was equal but that all were homogenized, deprived of their individuality.

The sense of group homogeneity reminds us of the antisemitic demand for racial purity. The ideological fraternity assumes control over the nation and imposes its ideology upon it. The "purely" Aryan Nazis and Freikorps men demand that their people and their country be purified. There had to be no heterogeneity, no "alien" elements. The Nazis "purified" Germany of mental defectives, homosexuals, and Gypsies as well as Jews. As I write, the Serbs are engaging in what they call "ethnic cleansing" in Bosnia.

In chapter 2, we discussed family romance, the reorientation of the child away from his or her parents and toward others who are considered more loving or more generous parents. I related the oscillations between philosemitism and antisemitism to shifts in the direction of the family romance. Jews were valued by some gentiles, as superior to one's own family, more loving, more generous, more interesting, more exotic. At a given point, however, stimulated by some external event or by some shift in inner dynamics, Jews were seen as unworthy intruders, alienating the gentile's natural affection from his own true parents, and the philosemitism gave way to antisemitism. The racial purification program of the Nazis demanded that gentiles withdraw from their identification with and concern for the Jewish "aliens" and return to the original German family. In fact, it is a kind of negative or centripetal family romance. The individual is encouraged to withdraw even from his natural family into the bosom of the German *Volk*, the Ur-mother.

## The Cause of Fraternal Group Formation

Although history is replete with instances of aggressive fraternal groups like the Freikorps and the Nazis, the factors that trigger their formation are not easy to apprehend. The immediately preceding circumstances are less well known as we go back in history. It is seldom a single overwhelming event—more often a group of stressful events, such as natural disasters, famine, war, social dislocation. Michael Barkun (1974) contends that disasters and upheavals are necessary but not sufficient conditions. He includes culture clash, economic depression, revolution, war, and natural catastrophes. He adds four additional variables as necessary conditions for the evolution of a defensive millenarian movement: an agrarian society, a multiplicity of disasters, a millenarian ideology, and the availability of a charismatic leader. Peter Loewenberg (1969) has given us a splendid account of the "psychohistorical origins of the Nazi youth cohort." He delineated with great care the deprivation of food and parental care during World War I of the generation that subsequently became the young Nazis, and quotes approvingly Martin Wangh's account (1964) of the psycho-sexual stresses affecting that generation.

I find these arguments persuasive but they do not tell why the traumata, described both as events in the external world, and by their impact on the mental state of the individuals, should have issued in just this kind of attempted resolution. James A. Aho (1990) in his report on the militant Christian right of the American northwest, observes that surges in extremism do not at all correlate with economic depression. They seem to occur at fairly regular intervals of about thirty years on the basis of generational dynamics. Each generation of militants is gradually co-opted into mainstream conservatism and thirty years after the origin of the previous movement, a new one starts. (p. 216ff.). At the end we are left with general and nonspecific items such as deprivation, stress, misery, dislocation, demoralization. Perhaps that very fact tells us that the common factor is human anguish, no matter how that is brought about.

But perhaps we can be a little more specific. Reviewing the history of fundamentalist movements in general and of pogroms in particular, one predisposing element appears salient, that is, chaos. While some of us are more preoccupied with order than others, I doubt that anyone can feel comfortable in the presence of chaos. Chaos means unpredictability, complete subordination to chance. Unpredictability was more common in the ancient world and only slightly less so in premodern times because of limited ability to communicate over distances. That is why revelations, prophecies, omens, and portents were sought. But information can also create anxiety if the information is unsettling—if it conveys the realization that there is no order.

In chapter 1, I observed that the novel, the unfamiliar provokes anxiety in the infant, the anomalous, discordant, weird provokes anxiety in the older child and in many adults. But chaos I believe provokes anxiety in all, and motivates a closing of ranks. Infants cling to mothers, families cohere, social groups organize more tightly—and fundamentalism is encouraged.

All of the students of this phenomenon speak of the need for a charismatic leader. In our discussions, it was observed that the leader was not always charismatic, Josef Stalin, for example. With respect to the Freikorps, the individual units were led by men with variable degrees of charisma, but we know of no overall leader who stood head and shoulders above the others. Perhaps most of the time the leader creates the group, and at other times the group encourages leadership. In many instances, the leader does take an active initiative and *entrains* a group, invoking their apocalyptic feelings to resonate with his oratory.

The charismatic leader usually possesses some distinctive and unusual quality, a special capacity that verifies his superiority, for example a remarkable memory, an unusual appearance, or a special toughness in the face of hardship. He always exhibits a pronounced self-confidence. He articulates some sentiments that are plainly contrary to fact, that violate secondary process thinking but conform to primary process. Thereby he validates the primary process thinking of his followers. In that sense he is more of a misleader than a leader.

Psychologically the charismatic leader need not represent the father. He may represent the mother or he can stand for a heroic sibling. He may represent the "antifather," that is, the wished for, ideal father, rather than the perceived father. The family paradigm may not correctly represent the relation between the leader and the group. The leader, says Chasseguet-Smirgel, is the person who activates the primitive wish for the union of ego and ideal: "He is the promoter of illusion, he who makes it shimmer before men's dazzled eyes, he who will bring it to fruition." She continues "There is no absolute ruler who is not the bearer of an ideology. He is in fact the intermediary between the masses and the ideological illusion" (p.82).

While the group is held together by a combination of mutual love among themselves and hatred for the outsider, these feelings must be verbalized and rationalized in a formula. The formula becomes a doctrine and a banner that can be waved, so to speak, so that it attracts group loyalty and commitment.

For the antisemitic groups that we are studying, the ideology is specifically antisemitism. The group's welfare and life are said to be threatened by the Jews who are trying to poison them, infect them, steal their money, gain control over them, humiliate them. That the Jews cannot be seen to be doing all of these things means nothing. They are engaging in secret conspiracies, invisible. Every now and then, immoral Jewish behavior is publicly uncovered but that is merely a trivial trace of the full mischief. The leader has come to disclose this masked danger and to organize the community to recognize it and to defend itself by fighting back, denouncing, punishing, isolating, exiling, or murdering these Jewish criminals. The community must save itself by responding to the leader and, renouncing all normal feelings of compassion, proceed to stamp out this danger. In this way the community will be saved and permitted to flourish and rise to new heights of strength and gratification.

The ideology makes much of feelings of amity and mutual love and identification. The love community involves not only current members, but also the hallowed and celebrated patriots of the past, the mythological gods of the community, and the land itself, variously referred to as the Motherland or the Fatherland. They are all combined into a coherent matrix that conveys a feeling of continuity, of parental comfort and protection. The affective resonance of the myth, the feeling of relief and salvation from fear and despair overrides all objections based upon reason or fact or guilt.

Analytic discussions of the militant, fraternal group inform us about the dynamic mechanisms that hold the group together, the libidinal and aggressive forces, and how the group relates to the organizing experiences of childhood. However, the biologic basis of this type of group formation is more obscure. How does this phenomenon develop? What biologic or psychologic influences mold it into this shape? One can compare these adult groups to adolescent or even latency, same sex, groups, in which the participants affiliate with each other and the group to permit them to consolidate their emancipation from their parents and at the same time to protect each other against the dangers of individual responsibility and of heterosexual expectations and demands. The elements of uniformity and synchronicity in appearance and behavior, the propensity for mass displays suggest to me the type of multiindividual organism that one sees in schools of fish or flocks of birds, that function as though they were members of one body, so perfectly do they synchronize their movements. I am not prepared to propose that the two situations are indeed homologous in origin, but they do resemble each other functionally, that is, the behaviors converge. This device whereby many individuals coalesce into a pseudoorganism is called into play when the situation requires more strength, real and apparent, than the individual can muster. In that case, the psychodynamics of identification and mutual love and mutually agreed upon hatred, prevail in *response* to the group formation, or as its psychic mechanism, not necessarily as its cause. The group, when it is organized in response to a felt threat, must respond by attacking a target, a fictitious one if a real one does not exist or cannot be found. Primary process thinking is determined by the biologic forces, and the myth attempts to reconcile it with reality, to create the impression of secondary process. The myth makes it seem as though the hatred and determination to destroy were legitimate and appropriate to the situation, rather than an archaic response to a stress of entirely different origin.

The members of the Freikorps were clearly unusually aggressive. As for the Nazis, *Triumph of the Will* deliberately plays down aggressiveness and emphasizes mutual love, cooperation and hard work. Judging from their behavior, however, one must conclude that they incorporated a core of vicious sadists and a larger number of followers, perhaps no more sadistic and vicious than absolutely necessary—though the expression of that aspect of their character was encouraged by their leaders by both precept and example.

## The Fraternal Group and Apocalypse

Reviewing the historical apocalypses as they are represented in Scriptural and apocryphal accounts and in historical reports, I recognize three types of social apocalypse, homologous to the three types of individual apocalypse that I mentioned above (pp.158ff.). First, the Book of Revelation and the second half of Daniel include apocalypses that are intended to comfort an oppressed population. The oppressors will be utterly eradicated in a widespread destruction, but the suffering population will be saved and permitted to flourish.

Second, the prophets of Israel voiced punitive threats against their own people for engaging in sinful and dissolute behavior. They and their habitation will be destroyed, and only a righteous remnant will remain (see especially the Book of Amos).

The third type of apocalypse became prominent in the Middle Ages. Militant movements appeared, probably in response to perceived distress or abuse or demoralization. They are well described by Norman Cohn in his important book, *The Pursuit of the Millennium* (1957, 1970). The aggressive outbursts, the revolutionary battles, were not simply efforts by the impoverished and disadvantaged to better their own lives. They were not just social and political revolutions. They were campaigns believed by the participants to have cosmic significance, to anticipate the last days and to hasten the return of Christ and the arrival of the millennium. The leaders were inspired by the classical Biblical apocalypses; they thought that they were doing the Lord's work. Those whom they labeled as the enemies of the Lord were to be eradicated. Their apocalypse represented a rebirth for them, but apocalyptic destruction for their victims.

There can be no question but that the Holocaust was such a religious, millenarian movement, intended to eradicate the cosmic enemy, the Jews, to make way for the "thousand-year Reich." While some millenarian leaders have been imposters, utilizing mass agitation for personal profit, Hitler's irrational behavior, sacrificing the entire nation and finally himself in response to his delusions about Jews, leaves no doubt that he saw himself as a divinely inspired leader. The inspiration was not religious as the medieval apocalypses were, but utilized the Christian myths that stigmatized the Jew as the cosmic enemy.

Let us look again at the components of apocalypse. The revelation is the myth that is circulated by the leader, that is presumed to originate from a divine source. It is often presented as a prophecy, as the words of an oracle, as a newly inspired reinterpretation of Scriptures. It is widely credited among the population. The leader of an apocalyptic movement may also be the source of the revelation, or the messiah, although these may be personified by other individuals. As we observed above, the leader may or may not be a current representation of a parent or a heroic sibling.

The element of destruction here is experienced not only in the anguish of the apocalyptic community but also in the savage attacks on the designated opponent. Presumably anger has been aroused by any of the usual precipitants of discontent. But whatever the real source, the individual sees his suffering as the consequence of having been abandoned by his god, or more accurately, by his having lost divine protection as the result of the hostile intrusion of a malignant element. The attacks on the Jews or others are seen as attempts to clear the way to a reunion with the divinity, to acquire the benefit of his unobstructed beneficence.

It follows then, that the anticipated result of the militant campaign constitutes the rebirth, the millennium, the divine reward.

However, in addition, the mobilization, effecting mass mutual identification and love, and crediting the leader's promise of salvation, is itself experienced as a rebirth. The battle brings exhilaration, the enjoyment of fraternal love, and the love of a leader. It creates a sensation of a clear and present rebirth, more vivid even than the promised rebirth of the future.

It is ironic that the apocalyptic violence that is intended to achieve his own rebirth by the aggressor, does so by imposing apocalyptic destruction upon the designated enemy. On the other hand, given its origins as an attempt to avoid suicide by displacing the violence outward, the attack is often so contrived as to result in the ultimate defeat and demise of its instigator. The Nazi Holocaust destroyed six million Jews but in the end destroyed itself.

Revelations, messiahs, anticipation of divine retribution and of human campaigns of destruction, and the process of salvation and renewal clearly label all of these destructive movements as apocalyptic in nature. A full understanding of the phenomenon of the militant fraternity cannot be achieved without acknowledging this pattern.

### Fundamentalism

The Nazi Holocaust in a sense is unique, by virtue of the magnitude of its grasp and the relentless persecution of the Jews in the hope of eradicating them from the face of the earth. However in quality, it probably exemplifies the essential features of what we may call the pogrom mentality. To round out the picture we can take note of other movements characterized by hatred of the outside and mutual love among the inside fraternity.

In 1990, I published an essay on fundamentalism in which I tried to discern the psychologic basis for the fundamentalist movement. The characteristics of the Nazi movement as we have discussed them closely resemble those of fundamentalist movements. Nancy T. Ammerman, in her book, *Bible Believers: Fundamentalists in the Modern World,* (1989) notes the following characteristics. Fundamentalists cannot tolerate uncertainty or disorder and require the certainty of an unambiguous Scripture that makes the world predictable, anticipating the future as well as recording the past. The world outside the community of the fundamentalists is wicked, depraved, and doomed to apocalyptic destruction. The fundamentalist community stands alone and apart as an island of righteousness that will be saved. Its members submit passively to authority. Optimism is cultivated. Fundamentalists think in terms of polarities, good and evil, black and white, God and Satan, darkness and light. (These polarities reflect the basic polarity of apocalypse, death and rebirth.—M.O.) The pastor is recognized as leader and idealized. Unison singing plays an important role in religious service. Fundamentalists use whatever power and influence they have to impose their view of proper behavior and proper belief upon the rest of the community.

In his book, *Anti-Intellectualism In American Life,* Richard Hofstadter (1962) lists similar traits. Fundamentalists oppose intellectuality. They exhibit a paranoid attitude. They are militant and oppositional. They do not tolerate sexual language or behavior outside family channels. Fundamentalists separate themselves from the surrounding modern society. They reject the political state and political democracy, and yearn for their version of a theocratic state. They resist institutional religion, traditional religious scholarship, and traditional religious leadership. They reject science and especially theories of evolution. They believe in the power of Satan and subscribe to simplistic principles of reward and punishment. They credit miracles in a literal way.

There are obvious differences between Nazism and what we know as fundamentalism. Fundamentalism characterizes a number of different groups with somewhat different central doctrines, while Nazism was monolithic. Fundamentalists are aggressive and sometimes militant, but except for some radical rightists, not as vicious or destructive as the Nazis. This statement applies to Christian and Jewish fundamentalists. Many Islamic fundamentalists seem to be quite as ruthless and destructive as the Nazis, judging from the terrorism that they sponsor. The Nazis targeted the Jew as their principle antagonists and the source of the major threat to the German people, and in fact, the whole world, whereas some Christian and Islamic fundamentalists are vigorously antisemitic, some philosemitic, and many indifferent to Jews. Most of these differences are differences of degree rather than of quality. Essentially it seems to me that Nazism and religious fundamentalism are congruent in most respects.

On the basis of the observations given above, I propose that the apocalyptic complex forms an essential part of both movements. In both, one finds a central myth to the effect that civilization is being destroyed by an insidious, cosmic enemy, that the remedy consists of destroying that enemy, and that the outcome will be a millennium of bliss and blessedness. In both, one finds a determination to overcome or destroy opposition. In both, celebration of unity and coordinated worship (both religious and its Nazi equivalent) create a feeling of exhilaration experienced as rebirth. In both we find primary process thinking as the dominant mode of thought. Science and all other objective knowledge are disparaged, though their fruits, especially technology, are exploited. Only that "wisdom" that is revealed by cultic authority is valid.

Among the fundamentalists, the radical rightists correspond more closely to the Nazis although their religious orientation differs. James Aho (1990) has described the various movements in the category that he calls Christian patriotism. He lists (pp. 16ff.) the central beliefs that characterize that movement. As he summarizes it, the "Christian patriot" commits himself to belief in Jesus Christ as savior, believes the promise of salvation and that only through Jesus can salvation be obtained. He feels obligated to transform the world according to his perception of God's will which is manifest in his own interpretation of the Bible and in a limited portion of the Constitution of the United States. He is obligated, he believes, to accept secular authority but accepts only the Christian patriot's reading of the Bible and the Constitution. He believes that America's major institutions have been invaded by a secret satanic conspiracy and he believes that the corrupted institutions must be attacked from the point of view of the patriot's righteousness. Here again the elements of revelation, destructiveness, and rebirth establish this as basically an apocalyptic movement.

It follows that although the Nazi movement was really *sui generis* with respect to the amount of damage done, nevertheless with respect to its social psychology, it was nothing other than an apocalyptic movement like those recorded in history and prevailing elsewhere even now, and which has recurrently formed the basis for the pogrom mentality.

## How do Such Movements Come into Existence?

Apocalyptic movements tend to homogenize their members psychologically, members who were not necessarily homogeneous to start with. Most likely the movement starts with a leader who provides the myth, the illusion that promises relief from distress, to a small number of followers to whom the myth appeals. As the core following enlarges, its power seems to depend on its ability to recruit others whose frame of mind is not necessarily apocalyptic but who can sympathize and identify with that *Weltanschauung* under circumstances that favor it. One can say that first the leader and then the central core entrain the latent apocalyptic readiness that exists among the followers. The apocalyptic can be sponsored by either the political left or right, or the religious left or right.

One of the members of our study group, Dr. Peter B. Neubauer, described recruitment of Nazis as he saw it as a child in Austria among his high school classmates. The first to be attracted to the Nazi party were adolescents who were clearly recognized as eccentric and psychologically deviant. They were joined by others who sympathized with the first group, but without it would not themselves have become involved. The third to join were those young people who had no strong political convictions but who were not able to withstand the pressure to join the others. A fourth group, composed mostly of Catholics, actively resisted the Nazi influence as a matter of religious principle.

### Recruitment

Loewenberg (1969) tells us that most of the recruits to the Nazi party were young people, actually the cohort who were young children during the World War I and who had suffered starvation, absence or loss of their fathers and the relative inattention of working mothers. He reminds us that the years between 1928 and 1933 saw remarkably rapid recruitment. Two students of personal experience in the Nazi movement gave examples of the importance of friendship, comradeship, in recruiting members to the Nazis. (Abel, 1938 and Merkl, 1975). According to Merkl (p. 35) people in his sample were introduced to the Nazi party as they witnessed demonstrations or violence in the streets or at party rallies, or by reading about the party's ideology, or often through a friend or colleague. Merkl refers to finding "real comradeship" in the Hitler Youth and a sense of belonging (p. 571). Abel cites autobiographical accounts that included expressions such as "joyous acknowledgment," "bright enthusiasm," "pure faith" (p. 212).

Tom Segev (1987) reports the comments of the widow of one executed concentration camp guard. Her husband, she said, had joined the Nazi party out of despair, identifying with the party and with individual members. The Nazi movement offered him faith and the opportunity to make close friends with other young men (p. 49). Another widow reported that her husband discovered a new kind of friendship in the party, a friendship that became very important and that created a fraternal feeling (p.139). The idea of rebirth is already implied. In other words we hear of attraction because of the "ideology," that is, the myths of the party and because of the comradeship, that is, the mutual love and identification offered by membership in the party. Of course, it is likely that more than one of these considerations prevailed and contributed to the motivation, but a frame of mind that was hospitable to apocalyptic thinking found ideology, mutual love, and also group aggressiveness in Nazi party membership.

Aho (1990) reports that personal contact, friendship, family ties in very many cases, opened the channels of communication between the candidate and the religious extremist group. He suggests that what distinguished Christian patriots from their fellow citizens is their access to what he calls a "patriot" opportunity structure. This structure provides a body of patriot exemplars, a sophisticated ideology, justificatory motives, a support network with emotional surcease, physical retreat, and protection from authorities (p. 209). But he emphasizes that the essential motivation for joining lies in establishing and expanding love relationships, family ties as well as friendship and a hospitable work environment (p. 191).

## Indoctrinating Children

In Nazi Germany and in other totalitarian cultures, children were subjected to propaganda in books prepared for them. Professor Yosef Yerushalmi has examined children's literature in Nazi Germany and was able to show us examples. Such books deal with stereotypical distinctions between Jews and Aryans, with the theme of the Wandering Jew, the grotesqueness of Jewish features, Jewish dishonesty and untrustworthiness, Jewish avarice and abuse of German peasants, taking the peasants' land, Jews as predatory strangers, Jewish doctors who abuse German children sexually, blood and Jewish animal slaughter, Jewish worship of money, and the need to get rid of the Jews.

Our group was especially struck by the subtle but definite encouragement of children to replace respect for parents with idealization of Hitler. This is the equivalent of the negative or centripetal family romance mentioned above. The child is urged not merely to withdraw from the alien back to the family but from the family to the Ur-family, that is German mythic heroes and current Nazi leaders.

A more systematic study of children's literature in Hitler's Germany is found in a book by that name by Christa Kamenetsky (1984). Children's literature is used to imprint the group myth in the mind of the child or young adolescent when it is most receptive.

We have already commented briefly on parent-child, teacher-child, religious teacher-child, and child-child modes of communicating prejudice via the transmission of myths. For the purpose of combatting prejudice, the prejudice inspiring potency of these channels should be carefully studied.

## The Instigation of Pogroms

In addition to mythic propaganda, pogroms require more immediate stimulation. While we know of individual clusters of pogroms of the past, the psychosocial background against which they occurred can only be guessed at. Few if any pogroms were as well organized as the Nazi persecution. Most were probably the result of organized agitation in a population prepared by prevailing antisemitic myths activated by current incitement. The population is more susceptible to current agitation if what they hear is a repetition of what they have already heard in childhood. At any rate, a pogrom is not likely to be carried out by a population that does not take the antisemitic myths seriously, that is, that does not believe that the eradication of the Jews would achieve their salvation. To be effective in inspiring a pogrom, antisemitic propaganda must not only convey antisemitic ideas, but also encourage the apocalyptic frame of mind.

Antisemitic attacks do not require an actual conflict of interest between the perpetrators and the Jews but such a conflict makes the rationalization of antisemitism easier and also reinforces the motivation. If Jews are tax farmers in Europe's Dark Ages, or moneylenders in medieval Europe, or immigrants competing for jobs, or landlords in Harlem, then non-Jewish antagonists will have reason to feel anger, resentment, or at least rivalry. Even when there is no active rivalry, when Jewish success becomes visible, others become envious. Both rivalry and envy contribute to the antisemitic climate and to the readiness for persecution. Conventional histories of antisemitism dwell on these material factors (cf. Baron, Ginsberg cited above).

However, even on those occasions when no realistic basis for enmity or rivalry existed, antisemitism was mobilized for the purpose of directing popular attention to what the antisemitic leaders saw as a realistic danger. Cohn (1981) writes that the Black Hundreds ("armed bands recruited for purposes of terror by the union of the Russian people and similar political organizations") and other right-wing political leaders aimed to "fight liberalization of Russia by presenting it as a Jewish plot, to get Jews massacred to show how real the plot was."

> Henry Louis Gates, Jr., professor of English and chairman of the African-American Studies department at Harvard wrote in the *New York Times* on 20 July 1992, "The answer [to the question, "Why Target the Jews?"] requires us to go beyond the usual shibboleths about bigotry and view the matter from the demagogues' perspective, strategically: as the bid of one black elite to supplant another. It requires us, in short, to see antisemitism as a weapon in the raging battle of who will speak for black America—those who have sought common cause with others or those who preach a barricaded withdrawal into racial authenticity. The strategy of these apostles of hate, I believe, is best understood as ethnic isolationism—they know that the more isolated black America becomes, the greater their power. And what is the most efficient way to begin to sever black America from its allies? Bash the Jews, these demagogues apparently calculate, and you are halfway there."

Active, aggressive, and effectual leadership of an antisemitic movement greatly increases the likelihood that the pogrom will happen. Emicho of Leiningen, Bogdan Chmielnicki, Simon Petlyura, Adolf Hitler are all names that have become associated with massive persecution of Jews. They reinforced the antisemitic preparedness of the people they led and at a given point galvanized them into murderous action. In each case there were two enemies, a real enemy and a fantasy enemy, a secondary process enemy and a primary process enemy. In each case the Jews were held responsible for whatever evil existed. Individual and more local pogroms were organized by leaders whose names appear only in history books and are not recognized by the average reader. Pogroms of any degree of severity seldom occur without leadership.

A specific crisis, real or fabricated, serves to trigger the actual attack. It might have been the discovery of the corpse of a child whose death was attributed to the Jews. It might have been an epidemic, or famine, or economic depression, or a political revolution. When a population is prepared with antisemitic mythology, when there is an effective and dedicated leader, and especially if there is a real grievance, the crisis can initiate an outbreak.

Finally, a pogrom does not come about unless there is no source of power able or willing to prevent it. In the absence of a potent government that wishes to protect its citizens, the potential of *pogromchiki* to commit murder, rape, looting, and general mayhem is unlimited. It is no secret that Jews were persecuted when they were weak, when they depended upon the generosity of others but were not in a position to defend themselves, whether because of small numbers or because they were not permitted to bear arms. With the formation of the State of Israel, the regnant myth among the Jews has changed. Until then Jews revered Yohanan ben Zakkai who, it was said, escaped from besieged Jerusalem, surrendered to the Romans, obtained safe passage from them and permission to found a school at Yavneh. Since 1948, the Jews of Masada, who fought the Romans until in desperation they committed suicide (73 C.E.), have become idealized. The Jews of Israel have to defend themselves against Arab military and economic attacks, but not against antisemitic persecution. The Jewish state became itself a defense against antisemitism for Jews all over the world. One aspect of the defense is accepting impoverished and endangered Jews, black and white, skilled and unskilled, poor and rich, religious and secular. The other aspect of the defense is the moral strengthening of all Jewish communities of the West.

On 19 August, 1991, a car being driven by one of the attendants of the Lubavitch Rebbe, accidentally struck and killed a young African-American child in Brooklyn, New York. There followed a night of rioting, looting, fire setting, and window breaking by African-Americans attacking the homes and stores of the Lubavitch Hasidim. Throngs of African-Americans shouted "Heil Hitler" in front of the Lubavitch headquarters. Ultimately a Hasidic Jew was stabbed by a mob shouting "Kill the Jew." The victim died shortly thereafter in the emergency room of a local hospital. (It was later claimed that he would not have died but for the incompetence of the emergency room surgeon.) Since the incident, a "shrine" has been devised at the site of the automobile accident, just as the mythic victims of the blood libels of the Middle Ages were memorialized by shrines, some of which exist to this day.

So how does our schematic ideologic system apply to this small pogrom? The African-American community of Crown Heights, surely among the most unfortunate citizens of the city because of the history of discrimination that they suffered, poor education, unemployment, weak family structure, and bad morale, envy the Lubavitch Hasidim. The latter, although they too have suffered discrimination and have had a limited secular education, have achieved relative comfort by virtue of their industry, sobriety, tight and mutually supportive community organization, and religiously inspired morale. Their African-American neighbors attribute the difference in comfort and status to a white-inspired conspiracy and to discrimination by the police who accommodate the Hasidim by modifying traffic regulations on religious holidays.

The African-Americans of New York City, whatever other exposure to antisemitic mythology they may have experienced as children, had in recent years been subjected to antisemitic propaganda by "community organizers," black newspapers, and African-American pseudointellectuals. At the time that this happened, the blacks and Jews of New York had both been agitated by the enunciation of antisemitic canards by the chairman of African-American Studies at City University, presented as authentic historical scholarship.

We have then a population prepared for antisemitism and propagandized more intensely recently. We have envy and perceived injustice and discrimination. We have an acute crisis. This situation would have escalated into greater loss of life and more widespread rioting but for two factors. In the first place, effective black antisemitic leadership was lacking. Even the bumbling, swaggering "community organizers" were absent until the third day. Had there been effective black antisemitic leadership on the spot, matters could have escaped far beyond control.

Second we had here what Jews in no other pogrom situations had, namely, effective official government determination to prevent violence, delayed though it was. In the serious pogroms of history, government lacked either the will or the power to prevent a pogrom.

Having reviewed the various factors that must be added to the antisemitic myth in order to create murderous pogroms, let us consider what use we can make of these discussions.

# 6

# Conclusions

Looking back at the ground we have covered, it becomes evident that we have considered many incidents over long stretches of Jewish history, none in depth. Recognizing the hazards of doing so, nevertheless, I consider this procedure necessary in order to learn what are the constants of antisemitism.

What have we learned? Antisemitic sentiments are not to be correlated with any psychopathologic entity, or any of the commonly considered psychodynamic complexes. We have encountered antisemitism associated with the problems in the resolution of the Oedipus complex, sibling rivalry, family romance, sexual perversion. Antisemitism was not correlated with diagnosis; it was not specifically associated with schizophrenia, manic-depressive disease, or neurosis. In the case of those individuals who had difficulty in controlling aggression, their antisemitism seemed to be more pronounced than it was among others who had less aggression to dispose of.

For many of the individuals whose cases we considered, antisemitism was a phasic phenomenon, alternating at various intervals with philosemitism. In a philosemitic mood, the individual entered into a family romance fantasy with the Jew as the new family, and then withdrew from that relation into an antisemitic rejection of the Jews.

Historically, we have found that there are no specific social or political conditions that favor antisemitism, though unrest or distress of any kind and arising from whatever source, does favor it. No specific accusations characterize antisemitism, even though certain types of myths have tended to recur, for example, those relating Jews to blood and to money. The influence of the early Christian Church and Church fathers certainly created the religious basis of antisemitic myths. Having done so, they proceeded to penalize Jews, but only to a limited degree. On

175

many occasions, groups of Christians took the anti-Jewish mythology and ran with the ball themselves, ignoring and overriding the limits placed by the Church on harassment and persecution. Even after the subsidence of Church influence, that is, even among the deists of the seventeenth and eighteenth centuries, and certainly among the Nazis, Christian demonization of the Jews was accepted, exploited, and elaborated.

Among most antisemites, we found that their irrational hatred was the expression of primary process thinking, that is, thought that is driven by feeling and not subjected to the discipline of reason, logic, or reality testing.

The psychologic issue in every case dealt with the need to understand the sources of personal unhappiness. The individual is looking for a principle of evil, an explanation less farfetched than invisible demons but something more tangible than what Talmudic literature calls God's severe judgment. Early Christian teachings to the effect that the principle of evil is the Jew, have been passed on through the ages and have remained active even among "post-Christian" antisemites. Other religions have offered religious dualism and polytheism as explanations for evil. The monotheistic religions had to find room for evil within their own domain. The explanation offered by Christianity was that the flow of God's benevolence was obstructed by the Jews. Because what was proposed did not square with what could be seen of Jews, considering their poverty, lack of power, and usually unexceptional behavior, it was proposed that Jewish power and malevolence operated secretly. Jews conspired to destroy Christendom, which was therefore justified in persecuting Jews even in the absence of visible evidence of malevolence.

This assignment of blame for misfortune to the Jews was congenial to those of an apocalyptic frame of mind, either because of their own temperament, or because they were drawn into it under the influence of individual or community misfortune. Apocalypse combines the illusion of Jewish fault with the need to attack and destroy, and yields the illusion of rebirth. The apocalyptic frame of mind, when it is present, makes the difference between antisemitic prejudice and antisemitic persecution, though not all persecution is apocalyptic.

Finally we considered the conditions that had to accompany this disposition before actual pogroms were initiated. We spoke of early mythologic indoctrination, adult reinforcement of that mythology, actual conflict of interest, antisemitic leadership, and acute crisis, and the absence of effective defense by the Jews or intervention by the government.

On the basis of these considerations, what can we say about prevention? Let us consider the several conditions for antisemitism that we have already noted. Inasmuch as psychoanalysis helps people by teaching them how to recognize and undo the personal myths that account for their irrational behavior and their unhappiness, one might propose that we teach antisemites the mythologic quality of their views of Jews. However, anyone who has had experience with this procedure clinically, with actual patients, knows how difficult it can be even when the patient starts with a consciously completely cooperative frame of mind; and how frequently the procedure is undermined by the patient's resistance. How can we hope to convey such insight to someone who would not accept the idea of submitting himself to a demythologizing process, someone who needs his myths? Nevertheless the exposure of the mythologic quality of certain beliefs can penetrate fairly widely and exert a not inconsiderable influence. Notwithstanding what he might think of it, who in Western literate society has not heard of the Oedipus complex or of sibling rivalry? Moreover demythologizing the public can only be useful. It would contribute to the process of making man independent of superstition, fantasy, and prejudice, begun with the Enlightenment. Freud proposed to extend that process by means of psychoanalysis. Where id was, ego shall be.

The Gates essay from which I quoted is an excellent example of demythologizing. It identifies the problem: the top down promotion of antisemitism in the black community in the face of waning antisemitism in the white community. He quoted a distinguished African-American authority, Professor Cornell West, to the effect that black antisemitism undermines the credibility of the black struggle against racism. He invokes the authority of Dr. Martin Luther King, Jr. in opposition to the promotion of enmity by invoking pseudo-memory. He locates the source of black antisemitism in black academia whose members are not above using *The Protocols of the Elders of Zion* again. He calls attention to a canard circulated in a pseudo-scholarly work called "The Secret Relationship Between Blacks and Jews." (Note again the use of the concept of the secret to explain the absence of evidence for the antisemitic argument.) He calls attention to the distortions and deceptions given in the book and cites the true facts which are virtually the opposite of what is claimed. For example, he makes it clear that whatever the participation of Jews in African slave trade, it was no more than a very small fraction of the participation of gentiles, though the book claims that the opposite is true. He explains that the antisemitic campaign is being promoted as a ploy in the struggle to obtain control of the black community. The true involvement of Jews with blacks, disproportionately, lies in their partnership in the civil rights movement. Many black leaders who know better, he continues, withhold criticism even though to do so is to capitulate to the isolationist agenda. Finally, he quotes Dr. King again: "We are caught in an inescapable network of mutuality. Whatever affects one directly, affects all indirectly."

Nevertheless one of the published replies to Dr. Gates was a letter signed by two distinguished African-American scholars, one from Harvard and one from Columbia, praising the Gates article but asking for a reciprocal definition of the Jewish contribution to the dissension, implying that the Jews are equally culpable. They seem in fact to be reinforcing the very same antisemitic myths that Gates was deploring.

Unfortunately we cannot rely on the press. Although they do not speak with a single voice, there is often enough unanimity to make their prejudices sound convincingly like objective reality. The anti-Israel bias shown by many writers and television personalities suggests that a suppressed antisemitism has been released by the transition of Jews from powerless victim to a people able to look after itself militarily. International behavior that is ignored when it is exhibited by others, is magnified in the case of Israel. Although courageous demythologizing is a weak weapon, it is one of the few that we have and must be encouraged.

The apocalyptic frame of mind does not lend itself to easy control. For many people it expresses an inborn disposition. For others it is evoked by external stress. In psychiatry we now possess certain chemical agents that help us to control affective dispositions that do not respond to psychotherapeutic influences. That type of intervention is obviously inappropriate in a social setting, and certainly among people who do not recognize that they have a problem that needs remedy.

The apocalyptic frame of mind of course is not specific to antisemitism. It also brings about revolutions and social and political upheavals of other kinds. Very often the serious pogroms occur in association with these other disturbances, before, during and after. Our assignment then, is nothing less than to find a procedure that will prevent social unrest and disruption.

However, with respect to both mythology and apocalypse the issue is not only antisemitism but prejudice and persecution in general. (The purveyors of antisemitic myths to the black community are serving that community badly. While exploiting antisemitic mythology for their own personal ambitions, they are validating the concept of prejudice as a weapon.) Before the Holocaust, Freud suggested putting some trust in the "still small voice of reason." I doubt that he would repeat that statement. I would hope that the dissemination of the understanding of the nature of prejudicial mythology and apocalyptic persecution might ultimately make a small contribution to their containment. But perhaps I am being too optimistic.

In an attempt to preserve traditional messianism and the hope that it brings, without at the same time encouraging messianic adventure, Maimonides, the great twelfth century scholar, physician and philosopher, offered his view of the messianic age (following the view expressed in B.T. Sanhedrin 99a):

Let no one think that in the days of the Messiah any of the laws of nature will be set aside, or any innovation be introduced into creation. The world will follow its normal course. The words of Isaiah: And the wolf shall dwell with the lamb, and the leopard shall lie down with the kid (Isaiah 11:6) are to be understood figuratively, meaning that Israel will live securely among the wicked of the heathens who are likened to wolves and leopards, as it is written: A wolf of the deserts spoils them, a leopard watches over their cities (Jer.5:6). They will all accept the true religion, and will neither plunder nor destroy, and together with Israel earn a comfortable living in a legitimate way, as it is written: And the lion shall eat straw like the ox (Isaiah,2:6) (Maimonides,Mishneh Torah, Kings, 12:1)

The Messianic age will be the age when persecution of Jews comes to an end!

# Bibliography

Abel, T. *Why Hitler Came To Power.* New York: Prentice Hall, 1938.

Abraham, H.C. and Freud, E.L. *A Psychonalytic Dialogue: The Letters of Sigmund Freud and Karl Abraham, 1907–1926,* translated by B. Marsh and H.C. Abraham. New York: Basic Books, 1965.

Abraham, K. "The Day of Atonement: Some Observations on Reik's *Problems in Psychology of Religion.* " In *Clinical Papers and Essays on Psychoanalysis,* edited by H. Abraham, translated by H. Abraham and D.R. Ellison. New York: Basic Books, 1955.

Ackerman, N.W. and Jahoda, M. *Antisemitism and Emotional Disorder: A Psychoanalytic Interpretation,* New York: Harper, 1950.

Aho, J.A. *The Politics of Righteousness: Idaho Christian Patriotism.* Seattle: University of Washington Press, 1990.

Albright, W.F. and Mann, C.S. *Matthew, A New Translation with Introduction and Commentary (The Anchor Bible).* Garden City, NY: Doubleday, 1971.

Ammerman, N. *Bible Believers: Fundamentalists in the Modern World.* New Brunswick, NJ: Rutgers University Press, 1989.

Arlow, J. "Aggression and Prejudice: Some Psychoanalytic Observations on the Blood Libel Accusations Against the Jews." In *The Spectrum of Psychoanalysis,* edited by A.K. Richards and A.D. Richards. Madison, CT: International Universities Press, 1994.

Barkun, M. *Disorders and the Millenium.* New Haven, CT: Yale University Press, 1974.

Baron, S.W. *A Social and Religious History of the Jews,* vol. 15. New York: Columbia University Press, 1957, Philadelphia: Jewish Publication Society, 1973.

Baron, S.W. and Wise, G. *Violence and Defense in the Jewish Experience.* Philadelphia: Jewish Publication Society, 1977.

Baron, S.W. "Changing Patterns of Antisemitism: A Survey." *Jewish Social Studies,* vol. 38, pp. 5–38, 1976.

Bergmann, M. *In the Shadow of Moloch: The Sacrifice of Children and its Impact on Western Religion.* New York: Columbia University Press, 1992.

Bergmann, M. and Jucovy, M., eds. *Generations of the Holocaust.* New York: Basic Books, 1982.

Bornstein, B. "Fragments of an Analysis of an Obsessional Child." *Psycho-analytic Study of the Child*, vol. 8, pp. 313-32, 1953.

Chasseguet-Smirgel, J. *The Ego Ideal*, translated by Paul Barrows. London: Free Association Books, 1985.

Chrysostom, John. *Discourses Against Judaizing Pagans*, translated by T.W. Hawkins. Washington, DC: The Catholic University Press, 1979.

Cohn, N. *The Pursuit of the Millennium*. New York: Oxford University Press, 1970.

Cohn, N. *Europe's Inner Demons*. New York: Meridian, New American Library, 1975, 1977.

Cohn, N. *Warrant For Genocide*, Brown Judaica Studies 23. Chico, CA: Scholars Press, 1981.

Dawidowicz, L. *The War Against the Jews, 1933-1945*. New York: Holt, Rinehart and Winston, 1975.

Dinnerstein, L. *The Leo Franck Case*. Athens: University of Georgia Press, 1987.

Douglas, M. *Purity and Danger: An Analysis of Concepts of Pollution and Taboo*. London:Routledge and Kegan Paul, 1966.

Duby, G., ed. *A History of Private Life: Revelations of the Medieval World*. Cambridge, MA: Belknap, Harvard University Press, 1988.

Duckitt, J. "Psychology and Prejudice, An Historical Analysis and Integrated Framework." *American Psychologist*, vol. 27, no. 10, pp. 1182-93.

Emerson, R.L. "Deism" in *Dictionary of the History of Ideas*, vol.1, P.P.Wiener, ed. New York: Scribner's, 1968.

Erickson, E. "Hitler's Imagery and German Youth." *Psychiatry* 5:479-493.

Federn, Paul and Herman Nunberg. *Minutes of the Vienna Psychoanalytic Society*, 4 vols. New York: International Universities Press, 1962-1975.

Fenichel, O. "Elements of a Psychoanalytic Theory of Antisemitism." In *Antisemitism, A Social Disease*, E. Simmel, ed. New York: International Universities Press, 1946.

Frenkel-Brunswick, E. and N. Sanford. "The Anti-Semitic Personality: A Research Report." In *Antisemitism, A Social Disease*, E.Simmel, ed. 1946.

Freud, Anna. "Insight." *Psychoanalytic Study of the Child*, vol. 36, 1981, pp. 241-249.

Freud, S. *The Interpretation of Dreams* (1900). The Standard Edition of the Complete Psychological Works of Sigmund Freud, vols. 4 and 5, James Strachey, ed. London: Hogarth Press, 1953-74.

Freud, S. *Psychoanalytic Notes On An Autobiographical Account Of A Case Of Paranoia (Dementia Paranoides)* (1911). Standard Edition, vol. 12.

Freud, S. *The Theme of the Three Caskets* (1913). Standard Edition, vol. 12.

Freud, S. *Totem and Taboo* (1913). Standard Edition, vol. 13.

Freud, S. *Jokes and Their Relation to the Unconscious* (1905). Standard Edition, vol. 5.

Freud, S. *Group Psychology and the Analysis of the Ego* (1921). Standard Edition, vol. 18.

Freud, S. *An Autobiographical Study* (1925). Standard Edition, vol. 20.

Freud, S. *Address to B'nai B'rith* (1941). Standard Edition, vol. 20.

Freud, S. *Civilization and Its Discontents* (1930). Standard Edition, vol. 21.

Freud, S. *Family Romances* (1909). Standard Edition, vol. 9.

Freud, S. *Moses and Monotheism* (1939). Standard Edition, vol. 23.

Friedlander, S., Holton, G., Mark, L., Skolnikoff, E. *Visions of Apocalypse, End Or Rebirth?* New York: Holmes and Meier, 1985.

Gates, H.L. "Why Target the Jews?" *The New York Times*, 20 July, 1992.

Geller, S. "Blood Cult: Toward a Literary Theology of the Priestly Work of the Pentateuch." *Prooftexts*, vol. 12, no. 2, 1992.

Gilman, S.L. *Jewish Self-Hatred*. Baltimore: Johns Hopkins University Press, 1986.

Ginsberg, B. *The Fatal Embrace: Jews and the State*. Chicago: University of Chicago Press, 1993.

Goitein, S.D. *Jews and Arabs*. New York: Schocken, 1974.

Goldschmidt, D., ed. *Mahzor Leyamim Hanora'im Lefi Minhag B'nei Ashkenaz*, vol. 2. Jerusalem: Koren, 1970.

Grunberger, B. "The Anti-Semite and the Oedipal Conflict." *International Journal of Psycho-Analysis*, 45:380–385, 1964.

Hertzberg, A. *The Jews In America*. New York: Simon and Schuster, 1989.

Hertzberg, A. *The French Enlightenment and the Jews*. New York: Columbia University Press, 1968.

Hofstadter, R. *Anti-Intellectualism In American Life*. New York: Random House, Vintage, 1962.

Hsia, R.P. *The Myth Of Ritual Murder, Jews and Magic in Reformation Germany*. New Haven: Yale University Press, 1988.

Jones, E. "The Psychology of the Jewish Question." In *Essays in Applied Psycho-Analysis*, vol.1. London: Hogarth Press, 1951.

Kamenetsky, C. *Children's Literature in Hitler's Germany*. Athens: Ohio University Press, 1984.

Karp, A.J. *Haven and Home: A History of the Jews in America*. New York: Schocken, 1989.

Klein, D.B. *Jewish Origins of the Psychoanalytic Movement*. Chicago: University of Chicago, 1981.

Langmuir, G.I. *History, Religion, and Antisemitism*. Berkeley: University of California Press, 1990.

Langmuir, G.I. *Toward a Definition of Antisemitism*. Berkeley: University of California Press, 1990.

Lewis, B. "The Enemies of God." *The New York Review of Books*, vol.40, no. 6, 1993.

Lewis, B. *The Jews of Islam*. Princeton, NJ: Princeton University Press, 1984.

Lewis, B. *Semites and Anti-Semites*. New York: Norton, 1986.

Lewis, M. *Clinical Aspects of Child Development*. Phhiladelphia:Lea and Febiger, 1971.

Liebes, Y. *Studies in Jewish Myths and Mysticism*. Albany: State University of New York Press, 1993.

Loewenberg, P. *Decoding the Past: The Psychohistorical Approach*. Berkeley: University of California Press, 1969.

Loewenstein, R.M. *Christians and Jews: A Psychoanalytic Study*. New York:International University Press, 1951.

Maimonides. *Mishneh Torah*, Kings, XII:1.

Merkl, P.H. *Political Violence Under the Swastika*. Princeton, NJ: Princeton University Press, 1975.

Mintz, A. *Hurban: Response to Catastrophe in Hebrew Literature*. New York: Columbia University Press, 1984.

Modder, M.F. *The Jew in the Literature of England*. Philadelphia: Jewish Publication Society, 1944.

Nelson, B. *The Idea of Usury*. Princeton, NJ: Princeton University Press, 1949.

Nelson, B. and Starr, J."The Legend of the Divine Surety and the Jewish Moneylender." *Annuaire de L'Institut de Philologie et D'Histoires Orientales et Slaves*, vol. 7. New York: The Moretus Press, 1944.

Neubauer, P. "Rivalry, Envy and Jealousy." *Psychoanalytic Study of the Child*, vol. 37, pg. 121–142, 1982.

Nunberg, H. *On Curiosity*. New York: International University Press, 1961.

Nunberg, H. *Principles of Psychoanalysis*. New York: International University Press, 1955.

Orr, D. "Antisemitism and the Psychopathology of Daily Life." In Simmel, *Antisemitism, A Social Disease*, 1946.

Ostow, M. "A Psychological Contribution to the Study of Brain Function, II. The Temporal Lobe and III. Synthesis." *The Psychoanalytic Quarterly*, vol. 24, pg. 383, 1955.

Ostow, M. "The Psychodynamics of Merkevah Mysticism." In Ostow, M., *Ultimate Intimacy: The Psychodynamics of Jewish Mysticism*. London: Karnac, 1995.

Ostow, M. Discussion of "On Shylock and Shakespeare: An Empathic Failure in the Sixteenth Century", by Dr. Hyman I. Muslin. (Unpublished)

Ostow, M. *Judaism and Psychoanalysis*. New York: Ktav, 1982.

Ostow, M. "The Jewish Reponse to Crisis." In Ostow, 1982 and *Conservative Judaism*, vol. 33, no. 4, pp. 3-25, 1980.

Ostow, M. *Ultimate Intimacy: The Psychodynamics of Jewish Mysticism,* London: Karnac, 1995.

Ostow, M. "The Fundamentalist Phenomenon: A Psychological Perspective." In *The Fundamentalist Phenomenon,* N. Cohen, ed. Grand Rapids, MI: Erdmans, 1990.

Paley, V.G. *You Can't Say You Can't Play.* Cambridge, MA: Harvard University Press, 1992.

Parkes, J. *The Conflict of the Church and Synagogue.* New York: Atheneum, 1981.

Parkes, J. *The Jew in the Medieval Community.* New York: Hermon Press, 1976.

Poliakov, Leon, *The History of Antisemitism.* 3 vols., trans. R. Howard, N. Gerard, and M. Kochon. New York: Vanguard, 1961, 1974, 1975.

Reinharz, J. *Living With Antisemitism: Modern Jewish Responses.* Hanover, NH: University Press of New England, 1987.

Robinson, D. *American Apocalypses.* Baltimore: Johns Hopkins University Press, 1985.

Roskies, D.G. *Against the Apocalypse.* Cambridge, MA: Harvard University Press, 1984.

Rothman, S. and Isenberg, P. "Sigmund Freud and the Politics of Marginality." *Central European History*, vol 7, 58–78, 1974.

Russell, J.B. *Lucifer and the Devil in the Middle Ages.* Ithaca, NY: Cornell University Press, 1984.

Russell, J.B. *Satan: The Early Christian Tradition.* Ithaca, NY: Cornell University Press, 1981.

Russell, J.B. *The Devil: Perceptions of Evil From Antiquity to Primitive Christianity.* Ithaca, NY: Cornell University Press, 1977.

Scheidlinger, S. "Identification, the Sense of Belonging and of Identity in Small Groups." *International Journal of Group Psychotherapy,* vol. 4, no. 3, pp. 291–306, 1964.

Scheidlinger, S. "On the Concept of the Mother Group." *International Journal of Group Psychotherapy,* vol. 24, no. 4., pp. 417–428, 1974.

Scholem, G. *The Messianic Idea in Judaism.* New York: Schocken, 1971.

Schorsch, I. *Jewish Reactions to German Antisemitism, 1890–1914.* New York: Columbia University Press and Philadelphia: Jewish Publication Society, 1972.

Segev, T. *Soldiers of Evil:The Commandants of The Nazi Concentration Camps.* New York: McGraw Hill, 1987.

Simmel, E., ed. *Antisemitism, A Social Disease.* New York: International Universities Press, 1946.

Singerman, R. "The Jew as Racial Alien: The Genetic Component of American Antisemitism." In *Antisemitism In American History,* D.A. Gerber, ed. Urbana, IL: University of Illinois, 1986.

Smith, D. "The Property of Hunger." Unpublished thesis, 1993.

Stein, H.F. "The Binding of the Son: Psychoanalytic Reflections on the Symbiosis of Anti-Semitism and Anti-Gentilism." *Psychoanalytic Quarterly,* 46: 650-685, 1977.

Stern, M., *Greek and Latin Authors on Jews and Judaism.* Edited with introduction, translation and commentaries. Jerusalem: Israel Academy of Sciences and Humanities, 1980.

Stillman, N. *The Jews of Arab Lands. Philadelphia:* Jewish Publication Society, 1979.

Strauss, H. and Bergmann, W., eds. *Current Research on Antisemitism: Vol. 2, Error Without Trial: Psychological Research on Antisemitism.* New York: Walter de Gruyter, 1988.

Styron, W. *Sophie's Choice.* New York: Random House, 1979.

Styron, W. *Darkness Visible: A Memoir of Madness.* New York: Random House, 1990.

Theweleit, K. *Male Fantasies, Vol. I: Women, Floods, Bodies, History.* Translated by S. Conway. Minneapolis: University of Minnesota Press, 1987.

Trachtenberg, J. *The Devil and the Jew.* Philadelphia: Jewish Publication Society, 1983.

Tractenberg, M. "Circumcision, Crucifixion and Anti-Semitism: The Antithetical Character of Ideologies and Their Symbols Which Contain Crossed Lines." *International Review of Psychoanalysis,* 16:459-471.

Virgil, *The Aeneid,* translated by Allen Mandelbaum. Berkeley: University of California Press, 1971.

Vogt, R. *Psyche.* 3, March, 1984.

Von Rezzori, G. *Memoirs of An Antisemite.* New York: Penguin Books, 1982.

Wangh, M. "National Socialism and the Genocide of the Jews: A Psychoanalytic Study of a History Event." *International Journal of Psychoanalysis,* 45, pp. 386-395, 1964.

Yerushalmi, Y.H. *From Spanish Court to Italian Ghetto.* Seattle: University of Washington, 1981.

Yerushalmi, Y.H. *Freud's Moses: Judaism Terminable and Interminable.* New Haven: Yale University Press, 1990.

Yerushalmi, Y.H. "Assimilation and Racial Antisemitism, The Iberian and German Models", Leo Baeck Memorial Lecture No. 26, New York: Leo Baeck Institute, 1982.

Ziegler, P. *The Black Death.* Wolfboro Falls, NH: Allan Sutton, 1991.

Zimmerman, M. *Wilhelm Marr, The Patriarch of Anti-Semitism.* Oxford: Oxford University Press, 1986.

# Index

Abbé Barrud, 122
Abraham, Karl, 23, 25
Ackerman, N.W., 8-9
Adolescence, 77
Affect, regulation of, 81-83
African-Americans, 15-16, 67-68, 134, 173-74
Aho, James A., 161, 168, 170
*Akedah*, 73, 76, 101
Almoner, 116
Ammerman, Nancy T., 166-67
Angels, 78, 113
*Anti-Intellectualism In American Life* (Hofstadter), 167
Antiochus Epiphanes, 107
Antisemitic personality, 7-8
Antisemitism, 175-79
    of African-Americans, 67-68
    after Constantine, 105-6
    of Christian Scriptures and Church fathers, 98-105
    and criticism of Israel, 58-60
    currently, in U.S., 124-28
    definition of, 13-15
    of deists, 119-21
    developmental issues, 29-39
    endurance of, 1-2
    Jewish association with psychoanalysis, 20-26
    in Jewish Bible, 95-97
    in *Merchant of Venice*, 115-19
    in the Middle Ages, 106-15
    of Muslims, 144-48
    in mythology, 130-33
    nonreligious, 133-35
    pre-Christian, 97-98
    as a prejudice, 15-16
    *Protocols of the Elders of Zion*, 17, 51, 58, 121-24, 134, 146-48, 177
    psychoanalytic interpretations, 4-11
    and psychopathology, 16-17
    racial, 128-130
    transmission of, 57-58
*Antisemitism, A Social Disease* (Simmel), 6-8
*Antisemitism and Emotional Disorder: A Psychoanalytic Interpretion* (Jahoda & Ackerman), 8-9
"Antisemitism and Mass Psychopathology" (Simmel), 6-7
"Antisemitism and the Psychopathology of Daily Life" (Orr), 6
Apion, 107
Apocalypse, 80-92, 138-39, 164-68, 176, 178
Arabs, 58-60, 126, 144-48
Aristotle, 78
Arlow, Jacob A., 88, 113, 153, 159
Austria, 127

Babylonian exile, 96
Babylonian Talmud, 141-142
Badge (Jewish), 106-7
Barkun, Michael, 160
Baron, Salo, 3, 110
Ben Zakkai, Yohanan, 173
Bergmann, Martin, 10, 13, 73-74
*Bible Believers: Fundamentalists in the Modern World* (Ammerman), 166-67
Bible (Christian), 98-105
Bible (Jewish), 95-97
Binswanger, Ludwig, 22
Birth myths, 69
Black Death, 108
Blood libel, 145-47
Blood symbolism, 74-75, 156-57
B'nai B'rith Society, 5, 21-22
Book of Amos, 164
Book of Daniel, 164
Book of Esther, 95-96

Book of Exodus, 53
Book of Genesis, 76
Book of Job, 141
Book of Revelation, 86, 88, 138, 164
Borderline personality disorder, 60
Bornstein, Berta, 71-72

Cannibalistic fantasies, 101-3, 107-10
Chaos, 161
Chariot mysticism, 72, 78
Charismatic leader, 161-62
Chasseguet-Smirgel, Janine, 13, 32, 158,
    162
Children's Crusade, 79
Child sacrifice, 72-76
Christian Church antisemitism, 98-105
Christian patriot, 168
Christians, 8, 18, 20, 127, 132, 135-36,
    145, 176
Christians and Jews: A Psychoanalytic
    Study (Loewenstein), 8, 15
Christian Scriptures, 98-105
Circumcision, 73-74
City University of New York, 174
Civilization and Its Discontents (Freud),
    5
Cohn, Norman, 106, 113, 121-23, 164,
    172
Congress of the International Psycho-
    analytic Association, 23-24
Conspiracy theories, 147
Conversion, 111, 128, 133-34
Conversos, 111
Coughlin, Father Charles, 125
Cromwell, Oliver, 119
Cross symbolism, 126
Crusade of 1096, 106, 108
Cultural stereotyping, 61
Curent Research on Antisemitism, 10

Dawidowicz, Lucy, 133
Death fantasy, 80-81
Defense mechanisms, 30-31, 34-37
Deists, 119-21
Denial, 34-35
Devil, 112, 142-43, 147
The Devil (Russell), 142
Dhimmis, 144
Diaspora, 96
Displacement, 46-51

Double registration, 65
Douglas, Mary, 37-38, 130
Duby, G., 108
Duckitt, John, 9-10

Ego dystonic, 46
Ego ideal, 153
Ego syntonic, 44
"Elements of a Psychoanalytic Theory
    of Antisemitism" (Fenichel), 8
Elizabethan England, 115-19
Erickson, Erik, 6
Eschaton, 86
Eucharist, 109-10
Evil, 141-43, 148
Externalization, 30-31, 46-51

Family romance fantasies, 51-57
"Family Romances" (Freud), 51-52
Fenichel, O., 8
Filicide, 74
Fiorentino, Giovanni, 117
First Crusade, 106, 108, 117
Flood apocalypse, 88-90
Ford, Henry, 125
Fourth Lateran Council, 107, 110
France, 122-23
Frank, Leo, 125
Fraternal group, 157-60
    and apocalypse, 164-66
    formation of, 160-64
    indoctrination of children in, 170-71
    origin of, 168-69
    recruitment for, 169-70
Freikorps, 155-64
Frenkel-Brunswik, E., 7
Freud, Anna, 29-30, 34
Freud, Sigmund, 4-6, 65, 179
    on apocalyptic delusions, 87-88
    concern with antisemitism, 20-26
    on family romance, 51-52
    on primary process, 123-24
Fundamentalism, 148, 166-68

Gates, Henry Louis, 177-78
Gender homogeneous groups, 32-34
Germans, 6
Germany, 122, 127-30, 151-74
Ghetto, first, 107
Gilman, Sander, 19

Ginsberg, Benjamin, 3
Goitein, S.D., 145
Golden ages, 1, 125-26
Grant, Madison, 129
Group membership, 31-34, 153-54. *See also* Fraternal group
apocalyptic quality of, 154-55

Halevi, Yehudah, 145
Hartman, John, 12, 151-53
*Hekhaloth* mysticism, 72, 78
Hertzberg, A., 120
*History, Religion and Antisemitism* (Langmuir), 11
Hitler, Adolf, 30, 123, 135, 138, 151-55, 170
Hofstadter, Richard, 167
Holocaust, 5, 13, 23-24, 131, 148, 165-66, 179
Host, 80
Hsia, R.P., 109

Iblis, 147
Idealizing transference, 152
*Il Pecorone*, 117
Infanticide myth, 73
Intermediaries, 78-80, 112-13
*The Interpretation of Dreams* (Freud), 5
*In the Shadow of Moloch* (Bergmann), 73-74
Islam, 144-48
Israel, 15, 58-60, 126, 146-47, 173, 178

Jahoda, M., 8-9
Jesus, 100-1, 104
*Jewish Self-Hatred* (Gilman), 19
*The Jew of Malta* (Marlowe), 118
Jews
    American, 1
    association with psychoanalysis, 20-26
    responsibility for antisemitism, 17
    separatism of, 17-20
*The Jews and Modern capitalism* (Sombart), 6
John, Saint, of Alexandria, 116
Joly, Maurice, 122
Jones, Ernest, 8, 22
Jucovy, Milton, 13
Jung, Carl, 21-22

Kemenetsky, Christa, 171
King, Martin Luther, Jr., 177-78

Langmuir, Gavin, 11, 66, 109-10
Latency period, 30-33, 71, 77
Lebanese War, 58-59
"The Legend of the Divine Surety and the Jewish Moneylender" (Nelson & Starr), 115
Lewis, Bernard, 144, 146-47
Loewenberg, Peter, 160, 169
Loewenstein, Rudolph M., 8, 15, 45, 139
Lopez, Rodrigo, 118
Lubavitch Hasidim, 173-74
*Lucifer* (Russell), 142
Luke, Saint, 99
Luther, Martin, 14, 20, 51

Maimonides, 78, 179
*Malakh*, 78
Marlowe, Christopher, 118
Marr, Wilhelm, 13-15, 51
Marranos, 118
Masada, 173
Mass, Catholic, 102
Matthew, Saint, 99, 104
*Mein Kampf* (Hitler), 38, 123, 154
*Memoirs of an Anti-Semite* (Von Rezzori), 28, 54-57
*The Merchant of Venice* (Shakespeare), 18, 115-19, 133
*Merkavah* mysticism, 72
Merkl, P.H., 169
Messianism, 85
Middle Ages, 106-15, 143, 164
Moneylenders, 106
*Moses and Monotheism* (Freud), 5-6, 22
Mother and child myths, 69-70
Muhammad, 51, 144
Muslim antisemitism, 144-48
*Myth of the Twentieth Century* (Rosenberg), 123
Mythology, 63-64, 66-68, 92-93
    apocalypse, 80-92
    of birth, 69
    individual and group, 70
    intermediaries, 78-80, 112-13
    issues of, 68
    of mother and child, 69-70

Oedipus complex, 46-48, 50, 55, 60, 70-72, 77
  of origin, 69
  purpose of, 64-65
  sacrifice, 72-76
  sibling rivalry, 46-48, 60, 76-78

Napoleon Bonaparte, 122
Napoleon III, 122
Narcissistic object choices, 153
Nazism, 16, 22, 24, 27, 30, 52-53, 57, 123, 127, 129-30, 136, 146, 151-74
Nelson,Benjamin, 115
Neubauer, Peter, 77, 158, 169
*New York Times*, 53
Nunberg, H., 69

Oedipus complex, 46-48, 50, 55, 60, 70-72, 77
Oedipus myth, 80-81
Okhrana, 123
Olden, Christine, 153
"On Wit and Humour" (Freud), 21
Oral fixation, 50
Origin myths, 69
Orr, Douglas, 6

Paley, Vivian Gussin, 31
Parkes, J., 104
*The Passing of the Great Race: Or, the Racial Basis of European History* (Grant), 129
Passover symbolism, 110-11
Paul, Saint, 99
Pentateuch, 141
Phallic symbolism, 50
Philosemitism, 51-57, 61, 96, 139
Pied Piper of Hamelin, 79, 109
Plague of 1348, 30
Pogrom mentality
  fraternal group, 157-60
  and apocalypse, 164-66
  formation of, 160-64
  Freikorps, 155-57
  fundamentalism, 166-68
  indoctrination of children, 170-71
  instigation of, 171-74
  origin of, 168-69
  recruitment, 169-70
  *Triumph of the Will*, 151-55

Poland, 62
Poliakov, Leon, 3, 119
Pollution, 37-38, 147
Pre-Christian antisemitism, 97-98
Prejudice, 9-10, 15-16, 29
Primary process, 123-24, 137, 139, 164, 176
Projection, 46-51
Prophetic Scriptures, 86
*The Protocols of the Elders of Zion*, 17, 51, 58, 121-124, 131, 134, 146-48, 177
*Psyche*, 59
*Psychiatry*, 6
Psychoanalysis, Jewish association with, 20-26
"The Psychology of the Jewish Question" (Jones), 8
Puritans, 118
*Purity and Danger* (Douglas), 37-38
*The Pursuit of the Millennium* (Cohn), 164

Quotas, 125

Rabbi Akiba, 115
"The Rabbi's Speech," 122
*The Races of Europe: A Sociological Study* (Ripley), 129
Rachkovsky, P.R., 123
Racial antisemitism, 128-30
Racial purity, 128-30
Rashi, 115
Rebirth fantasy, 80-81
Revelation of St. John the Divine, 83-85
Riefenstahl, Leni, 151-55
Ripley, W.Z., 129
Ritual murder accusations, 65-66, 73-74, 107, 110
Rivalry, 35
Roman Empire, 97-98, 106
Roman exile, 96
Rosenberg, Alfred, 123
Russell, Jeffrey Burton, 142

Sachs, Hans, 159
Sacrifice, 72-76
Satan, 112, 142-43, 147
*Satan* (Russell), 142
Scheidlinger, S., 32, 158

Screen memory, 64
Scriptures, 98–105
Secondary process, 124, 137, 139
"The Secret Relationship Between Blacks and Jews," 177
Segev, Tom, 169
Seixas, Moses, 125
Sexuality, 159
Shakespeare, William, 18, 115–19, 133
Shiites, 147
*Shoah* (film), 57
Sibling rivalry, 46–48, 60, 76–78
Simmel, Ernst, 6–7
Smith, Gerald, 125
Sombart, Werner, 4, 6
*Sophie's Choice* (Styron), 28, 136–37
Soros, George, 50
Spain, 20, 38, 62, 128–30, 133–34
Stalin, Joseph, 161
Starr, Joshua, 115
Stereotyping, 61
Stranger anxiety, 35–37, 96–97
Strauss, Herbert A., 10
Styron, William, 28, 136–37

Tacitus, 65, 97–98
Talmud, 142, 176
Tertullian, 107
Theodore-Abraham story, 116
Theweleit, Klaus, 155–57
Third Reich, 151–55
Thomas of Monmouth, 66

*Toward a Definition of Antisemitism* (Langmuir), 11
Trachtenberg, J., 37
Transference, 46–51, 152
Transubstantiation, 109–10
*Triumph of the Will* (film), 151–55, 157–58, 164

United States, 124–28
Urbantschitsch, Rudolf, 22

Vienna, 20
Vienna Psychoanalytic Society, 23
Voltaire, 120–21
Von Rezzori, Gregor, 28, 54–57, 114, 139

Wangh, Martin, 24, 161
Washington, George, 125–26
Weimar Republic, 123
West, Cornell, 177
Wiedeman, George, 157
William of Norwich, 66
Winrod, George, 125
World War I, 155
World War II, 146

Yerushalmi, Yosef, 12, 37, 104, 170
*You Can't Say You Can't Play* (Paley), 31

Zionism, 24